Language, Society and Power

Language, Society and Power is the essential introductory text for students studying language in a variety of social contexts.

This book examines the ways in which language functions, how it influences thought and how it varies according to age, ethnicity, class and gender. It seeks to answer such questions as: How can a language reflect the status of children and older people? Do men and women talk differently? How can our use of language mark our ethnic identity? It also looks at language use in politics and the media and investigates how language affects and constructs our identities, exploring notions of correctness and attitudes towards language use.

This third edition of this bestselling book has been completely revised to include recent developments in theory and research and offers the following features:

- a range of new and engaging international examples drawn from everyday life – beauty advertisements, conversation transcripts, newspaper headlines reporting on asylum seekers, language-themed cartoons, and excerpts from the television programme *South Park* and satirical news website *The Onion*
- new activities designed to give students a real understanding of the topic
- an additional chapter covering Student Projects – giving readers suggestions on how to further explore the topics covered in the book
- updated and expanded further reading sections for each chapter and a glossary.

While it can be used as a stand-alone text, this edition of *Language, Society and Power* has also been fully cross-referenced with the new companion title: *The Language, Society and Power Reader*. Together these books provide the complete resource for students of English language and linguistics, media, communication, cultural studies, sociology and psychology.

Annabelle Mooney is a Reader in English Language and Linguistics at Roehampton University, UK.

Jean Stilwell Peccei was formerly a Visiting Lecturer in the English Language & Linguistics programme at Roehampton University, UK.

Suzanne LaBelle is a Lecturer in English Language and Communication at Kingston University, UK.

Berit Engøy Henriksen attended The Norwegian University of Science and Technology (NTNU). She then studied at Roehampton University, graduating with an MRes in Sociolinguistics in 2009.

Eva Eppler is Senior Lecturer and convenor of the MRes in Sociolinguistics at Roehampton University, UK.

Anthea Irwin is Programme Leader of the BA (Hons.) Media & Communication degree at Glasgow Caledonian University, UK.

Pia Pichler is a Senior Lecturer in Linguistics at Goldsmiths, University of London, UK.

Siân Preece is Lecturer in TESOL Education at the Institute of Education, University of London.

Satori Soden has taught at both Roehampton and Goldsmiths, University of London, UK.

Language, Society and Power

An introduction

Third edition

Annabelle Mooney, Jean Stilwell Peccei,
Suzanne LaBelle, Berit Engøy Henriksen, Eva Eppler,
Anthea Irwin, Pia Pichler, Siân Preece and
Satori Soden

Routledge
Taylor & Francis Group

LONDON AND NEW YORK

First published 1999
by Routledge
Reprinted twice in 2000, 2001, twice in 2002 and 2003

Second edition published 2004
by Routledge

This third edition published 2011
by Routledge
2 Park Square, Milton Park, Abingdon, Oxon OX14 4RN

Simultaneously published in the USA and Canada
by Routledge
270 Madison Ave, New York, NY 10016

Routledge is an imprint of the Taylor & Francis Group, an informa business

Typeset in 10 on 12 pt Akzidenz Grotesk by Saxon Graphics Ltd, Derby
Printed and bound in Great Britain by MPG Books Group, UK

British Library Cataloguing in Publication Data
A catalogue record for this book is available from the British Library

Library of Congress Cataloging-in-Publication Data
Language, society and power : an introduction / Annabelle Mooney, Jean Stilwell Peccei, Suzanne LaBelle. -- 3rd ed.
p. cm.
1. Language and languages. 2. Sociolinguistics. I. Mooney, Annabelle, 1974- II. Peccei, Jean Stilwell. III. LaBelle, Suzanne.
P107.L36 2011
306.44--dc22
2010023020

ISBN 13: 978–0–415–57658–1 (hbk)
ISBN 13: 978–0–415–57659–8 (pbk)
ISBN 13: 978–0–203–83654–5 (ebk)

For Debbie and Jen

Contents

Figures

Tables

Permissions

The authors and publishers would like to thank the following for permission to reproduce copyright material:

Cartoon by Dave Coverly, Belfry Studio
Cartoon by Dainon Woudstra
Cartoon from www.cartoonstock.com
Cartoon from Knight Features

Every effort has been made to trace and contact copyright holders. The publishers would be pleased to hear from any copyright holders not acknowledged here so that this acknowledgements list may be amended at the earliest opportunity.

Newspapers

During the course of our discussions, reference is made to and data are taken from English language newspapers and magazines. A list of these publications is given below.

Associated Press	A news wire service
Boston Globe	Boston, MA, daily newspaper
Daily Mail	UK national daily newspaper
Evening Standard	London daily newspaper
Glasgow Evening Times	Scottish daily newspaper
Glasgow Herald	Scottish daily newspaper
Glasgow Herald	Scottish daily newspaper
Huffington Post	US online source of news
National Enquirer	US weekly tabloid news magazine
National Geographic	US monthly magazine
New York Times	US national daily newspaper
Newsweek	US weekly news magazine
NZPA (New Zealand Press Association)	New Zealand news wire agency
Reuters	A news wire service
Scottish Daily Express	Scottish daily newspaper
Seattle Times	Seatttle, WA, USA, daily newspaper
Sydney Morning Herald	Australian daily newspaper
The Daily Telegraph	UK national daily newspaper
The Guardian	UK national daily newspaper
The London Paper	UK free daily
The Mirror	UK daily newspaper

The Northern Ditrict Times	Australian local (northern Sydney suburbs) free weekly
The Onion	US satirical 'news' paper
The Sun	UK daily newspaper
The Sunday Times	UK national Sunday newspaper
The Times	UK national daily newspaper
Washington Post	Washington, DC daily newspaper

Transcription conventions

Detailed transcription conventions are as follows:

{laughter}	non-verbal information
<u>xxxxxx</u> *{laughing}*	paralinguistic information qualifying underlined utterance
[good evening] [hello]	beginning/end of simultaneous speech
(xxxxxxxx)	inaudible material
(......)	doubt about accuracy of transcription
'......'	speaker quotes/uses words of others
CAPITALS	increased volume
%......%	decreased volume
bold print	speaker emphasis
>...<	faster speed of utterance deliver
/	rising intonation
yeah:::::	lengthened sound
-	incomplete word or utterance
~	speaker intentionally leaves utterance incomplete
=	latching on (no gap between speakers' utterances)
(.)	micropause
(-)	pause shorter than one second
(1); (2)	timed pauses (longer than one second)
.hhh; hhh	in-breath; out-breath
*Bengali	translation of Bengali or Sylheti *utterance* into English

Contributors

Berit Engøy Henriksen attended The Norwegian University of Science and Technology (NTNU). She then studied at Roehampton University, graduating with an MRes in Sociolinguistics in 2009. Her Masters research examined the communicative norms which develop in video blogging. She continues to pursue research in the field of new media and language

Eva Eppler is Senior Lecturer and convenor of the MRes in Sociolinguistics at Roehampton University, London. Her research, based on data from the LIDES corpus, focuses on structural and processing aspects of bilingual language use. Recently she has been working on bilingual conversational structures in single- and mixed-sex groups and processing of bilingual speech, especially in heavily intra-sententially code-mixed utterances. Among her publications are *The LIDES Coding Manual* and the edited volume *Gender and Spoken Interaction* (McMillan 2009, with Pia Pichler), as well as numerous articles on bilingual code-switching. She is presently also working on a monograph entitled *Emigranto*.

Anthea Irwin is Programme Leader of the BA (Hons) Media & Communication degree at Glasgow Caledonian University. She researches discourse reproduction and identity construction in both conversational and media data. Her publications include: 'London adolescents reproducing power/knowledge: "you know" and "I know"', *Language in Society* 35: 04 (2006); 'Now you see me, now you don't: adolescents exploring deviant positions' in Pichler, P. and Eppler, E. (eds) *Gender and Spoken Interaction* (Palgrave Macmillan, 2009); 'Race and ethnicity in the media' in Blain, N. and Hutchison, D. (eds) *The Media in Scotland* (Edinburgh University Press, 2008).

Suzanne LaBelle studied sociolinguistics at the University of Pennsylvania and Essex University. She is a variationist sociolinguist, and a lecturer in English Language and Communication at Kingston University. Her research interests include language change in minority language communities, particularly Welsh, and perception of variation during sound change.

Annabelle Mooney is a Reader at Roehampton University in London. She teaches in fields of gender, narrative, sexist language and language and the law. She has published on the topics of health and HIV, globalisation, religion, gender and law. She is the author of *The Rhetoric of Religious Cults* (Palgrave, 2005) and co-editor, with Betsy Evans, of *Globalization: The Key Concepts* (Routledge, 2009). She is currently working on language and the law.

Jean Stilwell Peccei is a former Visiting Lecturer in the English Language and Linguistics programme at Roehampton University. She is the author of *Child Language*, second edition (Routledge Language Workbooks series, 1999), *Pragmatics* (Routledge Language Workbooks series, 1999), and *Child Language: A resource book for students* (Routledge English Language Introductions series, 2005).

Pia Pichler is Senior Lecturer in Linguistics at Goldsmiths, University of London. She has published work in the area of language and gender and on the linguistic construction of identity, with a particular focus on the interplay of local identity practices with gender, ethnicity and social class. She is co-editor of the second edition of *Language and Gender: A Reader* (Blackwell, 2011) with Jennifer Coates and of *Gender and Spoken Interaction* with Eva Eppler, author of *Talking Young Femininities* (both Palgrave Macmillan, 2009).

Siân Preece is a Lecturer in TESOL Education at the Institute of Education, University of London. She is interested in applied linguistics in educational settings and her research interests include language, gender and sexuality, linguistic and cultural diversity in post-16 education, language learning and multilingual identities in widening participation contexts. She is the author of the book *Posh Talk: Language and Identity in Higher Education* (Palgrave, 2009) and has published several articles on gendered and multilingual identities in post-16 education.

Satori Soden completed her PhD at Roehampton University in 2009 and has taught at both Roehampton and Goldsmiths University. Her research interests are media representations, the social construction of ageing, semiotics, advertising and workplace literacies.

Preface to the third edition

In this third edition, we have sought to continue the traditions so well established in the first and second editions. The course, out of which this book grew, is still running as required for students on the English Language and Linguistics programme at Roehampton University. While we have kept the structure and tone of previous editions, there have been some changes. The previous editions were authored by academics who had at some time taught at Roehampton. We have kept to this in as much as all of the authors of the present edition have either worked or studied at Roehampton. Indeed, some have done both. What we all have in common is an enthusiasm for the course.

As previously, authors come from all over the world. While we have continued to include material about global Englishes, in this edition we have sought to include examples from other languages. We have also tried to include material from internet sources. The internet is indeed a global phenomenon; we hope you will be able to find your own 'local' examples of the kind of material which we have indicated.

This book introduces students to the central concepts around the topics of language, society and power. Since the previous edition, things have changed in the world of sociolinguistics, and we have tried to capture some of these changes as well as indicating where the field has come from. It is our belief that it is impossible to understand some of the current issues in the field of sociolinguistics without having a sense of how the various topics developed. Certainly the material is only indicative of these changes; we have tried to keep material accessible to students without a background in linguistics, while also wanting to whet the appetite of students and encourage them to take forward their studies in the area.

The importance of language is something that will never go away. The increasingly mediated nature of contemporary society means that it is important to be aware of issues related to representation and ideology. This critical stance is common in many disciplines; we understand it as crucial for meaningful engagement with the world in all areas. Because of this, in the first four chapters, we spend time on the concepts of ideology and representation.

The first two chapters set out our approach to language, society and power. The tools and concepts introduced in these chapters recur throughout the book. While we have indicated, by way of cross-referencing, particular topic links between chapters, the core ideas of ideology and discourse are relevant throughout the text. We have kept to the structure of the book from previous editions with some minor changes. In the chapters on politics (Chapter 3) and media (Chapter 4) we have worked with a broad understanding of these concepts, in order to highlight the importance of power and the ideological choices that are made with any representation. We hope that such a broad focus will assist in developing critical skills and the 'making strange' of the familiar. The other topics we cover were chosen as we understand them to be the 'classic' sociolinguistic variables. We start with gender (Chapter 5), moving on to ethnicity (Chapter 6), age (Chapter 7), and class (Chapter 8). While each of these are areas of change in terms of the questions they ask, they have all, to some degree, also become implicated in a more general discussion of identity. We cover this in Chapter 9 and hope that the topics and issues from previous chapters will be borne in mind when thinking about identity. The final chapter has been altered slightly to address the issue of standard languages and attitudes towards language. While standard English is still an important area, and is included in this section, we thought it important to highlight the work conducted in the area of language attitudes. Further, we see this discussion as bringing the discussion back to where we start, that is, the question of what 'language' means and what ideas we already have about language.

A new addition is the projects chapter. We have sought to provide ideas for investigation of real language, building on the areas covered in the chapters. Included in this chapter is material to encourage students to think about research, issues around gathering and analysing data, as well as information about ongoing research and resources that may be useful in exploring some of the concepts introduced in this book.

As there is a companion Reader for the textbook (*Language, Society and Power: A Reader*, Routledge, 2011), we have indicated in the Further Reading sections any texts which are included in the Reader. The book icon 📖 is placed next to these readings.

Many of the changes have come about as a result of teaching the course. We would like to thank the students we have taught for their engagement, the sharing of their own thoughts and language, and their questions. The latter especially have helped us enormously in the writing of this book. Part of the reason for continuing to address our readers as 'you' is to try to capture the dialogue that we experience when teaching the course. Thinking about language is, for us, something which benefits from conversation, discussion and debate. We all have our own biases (something you should bear in mind when reading the book); reflecting on these in the company of others is, for us, an essential part of learning. In this spirit, as authors, we have benefitted from the input of a number of people. Thus, alterations, at various stages, were prompted by incredibly helpful suggestions from current users of the second edition as well as reviewers of the draft of this edition. This detailed and constructive advice has been very useful and we are grateful for it.

We hope you enjoy thinking about language. While it can be challenging to develop the critical skills we believe are central to working with language, there is also a great deal of fun to be had.

Preface to the second edition

The first edition of *Language, Society and Power* was published in 1999, when the majority of the contributing authors were lecturers at Roehampton University of Surrey (then Roehampton Institute London). The book had evolved out of an identically titled course on which we had all taught, and which is still running as a required course for students on the English Language and Linguistics programme, and as a popular option for students in other departments. Since that first edition, several of us have moved to other universities and colleges, but we have all maintained an interest in studying language as a social entity. Thus, even though producing this second edition has required a great deal more co-ordination than the last time, we were all willing to be involved in revising and updating a project which has not only been enjoyable for us but which has also had a favourable reception from its intended audience.

The second edition has remained faithful to the first in many ways. We have maintained a focus on English (primarily British and American varieties). The first edition's glossary of terms potentially new to the reader (printed in bold in each chapter) has been retained but also updated. We have continued to make use of personal reference (something not typically found in academic texts), addressing the reader as *you*, and referring to ourselves as *I* or *we* as appropriate. We have also continued to assume that our readers are generally not, or not yet, specialists in the areas of language study and linguistics, and therefore need an introduction to the kinds of topics which feed into a broader examination of language and society. As such, the book does not offer comprehensive coverage of every possible issue within this vast subject area but, instead, provides a stepping-stone to exploring and thinking about at least some of them. Thus, each of the chapters deals with a topic that has been the subject of academic sociolinguistic investigation, and is supplemented with references to useful reading and other sources of material. There are substantial Activities throughout the text to help the reader engage more actively with the ideas being presented.

We have maintained the distinctive authorial 'voices' of the first edition, since they make for a more varied and interesting approach to analysis and discussion. One of the things that the majority of the chapters do have in common, though, is that they seek to interpret the ways in which language and language issues can be deconstructed to reveal underlying ideologies, or beliefs. While all of the chapters have a solid academic grounding, it is important to bear in mind that any interpretation of what people do and say is necessarily going to contain a certain measure of bias. Thus, while we can justifiably analyse a newspaper headline about immigration, for example, and state that its 'slant' reveals an affiliation to politically left- or right-wing principles, it must be remembered that any such approach is in itself ideologically determined: it reveals the analyst's belief that language is not a neutral tool of communication but instead a channel for how we see and construct the world around us. This tenet will become clearer as you read through the text.

Each chapter of this book deals with a different area of language, although there are connections between many of the chapter topics. We have designed the book so that it can be read from cover to cover as a continuous text, but also so that individual chapters can stand alone and be read in their own right. We have divided chapters into subsections, partly to indicate the structure clearly with subtitles and partly to help you find the sections you need to read if you don't need to read the whole chapter.

Chapter 1 interrogates the notion of 'language', and raises some of the underlying questions and ideas that will be relevant as you move into the other chapters. Chapters 2–4 all concentrate on the ideological properties of language, and on how it can be used to influence the ways in which people think and behave. Chapter 2 is concerned with the connections between language, thought and representation, and considers the extent to which language can be said to shape and perpetuate our worldviews. Chapter 3 moves on from the conclusions of Chapter 2 to consider whether, and how, language can be used in politics, and in other fields, to persuade people of particular points of view. Chapter 4 considers how language is used, and to what effects, in media such as newspapers and television with particular reference to news reporting and advertising. Chapters 5–7 deal with language use in connection with particular subgroups within a population. The terms or 'labels' that can be or are applied to members of those groups, and the effect of those labels, are considered. The chapters also look at the kinds of language choices members of those groups sometimes make. Chapter 5 focuses on language and gender, Chapter 6 deals with language and ethnicity and Chapter 7 with language and age. Chapter 8 considers how a further set of subgroup divisions, namely those which go into the construction of social class, affect language use. The last three chapters, 9–11, are concerned with attitudes towards language, and the relationship between language and identity. Chapter 9 deals with language and social identity, and Chapter 10 with the debates that surround the use of standard English. Chapter 11 provides a conclusion to the whole book with an overview of attitudes towards language.

Finally, we hope that you will enjoy reading and using this second edition, and that it will add another dimension to how you think about language and language use. We have certainly enjoyed putting it together, and we hope that at least some measure of our passion and interest in this everyday but extraordinary faculty will prove infectious!

Preface to the first edition

This book is based on a course of the same name that runs in the English Language and Linguistics Programme at Roehampton Institute London, and on which all the authors have taught. It began life as Language, Power, Politics and Sexuality, a short (five-week) introduction to language issues for students studying literature. Over the years the course has grown as interest in language study has grown, and it is now an introductory course for students studying language and linguistics, while continuing in popularity with students of litera-ture. Many of the students taking the course are combining their studies with subjects such as sociology, media studies, women's studies, education and history, where they find that the issues raised are also relevant.

In preparing this book, we have assumed no prior knowledge of linguis-tics. We hope that students taking courses on the social and political dimen-sions of language use will find this a useful foundation text. Students of disciplines that include the study of language use, discourse and ideology, power relations, education, the rights of minority groups and equal opportuni-ties should also find this a helpful text. Learners of English may find this a useful route to a better understanding of language use. Since we see language use as being central to many, or most, human activities, we hope that students studying apparently unrelated disciplines may also find it helpful to have a book which covers the range of issues we deal with here. And we have tried to make the text appropriate and interesting for the general reader.

The ideas covered in this book have been explored and developed with groups of students since the early 1980s. They are presented here as eleven topics, currently covered in a modular course on a week-by-week basis. Although they may look it, the topics are not discrete, but have overlapping themes and common threads which we have tried to bring out. Nor are they exclusive. As you read, you may well think of other areas of language use which are worthy of investigation or consideration, such as the relationship between language and health, or language and the law. Issues such as these are not omitted because we think that they are unimportant but because in a book of this length there is not space to cover everything. We hope what we have covered will assist your thinking about the relationship between language and the different dimensions of the societies in which we live.

The authors have taught as a team the course from which this book was generated. We felt that as a group we shared common values both about the topics we taught and our approach to teaching, and that this provided us with a solid foundation for writing this book also as a team. We distributed the topics amongst the six of us, according to our areas of special interest, and met regularly to review the drafts of our chapters and to discuss revisions. Our aim was to produce a coherent text that still reflected the ideas and writing styles of individual team members. To some extent, the different 'voices' of the authors should still be apparent.

Amongst other decisions we had to make as a team of authors, we had to decide on how we would use pronouns such as *I, we* and *you*. We could, for example, have decided to write impersonally, and avoid using personal pronouns as much as possible, which is quite common in academic writing. We had to decide whether we should refer to ourselves in the chapters as *I* (the individual writing the chapter) or *we* (the team of writers). We also had to decide whether we should use *you* to address our readers. The conventional, impersonal academic style is often criticised by people with an interest in the social and political functions of language because, as is discussed in Chapter 3, it can be used to make ideas seem less accessible than they need be, and to increase the apparent status of the writers by making them seem 'cleverer' than the readers. In the end, we felt the most honest and sensible thing to do would be to use *we* to refer to the team of authors, to acknowledge the input we have all had in each other's thinking and writing, but to use *I* if we write about our personal experiences. We have addressed you the readers as *you*.

Throughout the book we concentrate on the English language, although we occasionally use another language to illustrate a particular point. The main varieties of English looked at are British and American English.

There is a glossary of terms with brief explanations at the back of the book. Words which appear in the glossary are printed in bold the first time they occur in a chapter. You will also find at the end of each chapter recommended further reading which you can follow up if you want to learn more about a topic. If you want to check whether a topic is covered in this book, and where, the index at the back gives page numbers.

We have included Activities throughout the text. Some ask you to reflect on your own use of, or feelings about, language. Some ask you to talk to other people, to elicit their language use or thoughts on certain issues. Some require you to collect data from other sources around you, such as the newspapers or television. Some you will be able to do alone, and some need group discussion. One of the main reasons we have included Activities is that we believe that the ideas we are discussing in this book really come alive when you begin to look for them in the language which goes on around you. We have seen students' attitudes change from mild interest, or even a lack of interest, to absolute fascination when they have started to investigate language use for themselves.

If the ideas we have presented here are ones you have come across before, we hope we have presented them in such a way as to provoke further thought, or make connections you hadn't previously made. If you haven't thought about some of the ideas we raise here before, we hope that you also find them exciting and spend the rest of your life listening to what people say, reading newspapers and watching television commercials differently.

Acknowledgements

As this is now the third edition of this book, some traditions have been established. While not all of us were involved in the production of previous editions, we have all taught from them. We would like to thank Deborah Cameron and Jennifer Coates who designed the original course. We retain the dedication to them as a tribute to their extensive work in establishing the programme and the course. We hope to have continued the traditions they established in a way that would please them.

The many students who have taken the course have also provided invaluable help in formulation of this text. We would also like to thank Routledge's anonymous reviewers and readers for their valuable suggestions at the start of the project and at the draft stage of composition. We'd like to thank our American consultant, Dr Betsy Evans, for extensive guidance and support. Our editors at Routledge, Eloise Cook and Nadia Seemungal, have been unstinting in their enthusiasm, support and patience. Thanks also to Pia Pichler for permission to use her transcription conventions.

Each of us have benefitted from support from our colleagues, family, friends and readers. They have our heartfelt thanks. We have also looked to previous editions, especially the second, for material, ideas and sensibility; this has been of great importance and we would like thank our colleagues who worked on these texts. We'd also like to thank Jean Stilwell Peccei for instigating and designing this third edition as well as providing extensive material from the previous edition to build on. Without her, the project would never have come about. Her experience, her advice and assistance at all stages of preparation – as well as her writing contribution – have been invaluable.

CHAPTER 1

What is language?

Annabelle Mooney

1.1 INTRODUCTION

Even though we use language constantly, we don't normally pay a great deal of attention to it. When we do, it's usually because something has gone wrong, or because we're passionate about the topic or speaker. While we will consider cases where things go wrong, in this book we focus more often on how language works, in common situations, in different ways, for different people. Before we do this, we need to think about what 'language' is. This is not an easy task. What counts as a language is a political, cultural and technical question. At the same time, while a group of people may share a language, they will each have their own individual way of using that language. To make matters even more complicated, individuals don't consistently use language in the same way. The language we use when we talk to our friends is not the same as the language we use to write a letter of complaint. Language varies depending on the people using it, the task at hand, and the society in which it all takes place.

While some linguists work to describe the rules of word order (**syntax**) or the sounds that make up words (**phonetics** and **morphology**), here, we'll be looking at what language can tell us about people as individuals, as members of groups, and about how people interact with other people. Before we start thinking about differences, it's worth considering why language is worth studying at all. As we'll see, linguists look at language for very different reasons, with various questions that they want to answer. Whatever path this work takes, it always treats language as a system. Studying systems might sound tedious, but linguists do more than that

– they describe the systems. Linguists are like spies, describing the rules of complex and changing systems, working with pieces of data from the everyday world. And this is not just any set of rules – language is a system that allows people to tell jokes, write poetry, make an arrest, sell you washing powder, pay a compliment and wish you good night. Language allows us to be precise and persuasive, ambiguous and evasive, charming and charismatic.

1.2 WHY STUDY LANGUAGE?

While not everyone studies language in a formal way, everyone has opinions about it. This is to be expected, given how central language is to our everyday life. If we canvass these opinions, we have an excellent starting place for the study of language generally and, more specifically, for thinking carefully and precisely about language. Norman Fairclough argues that a 'critical aware-ness of language … arises within the normal ways people reflect on their lives as part of their lives' (1999: 73). Such reflection is well worth encour-aging; Fairclough argues that the ability to understand how language functions, to think about it in different ways, is crucial to understanding society and other people. Critical awareness isn't important because it makes us more accomplished or more intelligent; there is much more at stake. Fairclough argues that to understand power, persuasion and how people live together, a conscious engagement with language is necessary. That is, critical thinking about language can assist in resisting oppression, protecting the powerless and building a good society. Ferdinand de Saussure, sometimes referred to as the founder of modern linguistics, puts it rather more starkly. He writes: 'in the lives of individuals and societies, speech is more important than anything else. That linguistics should continue to be the prerogative of a few specialists would be unthinkable – everyone is concerned with it in one way or another' (1966: 7). In a way, all people are linguists, whether they like it or not.

    If arguments about protecting people or challenging power seem abstract, consider a concrete case where language has a very precise value. In the first chapter of a recent book, Stephen Pinker describes 'the world's most expensive debate in semantics' (2008: 3).[1] After the events of 9/11 in the United States, the owners of the twin towers wanted to claim insurance for the catastrophic damage. They had insurance for 'destructive "events"', and the amount they were entitled to receive related to how many 'events' there had been. Was the crashing of hijacked planes into the twin towers one event or two? You might think this is an inappropriate or even trivial question to ask. After such a terrible event (or events) is it really important to make a decision about whether the 'event' was singular or plural? It certainly mattered to the owners, as a specific monetary amount was involved, 'in this case [Pinker] can put an exact value on it: three and a half billion dollars' (2008: 2). That is, for each 'event', the owners would receive three and a half billion dollars. Pinker concludes, 'There is nothing "mere" about semantics' (2008: 3). The case went to court, in two different trials. In one, the jury held there was one event; in the other, that there were two.

Semantics is just one of the areas of linguistics that looks at how we understand and construct meaning. But there are many others. Looking closely at language can tell us about:

- how our brains understand and process language (psycholinguistics)
- how we learn languages, and so how best to teach them (applied linguistics)
- how social factors (age, gender, class, ethnicity, etc) affect the way people use language (sociolinguistics)
- how it might be possible to have a realistic conversation with a computer (artificial intelligence)
- what it is distinctive about literature and poetry (stylistics)
- how people in different cultures use language to do things (anthropology)
- the relationship between words and meaning and the 'real' world (philosophy)
- whether someone is guilty of a criminal offence (forensic linguistics).

This is far from a full account of the various kinds of linguistics. The subfields here are much richer and further reaching than the bullet points suggest. The important point is to realise that language can be examined in a variety of ways with diverse and specific concerns in mind. It's also important to point out that these areas aren't completely separate. We may want to know something about how brains process language if we're interested in finding good teaching methods, for example. The way in which linguists in these areas go about looking at language may overlap. For example, the kind of analysis that is done in stylistics will be similar in some ways to the work done by forensic linguistics because there is a similar attention to the detail of language and some of the same tools of analysis are used.

1.2.1 The rules of language: prescription vs description

As mentioned, most people have opinions about language and language use. Looking at the letters pages in a newspaper, on blogs or even listening to the radio we notice that people have very strong ideas about language. There may be particular words or expressions that are commented on, perhaps because they cause offence, or because they are considered to be 'wrong'. Judgements about what is 'correct' language abound. Several amusing cases can be found on a blog dedicated to the use of 'literally' (http://literally.barelyfitz.com/). One striking example is from a man who plays Santa Claus in the United States, 'You see things behind the beard that nobody else will ever see or hear. I've had children just literally tear my heart out' (posted 30 March 2009). Clearly this is incorrect if we interpret 'literally' in a literal way; had the children actually torn Santa's heart, he would be dead. Nevertheless, we all understand 'literally' here as an intensifier, an exaggeration which we grasp immediately.

The disapproval of this use of 'literally' is echoed in a usage note in the online edition of the Oxford English Dictionary (OED): 'Now often improperly used to indicate that some conventional metaphorical or hyperbolical phrase is to be taken in the strongest admissible sense.' On the basis of this, you might conclude that the blogger is right: 'literally' shouldn't be used in this way, it's 'improper', even according to the OED. What do you think? Is Santa's use of 'literally' correct or not?

While it may seem to be a way of ducking a hard question, in deciding whether 'literally' is acceptable for Santa, we need to know what our definition of 'correct' is, or if we even have one. For linguists, meaning is use. That is, we don't judge a use of a word as correct or incorrect; rather, what the word means alters as it is used in different ways. This can be captured more precisely by talking about the difference between **description and prescription**. Linguists are concerned with describing what people are doing with language (description) while people who want to say that a certain use is incorrect are setting down rules for proper language use (prescription), quite apart from what people actually do.

But wait a minute; the OED said that it was an 'improper' use. You might be surprised to know that the OED note dates from 1903; the 2005 print edition is rather less dogmatic: 'This use … is not acceptable in standard English, though it is widespread'. Note how there is a distinction made between 'standard English' and something else: 'widespread' language use (see Chapter 10). While in 1903 the use of hyperbolic 'literally' appears to have been stigmatised to the extent of being considered 'improper', now it is only seen as unacceptable in 'standard English'. This is an excellent example of how language changes and how the rules of language change. The prescriptive rules don't seem to have changed; but usage rules have. While the prescriptivist would argue that the 'rules of English' dictate that you can't 'literally explode', a linguist would argue that given we all understand what it means for a person to 'literally explode' (without blood being involved) the rules about what 'literally' means must have changed. Prescriptivists seem to think that if language changes, if their rules are broken, that the heart of language will be torn out. For linguists, these changes are interesting and inevitable. As languages are used, they change; while old descriptive rules may no longer work, new ones can be found. Even though language changes, it is always systematic – that is, language remains part of a system that reorganises itself around changes in language use. This idea might take some getting used to; but it is fundamental for any study of language.

Many prescriptivist requests to respect the 'rules' also come with some kind of warning: breaking the rules will lead to breaking the language itself. 'The crisis is imminent,' we are told. 'Things have never been this bad, it's all the fault of young people, foreigners and poor schooling.' While language changes, the theme of prescriptivist arguments barely shifts. Disapproving of the way some people use language, especially in relation to grammar and

the meaning of words, has a very long history known as 'the complaint tradition' (Milroy and Milroy 1999). The idea that language is in decline and that
this is someone's fault dates back to at least the fourteenth century (Boletta
1992). You can find many contemporary examples of the complaint tradition
in newspapers or any mass media. The following, from a newspaper, relates
to spelling.

> There can be no doubt, I fear, that the newspapers are the great corrupt-
> ers of the English language. The ignorant Americanism *program* for
> *programme* is gradually creeping in through this source.

Here, print media is blamed for the problem as well as being the place
where the problem is identified! Obviously this is from a British newspaper;
blaming America for the destruction of the English language is rather
common. Note the use of 'corrupters' here, a word with particularly strong
emotional force. The underlying message in such letters is that language
has particular rules which should be followed. Those who don't adhere to
the rules are responsible for 'ruining' the language. As mentioned, this is
hardly new; this extract, from the *Pall Mall Gazette*, a London newspaper,
dates from 1891, and doubtless you could find the same argument today.

1.2.2 Bad language: jargon

Another complaint tradition, with a similar longevity, is that which bemoans
the use of 'jargon'. Depending on the context of use, this language problem
may also informally be called 'gobbledygook', 'management speak', and
when deception is involved, especially in politics, 'weasel words'. In such
expressions we also see complaint; the complaint is not so much about
rules being broken, but about language changing such that it becomes
overcomplicated or incomprehensible. If we remove the judgemental
aspects, we can define jargon as the use of specialised words and expressions that are difficult to understand for people not part of the specialised
group. It's important to remember that the use of specialised language is
sometimes necessary. You probably wouldn't want your doctor to try communicating with a surgeon in lay terms. It would be rather frightening to hear
a surgeon say to his colleagues, 'we're going to operate to get that nasty
bit out of her tummy' when what you need is to have your appendix
removed. Thus, whether or not something is jargon (especially in the
negative sense) depends very much on who is speaking to whom. As Crystal
argues:

> The difficulties arise only when others come into contact with [a special-
> ised variety of language], by accident or design, and find themselves
> threatened by its lack of familiarity or clarity, as happens so often in
> such fields as science, medicine, religion, and the law.
>
> (2005: ch 72)

There is also an important element of power involved in jargon that we need to be aware of. The issue of power and how to define and detect it with respect to language comes later in this chapter.

At this point, it is worth remembering that language has different kinds of power; one of these is the power to make us laugh. Here we examine a humorous passage which deals with jargon. The following 'news' story is taken from a satirical, comic publication, *The Onion* (www.theonion.com).

> CHARLOTTE, NC—During what was described to them as 'a look-forward meeting to discuss and evaluate the company's event-chain methodology,' MediaLine employees stood with mouths agape Wednesday as they witnessed the very moment at which project manager James Atkins attained complete mastery over the fine art of meaningless corporate doublespeak.
>
> According to his awed coworkers, Atkins' usage of vacuous administrative jargon reached an almost mythical apex with the pre-lunchtime announcement, during which a string of expertly crafted drivel rolled off the 28-year-old's tongue with the confidence of a seasoned executive.
>
> 'Due to the increased scope of the project vis-à-vis Tuesday's meeting, compounded with our aforementioned desire to maintain quality without increasing cost, an as-yet indeterminate amount of time will be allocated to our newest venture,' Atkins said without once stuttering. 'You should all be proud of the amount of effort and energy you have put forth thus far, and can be certain the project's conclusion will become more apparent as the tasks become increasingly more finite.'

Clearly *The Onion* is not a serious newspaper. This extract, however, points precisely to what people find frustrating and confusing about the use of jargon, especially in the workplace. There are a number of important points highlighted in this satirical piece. First, this language (jargon) is something that needs to be learnt, not just in terms of the words themselves but also how they are used. To attain 'complete mastery' requires that you are familiar with the terms and also how they go together in a sentence. Thus, there is a semantic and a syntactic element to learn. Second, this acquisition is not easy, but because of this, it is impressive. We can see this in the extract when we're told that the co-workers were 'awed'. The ability to provoke awe in an audience also points to the connection between jargon and power. People in positions of power often speak (and write) in a way that others find difficult to understand. At the same time, being able to use jargon is part of establishing and projecting power. The third issue, and one of the keys to the humour, is the inversion of the normal relationship between language and power. If powerful people speak in complex ways, perhaps speaking in complex ways also makes one powerful? Certainly our manager, Mr Atkins, has some real power over his colleagues. He is, after all, a manager. We've also noted that he impresses his audience. At the same time this language is described as 'drivel' and 'meaningless corporate doublespeak'. The clear message of the article is that while he has mastered the language style, he isn't using it effectively. He certainly breaks one of Orwell's guidelines for the clear use of language: 'Never use a foreign phrase, a scientific word, or a jargon word if you can think of an everyday English equivalent' (1946).

But can this style of language ever be used effectively? Recall the example of the doctor above. The use of specialist language between such professionals is necessary for good communication. Our manager, on the other hand, uses apparently specialised terms to make what is a simple message more difficult to understand. Some see the use of such jargon as typical of particular professions. In the following example, those who write advertisements for positions in the public sector are lampooned. The journalist's newspaper, *The Daily Mail*, has 'christened' the 'bloated public sector' with the name 'Jobzilla'.

> The ads can be identified by their ludicrously politically correct language. This is a mutant tongue, ungrammatical, littered with pointless and often meaningless words, where the simplest concepts are rendered impenetrable by the use of pseudo-scientific terms, corporatese and ugly management speak borrowed from the private sector.
>
> These people talk about 'performance targets', 'service delivery' and 'sustainability'. They are obsessed with something called 'strategy'. In Jobzilla-land people are not helped, they are 'empowered'.
>
> (Hanlon 2009)

We will return to the issue of political correctness later. Here, notice that some people seem to be allowed to make up new words while others are not. The newspaper seems to think that 'Jobzilla' is an important, or at least worthwhile, contribution to the language, while other new usages are not. It seems to be the case that new words and expressions are acceptable if they help make things clearer, or if they have a point, but not if they make messages more difficult to understand. That seems like a very reasonable argument. However, the question we need to think about is who gets to make decisions about which words are clear and thus acceptable.

---

1   Taking the extract from *The Onion* above, rewrite the last paragraph into non-jargon.
2   Make a list of jargon from the field that you are studying. Discuss the meaning of the term with a colleague. Do you agree on the meaning? Consider whether you think these terms are useful, or whether another term could do its work.
3   Make a list of words that you don't like because they are jargon. Include words and expressions that you have been told not to use (by your parents or teachers).
4   Look at the following collections of jargon and select twelve you've heard before. Provide a translation
    a   www.theofficelife.com
    b   www.jargondatabase.com

Activity 1.1

For the moment, we simply need to realise that people do have strong feelings about language generally, and their own language in particular. The words and practices that people find annoying or incorrect, and the reasons given for this, can tell us a great deal about our relationship with language and our ideas about communication. In the next section we'll look at how language will be approached in this book. When we have a way of examining language, we can better explore and understand what people say about language generally.

1.3 WHAT IS LANGUAGE?

Answering the question 'what is language?' can only be done once we know why we're asking it. In this book, we'll be looking at the way different groups of people are represented by and use language. To be able to do this, we need to understand what it means to say that language is a system.

1.3.1 Language: a system

If we look closely at language, we find that it is in fact a rule-governed system. This may make it sound like language is *controlled* by rules that prevent it from changing. However, this is not what we mean by system; we need to be clear about what kind of rules we're talking about. Language is not governed by rules in the same way that society is governed by laws. Linguists don't decide on rules and then try to make everyone follow them. Rather, linguists look at language to discover the rules that make it work – that is, the things that make communication possible. As language changes, new rules are described.

The rules in language tell speakers how to combine different parts of that language, as the comic in Figure 1.1 demonstrates. We all know that 'ngux' is not a word that is possible in English. The rules of English sounds (**phonemes**) tell us that we can't have 'ng' at the start of a word. In the same way, if I tell you that I recently bought a 'mert', you would be able to form the question, 'What is a mert?' Even though you don't know what a 'mert' is, if I tell you I bought one this lets you know 'mert' is a noun. You would already know how to make its plural ('merts') and how to ask what it was. This is because of the rules in English about where certain kinds of words go in sentences (syntax) and how to form plurals (morphology). Theoretical linguists work at discovering these rules for particular languages. This work can then be used to say something about language in general – that is, linguists can come to conclusions about all languages, grouping them according to certain structural criteria and even make arguments about how the language faculty itself works.

Other systems of communication have rules too. The light that tells us when it's safe to cross the road is green. Around the world, there are differences in the shape of the light. Sometimes a word is given, such as 'WALK',

Figure 1.1 Get Fuzzy cartoon

sometimes a picture shape that suggests a person moving. The red light (in whatever shape it happens to be) tells pedestrians to stop. There is variation from place to place. Some countries have a flashing red light, for example, indicating that you shouldn't start crossing the road. While there are differences in the way in which different countries configure their traffic signals, there is one thing that is the same: the traffic lights can't tell you to 'skip' or to 'watch out for the tiger' or any number of other things. They tell us only about whether or not we can cross the road. Even a new combination would not of itself provide a new message. For example, if both red and green lights were illuminated at the same time, you would probably conclude that the light was faulty, not that a new message was being communicated. Such lights are very limited in what can be communicated. In language, it's possible to talk about 'merts', to ask what they are, and to create the word. This tells us something very important: it is possible to create new meanings. This creativity is possible because of the rules that inform language use.

1.3.2 Rules in theory and practice

We won't be considering syntax and grammatical sentences as such in this book. But it is worth making a distinction between theoretical linguistics and the type of linguistics we focus on here – sociolinguistics. The theoretical linguist Noam Chomsky made an important distinction between **competence** and **performance**. To have competence in a language means to have knowledge of the grammar. Grammar is all rules that need to be followed in order to produce well-formed utterances. A competent speaker needs to know which word order to use (syntax), which form a word should take (morphology), what those words mean (semantics) and how to produce those words verbally (phonetics and **phonology**). All these rules make up the grammar of the language. Examining the rules, what linguists refer to as the grammar, of natural languages allows linguists to say something about language generally, and also about the way humans acquire language – that is, what might be innate and what has to be learned.

Competence explains well-formed sentences, and also how we can generate new meanings. The rules that speakers know (though not always consciously) allow new, acceptable and, most importantly, meaningful utterances. The rules allow speakers to generate new utterances but they exist at an abstract level. On the other hand, performance refers to the way individual speakers actually use language. Performance does not always faithfully reflect the rules described by competence. As such, performance is not of great interest to theoretical linguists. Dell Hymes argues that factors of performance 'are generally seen as things that limit the realization of grammatical possibilities' and thus actually are an impediment to the linguist interested in the grammar (1997: 13).

It is possible, however, for a well-formed utterance to be inappropriate because of rules of social relationships, taboo or other cultural convention. The speaker may have grammatical competence, but lack **communicative competence**. This has also been called 'sociolinguistic competence' or 'pragmatic competence'. Knowing how to greet someone or what constitutes appropriate 'small talk' are examples of this competence. Communicative competence allows speakers to avoid inappropriate utterances. Sociolinguistics looks at the variation that we find among speakers in their linguistic performance in order to understand the different forms of communicative competence that are required by speakers of different kinds. The variation that sociolinguists examine is systematic – that is, it appears to be amenable to description in terms of rules. Given that the variation isn't random, it is possible that it means something, that is, that the variation is motivated by a reason or factor – the standards and rules of communicative competence that apply in the particular speech community.

We can define sociolinguistics in contrast to theoretical linguistics, but there are two problems. First, we need to be more descriptive about what sociolinguistics is; second, to suggest such a contrast would also suggest that they are mutually exclusive endeavours. This is not to say that theoretical linguistics is not important; nor is it to suggest that there is no link between theoretical and sociolinguistics. It is rather that the questions that these disciplines try to answer are different. Because of this, different tools, approaches and even definitions of 'language' occur.

William Labov, one of the founders of sociolinguistics, noted in 1972 that he had 'resisted the term sociolinguistics for many years, since it implies that there can be a successful linguistic theory or practice which is not social' (1997 [1972]: 23). In the same text he writes:

> There is a growing realization that the basis of intersubjective knowledge in linguistics must be found in speech – language as it is used in everyday life by members of the social order, that vehicle of communication in which they argue with their wives, joke with their friends, and deceive their enemies.
>
> (1997: 23)

This seems to me to be an appropriate account of what we understand as sociolinguistics in this book. The way that language is used in normal life, by all kinds of people, to accomplish all manner of goals is the subject of our attention. The last, the doing of action, reminds us perhaps more than the other aspects that language lets us do things and, as such, can be used to exercise or resist power.

1.3.3 The potential to create new meanings

We've already seen in the discussion of jargon that new meanings can be created. It's not only possible to create new words, it is essential. When new objects are made, for example, we need to know what to call them. In deciding this, we follow the rules about how to construct an acceptable word in whatever language we're using. It's also possible to use existing words in a new way. The language that teenagers use is often like this. While 'cool' used to be how one expressed admiration for or pleasure about something, at other times 'sick' has been used in this way. Is this a misuse of language? Clearly 'sick' can still be used to mean 'unwell' as 'cool' could always be used to mean a low temperature, but using these terms in a specific sentence can change the meaning completely. 'What sick shoes' will never be understood as meaning that someone's footwear is unwell.

It's also possible to create new words by changing their function; for example, by changing them from a noun to a verb or from a verb to an adjective, as the following letter to the editor illustrates:

> SIR – I was unable to find a product in its usual place in our local supermarket recently, but a small notice redirected me to the shelf where it was now being 'marketized'.
> Peter Carney, Northwood, Middlesex (*Daily Telegraph* London 21 November 2007: 25)

It has become normal to use 'market' as a verb; here, the verb has been further transformed into an adjective. This letter writer may be objecting to this new use when the word 'sold' would serve the purpose. He may also be unhappy about the whole process of 'marketizing' – that is, a specific way of promoting an item by drawing it to consumers' attention in a specific way. Indeed, the verb here is derived from a noun, 'marketization', which according to the Oxford English Dictionary refers to a very different process than that suggested in this letter: 'the exposure of an industry or service to market forces' or 'the conversion of a national economy from a planned to a market economy'.[2] Nevertheless, new uses for old words and changes to the kind of word it is (noun, verb, etc) are far from unusual. Words that are altogether new obviously occur, but it is incredibly difficult to predict which new words will catch on and which won't. Each year the American Dialect Society nominates its 'words of the year'.[3] However, even these experts are not always right about which new words remain in use and which don't.

What's fascinating about new words is that most of the time we understand what they mean without having to look them up in a dictionary (where we probably wouldn't find them because they're so new). Consider the following: 'There was so much tannoyance on the train, I couldn't sleep'. This fusion of Tannoy (a public address system in the UK) and annoyance usefully encodes the meaning:

> Endless, semi-coherent burbling about beverages, station stops and remembering to take your legs with you – delivered through speakers that make everything sound like a bee in a jar – on trains. Scientists predict that by 2014 these announcements will take longer than the average railway journey.

(Wyse 2008)

Indeed, 'Tannoy' itself is an example of meaning change, as it is actually a trademark of a particular public address product that is now used in the UK as a generic term.

Activity 1.2

You probably use words that other people don't like or understand. Write down a definition of one and describe the ways in which it can be used. If it's an adjective, for example, can it be used about people or just things? Can it be used about all things or just a subset (such as clothes)? To find examples, think of informal terms that you use with your friends.

You can find examples of completely new words at www.unwords.com.

1.3.4 Language: multiple functions

We've already seen that language can have different functions. It can be used to refer to things, to demonstrate status and power and to amuse. A single utterance can do more than one thing. Roman Jakobson argues that 'Language must be investigated in all the variety of its functions' (2000: 335). It's helpful to look at Jakobson's functions in a bit more detail as it helps to have a framework to think about the different functions. Without this, it can be difficult to think about the various ways that we use language.

He starts by describing the features one needs to take into consideration. On one side of his schema we find the speaker, the person who is speaking. On the other, we find the addressee, or the person being spoken to. To fully account for the message from the addresser to the addressee we need to examine four things. For the message to be communicated, there has to be a medium of communication, which may be verbal, written or even visual (*contact*). This will have some influence on how the *message*, the content, is encoded; whether through words or hand signals for example.

Whatever *code* is chosen (words or hand signals), it must be one that both *addresser* and *addressee* have access to. The *message* will also be sent and received in a *context* – that is, there will be a social and linguistic environment that frames the message.

```
                    CONTEXT
ADDRESSER           MESSAGE            ADDRESSEE
                    CONTACT
                    CODE
```

'Each of these six factors determines a different function of language' (Jakobson 2000: 335). We can see these functions set out below, in the same format as the features just examined. The *emotive* (or expressive) function is in the position of the addresser, as it 'aims a direct expression of the speaker's attitude towards what he is speaking about' (2000: 336). The **referential** function of language is what we might normally think of as information, or the denotative function of language, but also includes the ideas, objects and conventions which speakers share knowledge of. The referential function allows us to ask someone to pass the salt, and receive the salt (rather than the pepper). Focused on the addressee is the **conative** function of language. This function helps us describe messages that are intended to have an effect on the audience. This might be anything from a command, an insult, or an attempt at persuasion.

```
                    REFERENTIAL
EMOTIVE             POETIC             CONATIVE
                    PHATIC
                    METALINGUAL
```

While we often start with the referential function of language in an attempt to find out what information is being communicated, we need to do more than this to account for the way in which language works. If a person says 'it's cold in here', you may understand this as simply being a comment about the level of air conditioning. If you're sitting near an open window, however, it would be reasonable to interpret this as a request to close the window. Thus it's a message where the conative function is highlighted. Common stereotypes about British speech describe a preoccupation with the weather. In such a situation, 'it's cold in here' may well be understood as small talk, or making conversation. This is the **phatic** function. The purpose is not so much to communicate information (anyone in the room can tell what the temperature is), but rather to communicate about something that while socially acceptable, is not of itself significant. That is, it is considered to be polite to make 'small talk'.

It's important at this stage to note that the conative function is different from connotation. **Connotation** is the subjective or personal aspect of meaning, which can be contrasted with denotation, which is the literal definition. While denotation is related to the referential function of language, connotation is more likely to be related to the emotive function. To come back to Jakobson's functions, remember that the conative function is about addressing someone, using **imperatives** or **vocatives**.

The poetic function was of great importance to Jakobson as he was looking specifically at language and literature. The poetic function is important in everyday language, though, and draws attention to the message for its own sake. The most obvious examples of messages with significant poetic function often also have an important conative (and indeed emotive) function. Advertising, whether spoken or written, often takes advantage of the poetic function of language. The same is true of political and other persuasive texts.

The final function that Jakobson draws our attention to is the **metalingual**. This is language that refers to language and communication while communicating. This function is vital for successful communication to continue to take place. When we ask someone to repeat or rephrase or explain again what their message is, we are exploiting the metalingual function of language. In short, we are able to talk about talking.

All these functions of language are always available. We can, for example, look at the poetic function of any piece of language, whether it's literature, advertising or a mathematics textbook. Generally, however, we only notice the poetic function when it's **foregrounded** – that is, when a message is particularly nicely phrased or, conversely, obviously devoid of any poetic interest. These functions are also central in understanding how people use language to do things, whether it is to get a window closed or to be elected to government. In the same way, the functions of language are the means by which power can be exercised over people.

Jakobson's account of six functions of language is not the only way of classifying the purposes of language. David Crystal (2005: ch 71) recognises the same kinds of tasks, but specifically mentions the following:

- expressing emotion
- expressing rapport
- expressing sounds
- playing
- controlling reality
- recording facts
- expressing thought processes
- expressing identity
- meeting technological demands.

Activity 1.3

Are the Jakobson and Crystal models the same, but with different labels? Which do you prefer and why? Do you think there are any functions of language they haven't included?

1.3.5 Language diversity

As mentioned above, how we decide what a language is really depends on the kind of question we're asking. Even though English is widely used around the world, there are many different varieties. We look at some of the variation here as it highlights issues central to the study of language. Variation in language is a challenge, as it prompts us to think about how we can classify different varieties in relation to each other.

How we choose to classify these varieties can vary according to linguistic and political considerations. We might think that a language variety can be identified geographically, such that everyone in England speaks English, while everyone in the United States speaks American English. But, if you listen to someone from Liverpool in England and then to someone from Brighton, it's clear that there are some important differences.[4]

There are differences in the way in which people pronounce words, which varies systematically and very often on the basis of geography. Such differences can be dealt with in terms of **accent**. There are other differences between speakers of English in relation to the words they use for particular things (vocabulary) and even the order in which words are placed (syntax); we can talk about this in terms of **dialect**. Especially when coupled with an unfamiliar accent, this can make understanding different dialects of English rather difficult. Because today many people move to other places, it's easy to find great variation in the same city. Language varies among people for reasons other than where they're from. In the following chapters we'll be looking at variables such as class, ethnicity, gender and age that may influence the way in which language is used differently.

The political dimension of how to describe or delimit a language should not be overlooked. To say, for example, that Australian English is not a variety in its own right but merely a dialect of British English, immediately places Australian English in a subordinate position to British English. Remember that language is closely connected to identity. Similarly, nationality is an important marker of identity; thus language and national borders are sometimes spoken of as if they conform (see Chapter 6). Different governments as well as people have distinct views on such issues. Ferdinand de Saussure comments, 'The internal politics of states is no less important to the life of languages; certain governments (like the Swiss) allow the coexistence of several idioms; others (like the French) strive for linguistic unity' (1966: 20).

Because language and identity are closely linked, people have strong views about their language, about what it should be called and how it should be used. We saw some evidence of this when dealing with jargon above. The terms of discussion around accent and dialect are very often those of beauty and correctness and thus related to something we're already discussed: **prescriptivism**. But if there are prescriptive rules, should these vary according to variety (see Chapter 10)? In the following, one letter writer connects Singaporean English (Singlish) to the particular culture of the country.

Singlish encapsulates culture

Let us abandon the belief that Singlish is bad English.

To me, it is a unique vocabulary that encapsulates decades of local culture. One could throw in the occasional 'lah' and jargon like 'bo chap' ('can't be bothered' in Hokkein) to retain a wonderfully local flavour and still keep to grammatical English.

Singaporeans using Singlish are no different from Britons using unfamiliar local slang.

('Good English – whose line is it anyway?' *The Straits Times* Singapore, 1 September 2008)

In the same letters page there were many other contributions that took different stances on the issue. One writer despairs of the standard of British English, 'When my British housemate's sister from Manchester came to visit last month, I was appalled by her poor grammar and thick accent. She had to repeat herself many times to be understood' (ibid). Both writers are preoccupied with what is grammatically correct. The first writer appears to accept a wider definition of what counts as 'grammatical', while the second takes as the measure some form of standard British English, one that is not even uniformly spoken in Great Britain.

How decisions about what is 'correct' and grammatical in language are taken and what languages should be called is very often related to power. There are different kinds of power that we might want to consider and which will be relevant in later chapters.

1.4 POWER

Finding a full definition of power with respect to language is not straightforward. The many functions of language mean that there are different ways in which power can be exercised. While there are some examples of power being used to change language directly, the relationship is generally more subtle.

The former president of Turkmenistan, Saparmurat Niyazov, exercised his political power directly over language. In 2002 'He decreed that the month of January should be named after him and April after his mother' (Parfitt 2006). He also named a town after himself (or more correctly the title he insisted upon – Turkmenbashi – 'leader of all Turkmen') and decreed that 'bread' also be called by his mother's name (Paton Walsh 2006). This is an example of straightforward legal and political power being used to change language. Such action is generally only possible where there is absolute singular authority, as was the case with this dictator.

Influence over language, and influence over people through language, is far more commonly achieved in less obvious and direct ways. Of course there are situations where physical or institutional power has a direct influence on how language is understood. When a police officer asks you to stop your car, for example, the institutional power (and perhaps even their weapon) lends a particular force to the request (Shon 2005). In fact, such a request would more likely be understood as a command, because of the context in which the speech takes place.

When a manager uses a particular form of language, however, the power comes partially from her position (as your boss) but perhaps also from the kind of language that is used. We can think about this not as physical power, or even institutional power, but as symbolic power. Calling it symbolic power draws our attention to the link between power and symbols – that is, between power and language. To call it 'symbolic power' is not to say that the power is ineffective. If you think about the things that people can do with language, this becomes clear. With language, it is possible to insult, persuade, command, compliment, encourage, or make a promise. While these can be seen as individual acts, it is possible, through engaging in repeated acts of this kind, to change a person's world view.

Thus, while language is important in the exercise of power at particular moments, we also need to understand that language can work across long stretches of time. I can be commanded to do something now, but I can also be influenced to think and behave in a certain way pretty much all the time. This certainly involves language, but we need something more. Fairclough puts it as follows:

> It is important to emphasize that I am not suggesting that power is *just* a matter of language. … Power exists in various modalities, including the concrete and unmistakable modality of physical force … It is perhaps helpful to make a broad distinction between the exercise of power through *coercion* of various sorts including physical violence, and the exercise of power through the manufacture of *consent* to or at least acquiescence towards it. Power relations depend on both, though in varying proportions. Ideology is the prime means of manufacturing consent.
>
> (2001: 3)

There are two new ideas here. The first is **ideology**, and the second that of manufacturing consent, which we will come to presently. The general idea is that language plus ideology can encourage us to do things, not because someone has commanded us at a particular point in time, but because we have internalised certain values that mean we *want* to do certain things. This internalising of values takes place over longer stretches of time. Language is crucial to the creation and maintenance of 'common-sense' ideology. But to understand how this works, we need to know what ideology means. You can think about it as a way of structuring how language is used to communicate a more general message involving values and beliefs, in short, a world view.

1.4.1 Ideology

In everyday contexts, 'ideology' is something negative or, at the very least, **marked**. We think that only groups such as terrorists have an ideology. But as an ideology is simply a way of describing a set of beliefs and behaviours that are thought of as natural, everyone has an ideology. There are things we take for granted, values that we hold and ideas that we believe in that seem perfectly natural. It is this common sense, this natural and normal way of thinking and acting which we can talk about in terms of the dominant ideology, or **hegemonic** ideology. Ideology is a way of talking about a whole set of these ways of thinking and acting. Moreover, ideologies aren't just efficient ways of seeing and thinking: they have another purpose. The French sociologist Pierre Bourdieu writes:

> ideologies serve particular interests which they tend to present as universal interests, shared by the group as a whole.
>
> (1991: 167)

Bourdieu's words remind us that every group has an ideology. Thus, 'ideology' is used in at least two ways as William J. Thomas Mitchell explains:

> The orthodox view is that ideology is false consciousness, a system of symbolic representations that reflects an historical situation of domination by a particular class, and which serves to conceal the historical character and class bias of that system under guises of naturalness and universality. The other meaning of 'ideology' tends to identify it simply with the structure of values and interests that informs any representation of reality; this meaning leaves untouched the question of whether the representation is false or oppressive. In this formulation, there would be no such thing as a position outside ideology.
>
> (1986: 4)

The critical linguists Gunther Kress and Robert Hodge define ideology 'as a systematic body of ideas, organized from a particular point of view' (1993: 6). Given that we all have a particular point of view, we all have ideologies. We tend to only talk about them with the term 'ideology' when we want to draw attention to their power or the particular interests they serve. To label another group's values as 'ideology' is common; to talk about one's own values in the same way is not common at all. However, thinking about our own 'taken for granted' values, as members of groups or as individuals, is an important task for critical thinking.

Ideology may seem a long way from jargon and 'incorrect' uses of language. But power, and especially symbolic power, is supported by ideologies. Looking at language closely allows us to map these ideologies. In the same way that we can deduce the structure of a language by looking at the way people use it, we can also map the structure and content of an ideology. In the following, we describe one such mapping, which generates a more general theory: the manufacture of consent.

1.4.2 The manufacture of consent

The notion of the manufacture of consent originates in the work of Noam Chomsky. While Chomsky is well known as a theoretical linguist, he also examines media and political representations of events. In a seminal book, written with Edward Herman, an argument about how propaganda works is made. Focusing on the mass media, they point to a number of factors that influence what stories we read and hear and in what form we receive them. They identify five 'filters' that influence the representations finally produced. *Media ownership* is one of these filters, along with the importance of *advertising income*. *Where our news stories come from* (from large news agencies, for example), how *groups and individuals respond to stories*, whether they complain, for example, are also filters. The fifth filter is that *communism must be avoided at all costs*. Since the end of the Cold War this looked like it was taking a detour. The new analogous filter for a while appeared to be terrorism. Whether this will persist is not clear. Indeed, at the time of writing, there is a distinct move to anti-socialist discourses in the USA in relation to some of President Obama's initiatives, suggesting the continued relevance of the fifth filter.

The manufacture of consent seeks to capture the effect of these five filters. The filters can be understood as structuring language at an ideological level. Though audiences are unaware of these filters when reading or watching the mass media, they are nevertheless important. These filters present what really happened in particular ways. Some events may not be covered at all; some may be given a great deal of importance. The way in which stories are told – for example, who is to blame or what the real issues are – is also influenced by these filters. Because we are only exposed to the filtered representations, over time audiences find the values of the mass media are normalised. For example, it is common sense that terrorists are bad and that we need to be protected from them. In effect, Chomsky and Herman argue that such 'common sense' is constructed by the sustained representations of the mass media and that these representations are a product of the five filters they identify.

Thinking about ownership of newspapers and television channels and the significance of advertising revenue to their success, it is tempting to think that this 'manufacturing' is consciously planned by powerful people behind the scenes. This may well happen. However, the choice of the term 'filters' points to the automatic processes that occur without conscious intervention being necessary on the part of the producers. Newspaper editors do not need to be told to print or to withhold particular stories that may make large advertisers unhappy. In terms of running the newspaper as a business, which it obviously is, it's common sense to keep advertisers content. This is how ideology works; the ideology acts like a filter to remove anything that doesn't fit its values. By looking at what is left behind, we can deduce what these values are. We do this by looking at the language used.

1.4.3 Ideology in action: advertising

Powerful words and slogans are common when companies want us to buy something. Advertisements are an excellent place to see the way in which language can have power as well as seeing certain ideologies at work. Further, the speaker in these advertisements is very often crucial to their persuasive effect.

You're probably familiar with the use of celebrities, film stars and models to advertise goods, especially cosmetics and hair care. They tell the audience how scientifically advanced the product is, often with animated sections to make this visually meaningful. A television advertisement from 1998 for a hairspray featured Jennifer Anniston, the American actor. She tells us that she is 'being held by an invisible force' as she floats on air. This 'invisible force' is also active in her hairspray. But she leaves it to the voice over to explain how it works: 'Here comes the science' she says. Just as she trusts her hair (and visually her body) to an invisible force, we are invited to trust the force of celebrity endorsement of a product.

The use of celebrities is not accidental. Audiences have a positive emotional connection with these famous people: they want to be successful and beautiful too. So when a supermodel says that she uses a particular face cream, audiences are inclined to believe her and the words she uses. The power here, to persuade people to buy the face cream too, is partly the words spoken and partly also who is speaking them. To connect this to ideology, we can say that for women to look a certain way – to have long shiny hair, and even tanned skin – is considered to be attractive in many Western countries. This is, for us, common sense. We are consistently told that these physical attributes are desirable. But this is not a 'natural' state of affairs; it is a set of naturalised beliefs – an ideology. This particular ideology serves the interests of those companies that manufacture products to make hair shiny and skin tanned.

It's not uncommon for advertising campaigns to be global in their reach. Advertisements may be translated or made to suit local audiences in other ways, but the basic message is constant. This suggests that some ideologies have a wide appeal. A recent (2009) campaign from Gillette uses the idea of 'the moment' when men need to have courage. The advertisement mixes celebrities and 'normal' men, showing them in various situations of stress: about to shoot a basketball, wanting to ask a woman out, and so on. At this crucial moment, the voice tells us, it's important to be confident. 'What's gonna win?' the male voice asks, before the men succeed in their various endeavours. 'Here's to confidence' it answers, before commanding viewers to 'Look your best. Feel your best. Be your Best'. As we should already know, Gillette is 'the best a man can get'.

The link between looking, feeling and being is implied but nevertheless important. This message is trying to persuade us, through simple **imperative** statements, that when you look good you will feel good and ultimately be good. There is an implied causality here and the company's products are at the start of this causal chain. While the voice acknowledges at the start of the advertisement that 'we all have confidence' and 'we all have doubt', the men included in this 'we' are nevertheless encouraged to have confidence. This shift from doubt to confidence mirrors the shift from real man to celebrity man.

> Choose an advertisement, either from television, radio, print media or the internet. Watch it or read it a few times. How is it trying to persuade the audience? What values is it endorsing? What arguments is it actually making?

Activity 1.4

You might think that advertisements are generally all the same. Here, we have focused on the kind that uses celebrities. But as Crystal argues, 'it is not an easy field to make generalizations about. Its boundaries blur with other forms of persuasive language such as speeches, sermons, and public announcements' (2005: ch 72). The boundaries may be even more blurred than this, with advertising often looking like a news story or a 'real' television programme (infomercials). Someone might even start a conversation with you that seems quite normal, but is really just a way of promoting a particular product. Such placement of products in everyday contexts is done by 'brand ambassadors'.

1.4.4 Interpellation

The way we use language in less commercial contexts also links to power and ideology. We'll look at this in some detail in later chapters. The way that language is used in relation to addressees can be thought of in terms of the way it positions that audience, the way they are addressed. Above, we noted that language has a number of different functions, one of these being the conative function – that is, oriented towards the addressee. This can have implications in terms of relations of power. Louis Althusser theorises this as the audience being 'hailed' in a particular way. This means that language is used to address people and thus position them in some way. We can take a police officer as an example. When an officer speaks to a person, that person is positioned in relation to the officer as an individual and also positioned in a relationship of power. Althusser calls this positioning **inter-pellation**. Thinking of an actual speech event, however, is merely an illustrative example of what Althusser is talking about. We can also be positioned by (or hailed by) an ideology. More specifically, Althusser describes the Ideological State Apparatus (or ISA), which comprises institutions which are not necessarily part of the state (that is, the government), but that nevertheless perpetuate the same ideological values. The church used to be an

Interpellation

From the work of Althusser, to describe the way people are addressed and positioned by ideologies.

important part of this ISA, and in some places still is. Perhaps the most powerful components now are educational institutions and the media.

For Althusser, ISA communicates and confirms the dominant ideology, most notably in relation to political and economic structure. Globally, we can argue that the dominant mode of political organisation is democracy and that of economic structure is a form of capitalism. Clearly there are alternatives to these; however, in most parts of the world these are the common-sense, taken-for-granted values that are sanctioned by education, the media and the government. We are hailed by the dominant ideology and asked to respond to it. The very fact of being hailed puts us in a particular position. To understand this position, and perhaps to challenge it, we need to look closely at the messages that hail us.

1.5 SUMMARY

In this chapter, I've introduced some of the themes and issues that are taken up throughout this book. Understanding language as a system, with rules, is important in exploring the kinds of variation that we find. Studying language allows us to understand the way in which people exercise power and, in turn, ways in which this can be resisted. The rules that we're interested in are those which explain what people actually do, rather than being rules about what people should do. While some people are uncomfortable about language change, it is inescapable and unstoppable. It is also exciting, as such change is possible exactly because of the creative possibilities that language provides. This is an important language function, but there are others. We started thinking about the relationship between language, ideology and power. This relationship is one that we take up again in the following chapters as it can take some time for this complex interaction to make sense. Studying language allows us to think critically about power and helps us see that what we might think of as 'common sense' is nevertheless, ideological. In the next chapter, we consider the tools we need to think about some of these questions in more depth.

FURTHER READING

Bauer, L. and Trudgill, P. (eds) (1998) *Language Myths*, Harmondsworth: Penguin.

Cameron, D. (1995) Preface in *Verbal Hygiene*, London: Routledge.

Crystal, D. (2005) *How Language Works: How Babies Babble, Words Change Meaning and Languages Live or Die*, Harmondsworth: Penguin, especially chapters 71 and 72.

Crystal, D. (2007) *Words, Words, Words*, Oxford: Oxford University Press.

Crystal, D. (2007) *The Fight for English: How language pundits ate, shot, and left*, Oxford: Oxford University Press.

Fairclough, N. (1999) 'Global capitalism and critical awareness of language', *Language Awareness*, 8 (2): 71–83.

Montgomery, M. (2008) *An Introduction to Language and Society*, 3rd edn, Oxford: Routledge.

Truss, L. (2003) *Eats Shoots and Leaves: The Zero Tolerance Approach to Punctuation*, London: Profile Books.

FURTHER EXPLORATION

Some online resources of different varieties of English

http://www.singlishdictionary.com/
Dictionary of American Regional English http://dare.wisc.edu/
Macquarie Dictionary of (Australian) English www.macquariedictionary.com.au
'Sounds Familiar? Accents and Dialects of the UK'. Multimedia pages at the British Library www.bl.uk/learning/langlit/sounds/index.html
The Speech Accent Archive. English accents from around the world. http://accent.gmu.edu/

NOTES

1   Semantics is the study of the meaning of words.
2   'Marketization *noun*' *The Oxford Dictionary of English* (revised edition). Ed Catherine Soanes and Angus Stevenson. Oxford University Press, 2005.
3   www.americandialect.org/index.php/amerdial/categories/C178.
4   You can listen to these at http://sounds.bl.uk/Browse.aspx?category= Accents-and-dialects&collection=Survey-of-English-dialects.

CHAPTER 2

Language thought and representation

Annabelle Mooney

2.1 INTRODUCTION

To be able to look in detail at the functions of language discussed in the last chapter, we need to have terms for talking about the way language works. In this chapter, we explore Ferdinand de Saussure's theory of signs which will provide a way of discussing how meaning is constructed at the level of the word, how this can change, how words fit together into larger structures (sentences) and what happens when we make choices in sentences. Thinking about words as signs may take a while to get used to; likewise, the use of 'sign' in the technical sense introduced in this chapter can also take some time to feel familiar. These models of meaning matter, though, as they help articulate the way in which small changes can have significant consequences for the meaning communicated. Only when we have this model is it possible to discuss what 'politically correct' means and how such language functions. We will also revisit jargon by exploring the concept of Newspeak, a way of thinking about language deriving from Orwell's novel *Nineteen Eighty-Four*.

2.2 LANGUAGE AS A SYSTEM OF REPRESENTATION

Language is one way of representing reality. There are other signs that we can use to do this: I could take a photograph of something, paint a picture or even write a piece of music. In the definition that we're working with, all 'signs' have two parts: a concept and something that is connected to the concept. The pedestrian signals that tell you when to walk or not are signs because of the connection between the red light and the concept of stopping. Without these two parts, the red light would just be a red light. When we know that red means 'stop', the red light becomes a sign.

Words in language, therefore, are **signs**. For de Saussure, a sign is made up of two things: a **signifier** and **signified**. His definition of the sign makes a distinction between the sound we hear (the signifier) and the concept this makes us think of (the signified). The word sound and the concept it invokes together form a sign. It is important to note 'A linguistic sign is not a link between a thing and a name, but between a concept and a sound pattern' (1966: 66). These cannot be separated in the sign; to try and do so would be like trying to cut only one side of a piece of paper (1966: 113). A signifier needs at least one signified for there to be a sign. If there is no such signified, the alleged signifier is merely a sound that *could* be a word; it is not a sign by de Saussure's definition.

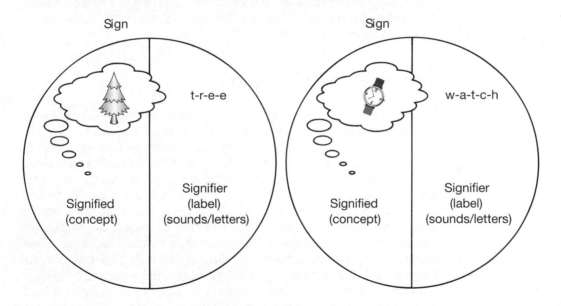

Figure 2.1 Signs are made of signifiers and signifieds

The connection between words and their meaning is accidental: there is no reason why bread should be called 'bread'. Indeed, in the previous chapter (section 1.4) we saw how one dictator renamed bread after his mother. The arbitrary connection between words and their meaning was one of Ferdinand de Saussure's great insights. Saying that the connection between the signifier and the signified is arbitrary doesn't suggest that words can mean whatever we like. 'The term [arbitrary] simply implies that the signal [signifier] is *unmotivated*: that is to say arbitrary in relation to its signification [signified], with which it has no natural connexion in relation' (de Saussure 1966: 69). You might be thinking that signifiers do have a natural connection with their signifieds; for example, in the case of onomatopoeic words or those we use for the sounds animals make. However, while a bee in English will 'buzz', in Japanese it makes the sound 'boon boon'. This shows that there is no straightforward connection between concepts and sounds. Even the sounds of the natural world that we might assume are heard in the same way by everybody are represented differently by different languages. At best, such examples of animal noises and the like are marginal cases and depend on conventional associations (especially when written) or the speaker's imitative ability (in speech).

There is more to de Saussure's work than his work on signs. He is also usually credited with being the founder of **structuralism**, which had great influence on linguistics, literary criticism and the social sciences. We'll look at structuralism when we consider signs later in the chapter. We've already established that language is a system (see section 1.3.1); systems have rules and these rules structure the language. The system of language allows us to talk about and represent the world around us. But just as the relationship between word and meaning is arbitrary, so too is the way in which language divides up the world.

2.2.1 Different kinds of language

De Saussure distinguishes three kinds of language. Recall in the previous chapter the difficulties of knowing exactly what we mean when we talk about 'language'. The three aspects de Saussure details help with some of these difficulties. The first of these is '*langage*' which has been translated as 'human speech' including its psychological and physical aspects, belonging both to the individual and to societies. It is the most general category and contains the following two, which will be our focus here. These two parts of langage are '*langue*' and '*parole*'. You can think of **langue** as competence and **parole** as performance (both in Chomsky's terms). The former is the overarching system, the latter being individual instances of language. While they are treated as separate by de Saussure, they are also closely linked.

Langue is the system that makes parole possible. In so far as langue makes speech possible, it has a social element. As we'll see when we look more at definitions of signs, the social and conventional agreement on how they are constructed is crucial. You can think of langue as the rules of the game, the entire system. A loose analogy would be the rules of chess. When you play chess, you don't play the rules, you play *by* the rules. The rules tell you what is an acceptable move to make and what isn't. You can also think of it in terms of performance and script. De Saussure provides a musical metaphor, comparing langue to a symphony; how good it is as a composition is not related to how a particular orchestra may perform it (1966: 18).

The point is that while individuals draw on langue every time they use language, people don't have direct access to langue. Langue is 'not complete in any speaker; it exists perfectly only within a collectivity' (de Saussure 1966: 12). We can only talk about langue sensibly if we have a community of speakers. You can't have a language all by yourself. This is why there is a social aspect to langue.

The analogy with chess breaks down when we move to the kind of language that we do actually speak – parole. Every instance of language in the world, all actual utterances, are parole. As speakers, we perform parole acts. While as speakers of a language we rely on shared understanding (accounted for by langue), as individuals we can do things in language that haven't been done before. You can construct a sentence that is so odd that you can be pretty confident that no one else has ever said or written it. For example, 'The surly clouds gathered their amusing faces and spat furiously on my new chartreuse coloured coat.' While this is a slightly poetic example (representing clouds as people, with faces and moods) because of langue, the system we all share, you should be able to understand this original parole act.

It is the relationship between langue and parole that is important. The system and rules of langue, unlike chess, can be changed. One way of changing is to legislate, like the dictator in Turkmenistan did. This is very uncommon. It is more usual for change to be slow and to involve many people. Individuals start using a new word, or an existing word in a new way (this is all parole), and other language users understand and adopt this (using it in their utterances). When this new linguistic behaviour is well enough established, we can say that it has become part of langue – that is, it has been accepted as a conventional rule of language, one that we all understand. The last part is important; the new behaviour has to become recognised and conventional, such that other people understand it. That is, acts of parole draw on *and* contribute to the abstract system of langue. As de Saussure puts it 'Language has an individual aspect and a social aspect. One is not conceivable without the other' (1966: 8). The distinction between langue and parole, however, allows us to think through their differences, while understanding that they are linked. It allows us to understand how language use can be individual and original and yet still be communicative.

While this is only a model, it is a useful one as it helps us understand how language works and how it changes. It is the level of parole that we are normally most concerned with in this book, at least as a starting point. There are a number of reasons for this. The first, and most important, is that we don't have direct access to langue. While it would be very convenient if it were the case, langue is not a big book somewhere with all the rules written down. The only access that we have to the rules of langue is through the particular uses of language – that is, parole. From this evidence, we can try and map what the rules are.

The second reason we focus on parole is that as sociolinguists we're primarily interested in how people use language. The creative aspect of language means that speakers will always do things that are different, new and surprising. The concept of langue and its relationship with parole allows us to describe and account for this.

Because instances of parole both draw on and contribute to langue, as individual speakers we have some power over what langue contains. Were we all to decide to call 'bread' 'dice', for example, eventually that would become part of langue. Yet, while many speakers might not make conscious decisions to change linguistic signs, change nevertheless occurs.

2.2.2 Signs and structure

We have described how a sign needs both a signifier and a signified to be a sign. But there is even more that the sign needs: it needs other signs. 'Signs function, then, not through their intrinsic value but through their relative position' (de Saussure 1966: 118). That is, the meaning of a linguistic sign depends on its relation to other signs. I find it useful to think of this relation in spatial terms, where the meaning of each sign is contained in a space. The space that signs occupy fits together, such that if a space is occupied by one sign, then that same space can't be occupied by another. If we take some signs that are related, that are in the same semantic field, it's possible to be clearer about this.

walk, march, stagger, amble, run, jog, dash, sprint

All these linguistic signs say something about moving on one's feet. We might group the first four together, as we can say that they're all kinds of walking. In the same way, we might group the other four together as they're all kinds of running. In semantics, we could look at the relationship between these words. We could argue that 'walk' and 'run' are more general than the others, in that marching, staggering and ambling can all be thought of as kinds of walking. We might want to represent this relationship as follows:

Walk   **Run**

march   stagger   amble   dash   jog   sprint

In any case, while 'ambling' is a kind of walking, it is slower than a 'walk'. 'Staggering' is also a kind of 'walking', but one less orderly and even than a 'walk'. What 'march', 'stagger' and 'amble' mean can be understood in relation to what they do *not* mean. The space that 'stagger' occupies is defined by the space that 'march' and 'amble' occupy. Given this metaphor of space, we can say that 'stagger' means what it does because it does *not* mean 'march', 'amble', 'run' or 'skip'. It also doesn't mean 'breakfast', 'butterfly', 'snore', 'kitten' and so on, but I find it easier to think of the structure of the system of signs in relation to concepts that are more similar to the word I'm looking at. We can say that the space a sign occupies – that is, what it means – is delineated by the spaces all other signs leave behind: 'In language … whatever distinguishes one sign from the others constitutes it' (de Saussure 1966: 121).

In terms of new signs, this means the whole system of signs, the space they occupy, will be reconfigured when a new sign is introduced. If we imagine that only 'run' and 'walk' are the signs available to describe someone moving in a rhythmic way, but not particularly fast, we would have to use the sign 'walk'. However, when we introduce 'march', some of the space that 'walk' occupied will be taken away by this new sign 'march'. That is, 'walk' will no longer be the best way to describe this rhythmic way of moving. This structured space is in the realm of langue. We can alter this space and the place of signs in it by what we do with language in the world, in parole.

The way in which we've been talking about langue makes it sound all encompassing and monolithic. We can, if it helps us in a particular task, talk about the langue of the whole English language. This would include parole from all the different varieties of English: British, American, Australian, Indian, Singaporean and so on. Depending on the kinds of question we're asking, this may make sense. But in thinking about how to use language in a particular context, it only really makes sense to include, for example, Indian English if that is available to those involved in a communicative event. In Indian English, 'wallah' is used to refer to a tradesperson or worker, usually of a particular kind that is specified as the first part of a compound. Thus, taxiwallah is a taxi driver. While in the abstract langue that encompasses all English, 'wallah' would jostle for semantic space with 'tradesperson' and other similar terms, in other parts of the English speaking world it may not be relevant as a sign at all. It would simply be a sound, as there would be no conventional linking of this signifier (wallah) to a signified.

Thus when considering the relationship between various signs, we need to know which signs and relationships are relevant in the communicative context we're looking at. In an environment where people from the Indian subcontinent are subjected to discrimination, it is entirely possible that 'wallah' will become an insult.[1] Indeed, insult terms, especially those linked to ethnicity and nationality, are notoriously diverse and difficult to negotiate for the newcomer to a speech community. We have also to remember that language changes. What were once 'neutral' linguistic signs are now highly insulting. For example, many people object to the use of the word 'niggardly' because of its aural similarity to another word. 'Niggardly' has a very different meaning, however, and is unrelated to ethnicity.[2]

We can talk about these changes over time with the following terms: **synchronic** and **diachronic**. The first, synchronic, refers to a particular point in time. The second, diachronic, allows us to talk about how language changes over time. We need to appreciate both aspects to understand language, as language 'always implies both an established system and an evolution; at every moment it is an existing institution and a product of the past' (de Saussure 1966: 8). We'll see in later chapters that changes over time and comparing variation in language at a particular time are crucial if we're to understand how people are using language and what the significance of any use may be.

Think back to words that you no longer use but that you once did. What did they mean? Do they mean the same now? Why did you stop using them? What would you think of someone who used them now?

2.3 THE SAPIR–WHORF HYPOTHESIS

2.3.1 Linguistic diversity

Because of the arbitrary relationship between signifier and signified, and because signs take their meaning from their relationship to other signs, there is no single way for languages to describe reality. We can call this linguistic diversity, and it is the first part of the Sapir–Whorf hypothesis. The world can be described in any number of ways and languages differ in terms of the signs that comprise them. Sapir was an anthropological linguist and, as such, encountered the different ways in which languages represent the world.

The familiar myth that 'Eskimos' have hundreds of words for snow is relevant here as this myth is based on the idea of linguistic diversity. In 'The Great Eskimo Vocabulary Hoax', Geoffrey Pullum traces the history of this myth and provides the necessary evidence to debunk it. Even if it were true, however, Pullum asks us to consider how interesting this would really be. 'Horsebreeders have various names for breeds, sizes and ages of horses; botanists have names for leaf shapes' (1991: 165). There does appear to be a fascination with multiple terms for the same thing in other languages, but if we look at the variation in a single language – for example, in special-ist fields of English – we also find various names for some things and differ-ent ways of representing reality.

Think of an area of your life where there are a lot of terms to make fine distinctions. This will probably be in an area in which you have expert knowledge, and you might not have noticed the variety of terms. You might refer to all contemporary music as 'pop music' or you might have a variety of words to designate differences. Discuss this with your colleagues; do you all have the same set of terms for different domains?

Figure 2.2 Speed Bump cartoon

2.3.2 Dyirbal

Just as languages encode semantic differences in various ways, grammatical systems also vary. It is the obligatory aspects of grammar that are interesting, the details that a speaker has to specify to have a well-formed, grammatically acceptable utterance. It is worth looking at an example of this. In the indigenous Australian language Dyirbal, whenever a noun is used, it must be accompanied by a noun-marker which indicates which class it belongs to. Nouns, then, are divided into four groups and this must be indicated when the nouns are used in a sentence. Dixon, who described this language, was initially puzzled as to how these groupings were made. He 'noticed that children learning the language did not have to learn the class [467] of each noun separately, but appeared to operate with a number of general principles. In addition, different speakers assigned noun class to new loan words in a consistent way' (2002: 466–7). Eventually, he was able to map these classes:

Class 1: human masculine; non-human animate
Class 2: human feminine; water; fire; fighting
Class 3: non-flesh food (including honey)
Class 4: everything else

(Dixon 2002: 467)

There are a number of other principles that help decide which noun class things belong to. Some of this is linked to Dyirbal mythology. The point here is twofold. First, the specification of noun class is compulsory; a well-formed Dyirbal utterance needs this information. Second, the Dyirbal language divides the world up in a particular way. In the example given here, it allocates nouns to specific classes.

The value of exploring this linguistic diversity – the way in which languages divide the world differently – is that it reminds us that linguistic signs are neither natural nor stable. While striking examples can be found in other languages' division of reality, we need to remember that our own division of reality is worth consideration. In a sense, we need to treat our own language as a foreign language, and examine the relationships between signs. In doing so, we can come to an appreciation of the representation of reality that language performs.

2.3.3 Linguistic relativism and determinism

The second part of the Sapir–Whorf hypothesis is somewhat more controversial as is the issue of what these scholars actually claimed the hypothesis meant. Because of this disagreement about what they meant, the hypothesis is variously labelled, depending on the strength of the arguments, as **linguistic relativism** or determinism. As the name suggests, this hypothesis argues that our language has a bearing on the way we think. The strong version of the hypothesis, **linguistic determinism**, is often called the prison house view of language – that is, the limits of language are the limits of the world.[3] The implication is that if a linguistic sign is not available for a particular concept, that concept is quite unthinkable. But, as we've seen, language allows us to create new meanings, whether these are words for new objects or examples of jargon to keep bureaucrats incomprehensible. If the strong version of linguistic determinism held, it would simply not be possible to do this. As a result, linguistic determinism is not a widely held view.

The question then becomes: does language influence thought and behaviour in any way at all? Benjamin Whorf, who was an amateur linguist and fire inspector, argued that there was some connection between them. In his work, he noticed that people behave according to the way things are labelled rather than in terms of what they really are. The best-known example from his work as a fire inspector is the way in which individuals threw cigarette butts into oil drums labelled 'empty'. Even though 'empty' may signal a benign absence, in the case of oil and other flammable materials, even a small amount of residual material in the functionally 'empty' container can be anything but benign. As Whorf puts it, 'the "empty" drums are perhaps the more dangerous, since they contain explosive vapour' (1954: 198). Despite the very real danger, the 'empty' sign appeared to encourage risky behaviour.

Linguistic relativism, the version of the Sapir–Whorf hypothesis that does seem plausible, is much less confining than linguistic determinism. It suggests that language, as in the case of 'empty' in Whorf's example, does influence the way we think. However, if the connection between language and thought is not absolute (as determinism would have it), then how far does it go? It might help to think of linguistic relativism as exploring the habits of thought that language produces. John Lucy is one academic who works in the field; he uses the phrase 'habitual cognition' to indicate that it is not the strong version of the theory that he is advocating. That is,

> the broader view taken here is not that languages completely or perma-nently blind speakers to other aspects of reality. Rather they provide speakers with a systematic default bias in their habitual response tendencies.
>
> (Lucy 2005: 307)

Lucy argues that the signs and structure of language influence thought. This is a much more modest argument than that of strong linguistic determinism. It is also incredibly useful, not just in considering languages as large entities (for example, the English language) but also in paying attention to more localised and specialised language use, such as the language of botanists. You can imagine that when a botanist sees flowers, she will think about them and (depending on her audience) speak about them in quite specific ways, influenced by the terms of botany. When I see a flower, it is all I can do to identify it as a flower and name its colour. That's not to say that I can't learn how the botanist sees flowers – with enough patience I'm sure she could explain the differences to me. But unless I had become an expert in the distinctions, until I had become fluent in the language of botany, I would most likely still think of all such flora simply as 'flowers'.

Having thought and language habits in relation to flowers may not seem particularly significant. In some areas, however, habitual modes of thinking can be very important. Obviously habits can be changed, but to do so takes effort and will. Moreover, generally, we're not aware of our habits of thought. Have you ever considered it unusual that we describe space in terms of 'left' and 'right', 'ahead' and 'behind' – that is, in relation to a forward facing body? You probably haven't, since this seems normal; it is habitual. In some languages, space and location are described in relation to compass points – that is, whether something is 'north' or 'south'. This is certainly a habit that we all could learn, but it would take time before it was habitual. Until then, we would probably think in terms of 'left' and 'right' and then (with the aid of a mental compass) 'translate' into the new system.

Research on exactly these different ways of dealing with space has been conducted, specifically on how people describe objects in relation to each other. It 'suggests that linguistic diversity aligns with cognitive diversity, as shown in people's language-independent solutions to spatial tasks and unselfconscious gestures accompanying speech' (Majid et al 2004: 113). We explore the habitual connection between language and thought with the example of what you might consider a very basic quality: colour.

2.3.4 Colour

The issue of colour has occupied a number of researchers over the years (Berlin and Kay 1969). You might be surprised to learn that not all languages have the same colour terms. Indeed, some linguists argue that colour itself is not a category found in all languages (Wierzbicka 2005). Here, we take just one example of a difference between two languages that do have colour terms: Russian and English. While English has one basic term for 'blue', Russian has two: 'goluboy' for lighter blues and 'siniy' for darker ones. Of course it is possible to make this distinction in English, but the point is that it is not an *obligatory* distinction. In Russian, a speaker has to decide whether something is 'goluboy' or 'siniy' as there is no less specific term for 'blue'. As Lera Boroditsky puts it, 'Languages force us to attend to certain aspects of our experience by making them grammatically obligatory. Therefore, speakers of different languages may be biased to attend to and encode different aspects of their experience while speaking' (2001: 2). With colour, we are dealing with a semantic rather than a grammatical category, but the argument is the same.

In psychology, the researcher Jonathan Winawer and colleagues investigated the case of blue in Russian and English in order to determine whether the difference in language can be said to lead to a difference in thought. The researchers first asked subjects to divide a spectrum of blue into light blue/goluboy and dark blue/siniy. That is, the experiments first established the boundary for each individual between the two categories. Despite the lack of basic terms for these two blues (English speakers have to qualify 'blue' in some way), the boundary for Russian and English speakers was about the same. The subjects were then given three squares of colour, two side by side and one square below these. They were asked which of the two squares was the same as the single square below. The time this took, and other information, was collected and analysed. Winawer and colleagues conclude:

> We found that Russian speakers were faster to discriminate two colors if they fell into different linguistic categories in Russian (one siniy and the other goluboy) than if the two colors were from the same category (both siniy or both goluboy).
>
> (2007: 7783)

Echoing the quotation from Boroditsky above:

> The critical difference in this case is not that English speakers cannot distinguish between light and dark blues, but rather that Russian speakers cannot avoid distinguishing them: they must do so to speak Russian in a conventional manner. This communicative requirement appears to cause Russian speakers to habitually make use of this distinction even when performing [7784] a perceptual task that does not require language.
>
> (2007: 7783–4)

This provides some support for the influence of language on thought. Remember that this is not an absolute determinism, but rather that we form particular *habits* of thinking based on our language.

2.4 ONE LANGUAGE, MANY WORLDS

Even in a single language like English there are many ways of representing the world. These representations are often the result of particular habitual ways of thinking, or worldviews. The example given above of the botanist is worth recalling here. The way a botanist thinks and talks about plants depends on the botanical language available to them. Obviously if a new plant is discovered, that will have to be named. But when deciding how to classify this plant, the botanist will look at the kinds of features considered important in their discipline. The features that matter to botanists are directly connected to the aims of this science: to categorise and understand plants, trees and other flora. The features that the discipline gives importance to can be understood as being structured by the botanist's (world) view of plants. Colour probably would not be important, but how the plant reproduces will be. We can say, then, that a particular set of values underlies this structure because some things are important and some are less important. Finally, we can call this world view the ideology of botany; that is, the values, ideas and features that define botany as a discipline; the things that are taken for granted in order to conduct the work of a botanist.

We don't tend to think of fields of science as having an 'ideology', as in everyday conversation 'ideology' tends to mean a false or misguided set of beliefs. If we take away the value judgement here, we're left with ideology being a set of beliefs. The reason we tend only to identify the beliefs of other people is because we consider our own (individual and group) beliefs to be normal, natural and obvious. Fairclough calls this 'naturalisation', which he defines as giving 'to particular ideological representations the status of common sense, and thereby mak[ing] them opaque, i.e. no longer visible as ideologies' (1995a: 42). For example, the concept and process of 'globalisation' can be understood as a result of a process of naturalisation in that globalisation is presented as a fact and a thing. We talk and write about globalisation as though it has an uncontroversial existence but, in fact, it has a variety of hotly contested meanings. As non-participants in these arguments, we usually only hear discussion of small details at the edges of globalisation – whether it's good or bad, for example. Its existence (whatever it is) appears to have been naturalised.

While noting there are many definitions of 'ideology' available, Simpson writes:

> An ideology therefore derives from the taken-for-granted assumptions, beliefs and value systems which are shared collectively by social groups. And when an ideology is the ideology of a particularly powerful social group, it is said to be dominant.   (1993: 5)

Here is where ideology links to power. We all have beliefs. Such beliefs become significant with respect to other people when the belief holders are in a position to get their point of view accepted as the norm.

If we look at language, we can see evidence of particular ideologies at work. As mentioned in the previous chapter, ideologies work like filters, changing the way things are represented according to the values of the ideology. You might have noticed that there has been a real shift in the way delivery of government services is described in recent years. Rather than being 'people' or 'citizens', we are now 'customers', 'service users' and 'clients'. This signals an ideological shift towards government services seeing (and speaking to and behaving towards) the public in the way a business or corporation would. The power of government means that it's very difficult to question or change this way of referring to members of the public. Further, particular ways of using language encourage certain kinds of behaviour. The customer–company relationship is different from, for example, that between doctor and patient. If you have to pay for medical care (a key feature of being a 'customer'), you will probably expect good customer service from your medical service provider. Thus, you will expect to get prompt service, to be able to choose your treatment and, if something goes wrong, you might be more likely to sue!

The idea that language influences the way we behave is perhaps most obvious in the case of certain metaphors. Lakoff and Johnson (1980) argue that our thought processes are structured along metaphorical lines. For example, when we describe a verbal argument, we are likely to use words such as 'attack', 'defend', 'won', 'lost' and so on. From evidence of the language we use to talk about arguments, Lakoff and Johnson suggest the existence of the metaphor ARGUMENT IS WAR. We use the language of war to describe arguments. They go further than this, and argue that this metaphor (ARGUMENT IS WAR) actually structures how we think about arguments. The words we use are thus evidence of the way we think for Lakoff and Johnson.

This way of speaking (and thinking) about arguments is probably so familiar that it doesn't seem particularly interesting. The familiarity of these expressions may hinder our attempts to explore any effect they may have. With newer linguistic signs it can be easier to look with a critical eye. At the time of writing, the 'credit crunch' is in full swing. In an article for the American publication *Newsweek*, Daniel Gross refers to George Orwell's famous essay 'Politics and the English Language' which argued against using misleading and imprecise language. Gross draws our attention to the renaming of some of the financial products that were said to be at the root of the credit crisis:

> Remember those toxic assets? The poorly performing mortgages and collateralized debt obligations festering on the books of banks that made truly execrable lending decisions? In the latest federal bank rescue plan, they've been transformed into 'legacy loans' and 'legacy securities'—safe for professional investors to purchase.
>
> (2009)

1 War metaphors are common. Make a list of war terms and then where they are used other than to talk about real battles.

2 As we saw above, some languages place things into different 'classes'. For this activity, it might help to work with some colleagues. Choose some objects around you, and either gather them in one place or mark them in some way. Develop a classification system that sorts the objects into classes. Try to develop some reasons for the classes. You may have trouble allocating objects to just one class! You'll need to think carefully about the objects and the features you use to construct your classes. You should give each class a name. Then, tell some colleagues which class each belongs to, but not what the classes are or how they are defined. They will need to try to figure out your classification system.

   This is exactly the kind of task that Dixon had to work through when mapping the noun class system of Dyirbal.

3 While the previous activity asked you to work as investigator, in this task, the idea is to get a proper sense of how easy or difficult it can be to change your habits of speech according to an unfamiliar convention of communicative competence.

   In the episode 'Utopia' of the British science fiction series *Doctor Who*, we encounter an alien whose speech community requires a very particular competence.[4] Chantho is an insect-like humanoid alien; Martha is a human.

MARTHA: Do you mind if I ask? Do you have to start every sentence with 'chan'?
CHANTHO: Chan—yes—tho.
MARTHA: And end every sentence with…
CHANTHO: Chan—tho—tho.
MARTHA: What would you happen if you didn't?
CHANTHO: Chan—that would be rude—tho.
MARTHA: What, like swearing?
CHANTHO: Chan—indeed—tho.
MARTHA: Go on, just once.
CHANTHO: (nervously) Chan—I can't—tho.
MARTHA: Oh, do it for me.
CHANTHO: No. (giggles)

Over the course of a seminar, or a day (as long as you can), start every utterance with the first syllable for your first name, and end every utterance with the second. If your name has only one syllable, you'll have to use it at the start and end of each utterance. You will probably need to ask people to monitor you, to remind you to do it. Does this start to feel 'natural'? How long does this take?

Naturally, the point in renaming 'toxic' assets is simply to make them appealing products for investors to buy. There is nothing negative about 'legacy', quite the contrary. Gross continues:

> More insidiously, the word [legacy] is frequently deployed to deflect blame. Legacy financial issues are, by definition, holdovers from prior regimes.

This renaming accomplishes a number of things. The assets, formerly toxic, now have an attractive hint of grandeur about them, making them more appealing to investors. Second, if something should go wrong with these assets, a historical past can be blamed: those responsible for providing the 'legacy'. Third, not only do the products sound more promising as a potential purchase, the renaming also remakes the financial news landscape. Instead of alarming reports of 'toxic assets', calling to mind a nuclear accident, audiences hear the reassuring mention of 'legacy loans'. Paying attention to language change can draw attention to ideological choices.

2.5 OTHER ANGLES OF TELLING

It's not necessary to create new words or expressions to convey ideological meanings. When speaking or writing, we constantly make choices. We decide which word to use from a number of possible alternatives, and we decide what kind of grammatical structure we'll use. The structuralist model of meaning that we encountered earlier, when looking at how the meaning of signs depends on their relationship with each other, also helps us to understand the significance of these grammatical choices.

There are two axes we refer to in order to discuss the choices that are made in a sentence. The **syntagmatic** axis describes the order in which words are placed; the **paradigmatic** axis is used to refer to all the other words that could have been chosen for a particular slot. We can think of the syntagmatic axis as being horizontal and the paradigmatic as vertical, as shown in figure 2.3.

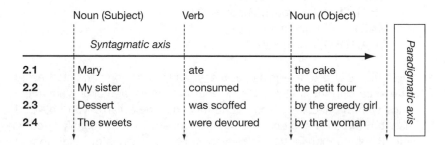

Figure 2.3 Paradigmatic and syntagmatic axis

If we take a simple sentence we see the number of choices available. As we can see from the form of the **verb**, the first two examples are in the active voice and the second two in the **passive**. The active sentences **foreground** – that is, draw attention to the person who ate the food. The passive sentences, on the other hand, foreground the food. Thus, choosing between the active and the passive has an effect on what the reader's attention is drawn to. What the choice of the active means can only be understood in relation to all the other choices that could have been made, in relation to the passive, for example.

The paradigmatic axis has been represented as running vertically. In each position a choice has to be made. Do we describe the woman's action as 'eating', 'consuming', 'scoffing' or 'devouring'? 'Eat' looks like the neutral choice; but it is still a choice. If 'scoffed' had been chosen, a negative attitude is immediately signalled. 'Scoffed' only has meaning because of the relationship it has to all other linguistic signs, and most importantly, in relation to the other signs (verbs) that could have been chosen in its place.

When these choices are made, we're making a decision not only about language and signs, but also about how we represent the world. By paying attention to the choices made along these two axes, we can begin to reconstruct the values and beliefs that constitute a particular ideology. It's important to note that whether or not the choices are conscious, in a kind of premeditated way, they are still meaningful as choices. Indeed, one insight in language and ideology is that what may not seem like a choice to an individual speaker, can nevertheless be said to be chosen by their own ideological position.

2.5.1 Transitivity

To pay this kind of close attention, we need a way of talking about different linguistic choices. There are a variety of theories that make this possible. Here, I provide a scaled down version of Simpson's transitivity analysis. Transitivity usually relates to whether or not a verb needs to take a direct object; 'hit' requires a direct object (someone being hit), while 'sit' does not. Thus, transitivity analysis is concerned with who does what to whom. The difference between this model and one with which you may be familiar is that it has a slightly different terminology. This is because rather than describing the rules for a well-formed sentence (which is what traditional grammars tend to do), this model includes information about the meaning of the clause.

If you look at example 2.1, you'll see that it has two nouns and one verb. If we change the active form of the verb to the passive form, we have to change things around a bit to end up with a well-formed sentence. We have to change the form of the verb (from 'ate' to 'was eaten') and we have to include a preposition ('by') before Mary.

2.1	Mary	ate	the cake
2.1b	The cake	was eaten	by Mary

As discussed above, example 2.1b starts with, and so focuses on, the cake. If we described these sentences in terms of nouns and verbs or subjects and objects they would look the same – that is, both are structured Noun, Verb, Noun, or Subject, Verb, Object. Basically, we need the terminology provided by transitivity analysis that tells us which noun is doing the action to what. The doer is the actor, and that which is done to is the goal. Verbs are always process.

	ACTOR	PROCESS	GOAL
2.1	Mary	ate	the cake

While for me cake is often a goal, you shouldn't think of the term 'goal' in the sense of something being aimed for. Dogs, broccoli and people can all occupy the goal position. The goal 'represents the person or entity affected by the process' (Simpson 1993: 89). Usually, sentences will have more than an actor, process and goal. The detail that is often given can be labelled 'circumstances'.

In more comprehensive versions of this transitivity model, there is specific terminology for different kinds of verbs. 'Thinking', for example, is a 'mental process'; while 'saying' is a 'verbal process'. In a similar way, the other roles have different terms in relation to these processes; for verbal processes, the 'actor' becomes the 'sayer' and the 'goal' the 'verbiage'.

The important thing is that even the stripped down terminology of actor, process, goal and circumstances allows us to describe the relevant difference between our two examples.

	ACTOR	PROCESS	GOAL	CIRCUMSTANCES
2.1	Mary	ate	the cake	in the rain
	GOAL	PROCESS	CIRCUMSTANCES	ACTOR
2.1b	The cake	was eaten	in the rain	by Mary

You probably know that in the passive form, the actor is not required for a well-formed sentence. If we take away the actor, we are left with:

	GOAL	PROCESS
2.4	The sweets	were devoured

Because the actor has been deleted, we call this choice 'actor deletion' or 'agent deletion'. Note that the 'circumstances' can be deleted too, but their removal is not quite the same as the deletion of the actor as circumstances provide additional information. When we are told that the sweets were devoured, we know that someone must have devoured them; they can't have been eaten without some actor intervention. Thus, the deletion of the actor serves to foreground the goal and background the person responsible. Sometimes such deletion may be because of lack of information; we know that the cake was eaten, but we don't know who did it. In other cases, it can be to deflect blame from the actor. Consider the following headlines:

Scientist denies linking H1N1 to NZ (Reuters, 2 June 2009)[5]
Scientist 'misquoted' on swine flu origin (NZPA, 2 June 2009)[6]

It looks like these headlines have a similar structure; but while the scientist is foregrounded in each (by virtue of being at the start), they have different roles.

Actor	Process	Circumstance
Scientist	denies	linking H1N1 to NZ
Goal	Process	Circumstance
Scientist	'misquoted'	on swine flu origin

In the second headline, we see an example of agent deletion (as well as the deletion of 'was' before 'misquoted' – this is common in headlines, so be careful when deciding whether you have an active or passive construction). Despite the surface similarities here, the transitive analysis reveals an important difference. In the first headline, the scientist is represented as doing something – that is, as denying something. In the second, the actor has been deleted. Someone misquoted the scientist, but we don't know who. In this headline, the scientist is, by his or her presence, somehow connected with the error of misquoting, even though he or she was the one to suffer the injustice of being linked to the mistake!

Look at headlines about the same event and compare using the transitivity model. What are the angles of telling?
From 4 June 2009

Al Qaeda says it has killed Briton (*New York Times*)
Fury as al-Qaeda 'behead' British hostage (Mirror.co.uk)
British hostage Edwin Dyer 'killed by al-Qaida' (*Guardian*)
British hostage executed by Islamists in Mali (*Sydney Morning Herald*)
Beheaded (*London Evening Standard*)
Briton beheaded by Al-Qaeda (*The London Paper*)

Activity 2.4

2.6 NEWSPEAK AND POLITICAL CORRECTNESS

Above, I noted that Gross invoked Orwell's essay 'Politics and the English Language'. Orwell is well known for his views on the connection between language and the political state of the world. In his novel *Nineteen Eighty-Four*, the state controls and limits language to produce a new language: '**Newspeak**'. The motivation behind this was that if the state could control language, it could also control thought. Thus, newspeak depends precisely on a version of linguistic determinism. The limiting of language was an actual paring down of words, a simplified version of (in this case) English. When jargon or other specialised language is criticised, usually on the basis that it impedes comprehension and indicates a lack of clear thinking on the part of the speaker, one often finds reference to Orwell's novel. But there is one important difference, noted by Nina Power in a recent article reflecting on Newspeak in the twenty-first century:

> We are certainly surrounded by (even trapped in) a language designed to bamboozle, baffle and blindside – a lexicon that serves the same purpose as Newspeak, namely to make impossible all modes of thought other than that of the reigning ideology. But here it is not so much a question of attenuating language as expanding it. Recent years have seen an astonishing proliferation of coinages, buzzwords and neologisms.
>
> (2009: 49)

While Power seems to allude to the strong version of the Sapir–Whorf hypothesis, speculating that we may be 'trapped' in language, it is important to note that there are different kinds of traps. The trap of linguistic determinism is an inability to think outside of the parameters of the language. One could argue that the trap of specialised language is the inability to think or communicate clearly. It is a subtle yet important difference. People expend so much energy in becoming fluent in what Power calls Nu-Language, that all attention must be focused on linguistic performance rather than, for example, problem solving: 'The Nu-Language that has so dominated the past decade is dangerously self-referential, and all too effective in enabling us to ignore urgent social issues' (2009: 50). This does suggest that there is some kind of reality that language refers to, and clearly at one level this is right. But language can also *create* things to refer to (ideas, qualities and perspectives) and this function (which doesn't depend on a 'real world' as such) can be an important tool in addressing social issues.

Specifically, what is often maligned as 'political correctness' may have at its heart a concern with what we could call representational justice; at least, it seems reasonable to think that language can be used such that it doesn't discriminate or demean. Here too, there are traces of linguistic determinism. If we start with a group that is discriminated against (let's call them 'martians') we could argue that the term 'martian' is pejorative. Then, one might argue that if the word used to refer to them is changed, for example to 'marsites', the discrimination will also end. As we've already seen in Chapter 1, people tend to have strong views about their own language, and may strongly resist any changes made to it, especially if it means that they have to change their own linguistic behaviour. Such resistance often uses the term 'political correctness', which has come to be associated with trivial and pointless changes in language that, as a strand of language reform, often prove offensive even when this is exactly what is trying to be avoided.

Deborah Cameron describes where the term 'political correctness' came from in her book *Verbal Hygiene* (1995). She argues that the history of the term is hidden because it was mainly used in verbal communication, rather than in print. It was originally used in an ironic way by the political left. It was a way to poke fun at themselves for not strictly adhering to their own political beliefs. Thus it was a way of humorously acknowledging the contradictions in their own lives. I might say 'I know it's politically incorrect, but I just had to have one of those cheap dresses; the images of the sweat shop couldn't stop my instinct for a bargain.'

Use of the term 'political correctness' was not to be confined to this group, however. Recall that meaning is use; how a term is used influences directly what it means. Cameron notes that the circulating definitions of 'political correctness' all come from those denouncing a particular 'politically correct' change or attacking the concept as a whole. This tends to be political too: 'the way right-wing commentators have established certain presuppositions about "political correctness" over the past few years is a triumph – as a sociolinguist I cannot help admiring it – of the politics of definition, or linguistic intervention' (1995: 123). Thus, 'political correctness' and what we understand it to mean is a direct result of more or less conscious effort directed at discrediting certain kinds of language reform and those who advocate it. At the same time, and related to people's views on their ownership of language, others argue that PC is an imposition of authority, a command to speak (and perhaps think) in a particular way. In this sense, they argue, it breaches rights to freedom of thought and speech.

Definitions and representations are important. We see this with Pinker's example of the definition of 'event' in the previous chapter (see section 1.2), and here again with the concept of 'political correctness'. While we've looked at the choices that can be made along the syntagmatic axis in some detail with transitivity analysis, we need to see the link between choices along the paradigmatic axis (the other words we could decide to put in any particular slot) and these issues of representation. We can explore this by noting the link between jargon and politically correct speech. Just as expert language

---

The following are some examples of 'politically correct' language: some are actually in common use, some have been reported by the media, but are not actually used at all. Which are 'real' examples. What issue is each addressing?

- Winterval
- Vertically challenged
- Ethnic minorities
- Coffee without milk
- Differently abled
- Thoughtshower
- Senior
- Non-denominational Winter Solstice Evergreen Tree
- Herstory

Activity 2.5

can change the way one represents and thus views the world, so does PC language. An exchange of letters in an Australian newspaper ('Too Young to Know', *The Northern District Times*, 22 April 2009, p 15) links political correctness with 'indoctrination' and a loss of 'innocence'. While one contributor points to the importance of awareness of 'political and social issues' the underlying attitude appears to be that one should 'speak plainly' and that limited or biased representations of the world only occur with politically correct language or jargon. In fact, all representations in language are partial. There is always an angle of telling.

2.7 SUMMARY

The way the world is represented matters. Every language choice, whether we intend it to or not, demonstrates an ideology. While we often consider ideology to be a bad thing, it's important to remember that we all have habitual ways of thinking about the world and this is reflected in the habitual choices we make in language. Because it's habitual, when we agree with the values expressed, we don't think about them. When we don't agree, we may well describe the language use as jargon or political correctness. To be able to think about these issues of representation we need tools such as transitivity analysis to describe these choices. We also have to be aware of the fact that arguments about language are very often political in the sense that they rely on certain assumptions about what is correct or standard. The way that correctness is defined is itself a political act as well as a way of exerting power.

FURTHER READING

Fowler, R. (1991) *Language in the News: Discourse and Ideology in the Press*, Oxford: Routledge

Lakoff, G. and Johnson, M. (1980) *Metaphors We Live By*, Chicago: University of Chicago Press.

Lucy, J. (1997) 'Linguistic relativity', *Annual Review of Anthropology*, 26: 291–312.

Lucy, J. (2005) 'Through the window of language: assessing the influence of language diversity on thought', *Theoria*, 54: 299–309.

Martin, L. (1986) '"Eskimo words for snow": a case study in the genesis and decay of an anthropological example', *American Anthropologist*, 88: 418–423.

Orwell, G. (1988 [1946]) 'Politics and the English language', in *Inside the Whale and Other Essays*, Harmondsworth: Penguin.

Pullum, G. (1991) 'The great Eskimo vocabulary hoax', in *The Great Eskimo Vocabulary Hoax and Other Irreverent Essays on the Study of Language*, Chicago: University of Chicago Press.

Reah, D. (2002) *The Language of Newspapers* (Intertext), Oxford: Routledge.

Whorf, B. L. (1954) 'The relation of habitual thought and behaviour to language', in S. I. Hayakawa (ed), *Language, Meaning and Maturity: selections from Etc., a review of general semantics*, 1943–1953, New York: Harper, 197–215.

You may enjoy a comedy sketch by Stephen Fry and Hugh Laurie which you can find on www.youtube.com 'A Bit of Fry and Laurie...Tricky Linguistics'.

NOTES

1   In fact, in a British version of Celebrity Big Brother, 'wallah' was used in a racist insult to an Indian actress.
2   'Niggardly' means ungenerous and miserly and is not etymologically related to racial terms.
3   The phrase 'prison house' is attributable to the philosopher Friedrich Nietzsche. The philosopher Ludwig Wittgenstein is also associated with the idea. Though he phrases it differently, '*The limits of my language* mean the limits of my world' (proposition 5.6, 1963: 115, emphasis in original).
4   http://who-transcripts.atspace.com/2007/transcripts/311_utopia.html.
5   http://tvnz.co.nz/health-news/scientist-denies-linking-h1n1-nz-2765970 (accessed 2 May 2010).
6   www.3news.co.nz/Scientist-misquoted-on-swine-flu-origin/tabid/420/articleID/106729/Default.aspx (accessed 2 May 2010).

CHAPTER 3

Language and politics

Berit Engøy Henriksen

3.1 INTRODUCTION

In this chapter I look at politics and what this term might mean. I take a broad definition of politics and thus I examine political speeches, the politics of families as well as the politics we find in everyday conversations and in new media. We have already encountered the concept of ideology (Chapters 1 and 2) but it can be a difficult concept to fully understand. It is also important to remember that ideology and power are enacted through specific choices made in language; so ideology will be a point of discussion in relation to the issues in this chapter too. While we can often tell where someone's ideas and comments are 'coming from', in this chapter I introduce some linguistic tools that help us to be more specific about how persuasion works and how power relations are built and sustained.

3.2 WHAT DO WE MEAN BY 'POLITICS'?

We hear the word 'politics' every day, in relation to politicians, governments, law making and international conflicts. It is a term most often connected to those who run nations, states and cities. But how do we define politics, if we define it at all? A narrow definition says that politics deals with decision making and government. In these terms, politics is carried out by politicians. In a democracy, politicians have the power to make decisions on behalf of the public, and the government creates laws that the public have to live by. We have seen that in rare cases, this institutional power is used to change the language (see section 1.4). The notion of power is therefore important when defining politics. The two concepts are closely linked. But while politicians have the power to make decisions that affect a nation as a whole, relations of power are also apparent in our daily life. A broader definition of politics is not limited to the activities of politicians and government. If we take a broader view, politics can be understood as any social relationship which deals with power, governing and authority. This definition includes a range of other relationships in addition to that between government officials and the public: a doctor has authority over a patient, friends can have power over friends, and parents have the authority and power to 'govern' the family. As we will see in this chapter, politics is not just limited to institutions. We might not always notice, but we engage in politics every day.

> What does politics mean to you? Think of your everyday life – what situations do you engage in that can be described as dealing with power, governing and authority relations?

Activity 3.1

3.3 TOOLS FOR PERSUASION

'Yes we can'

What do you think of when you see these words? What associations does this phrase make? 'Yes we can' was a catch-phrase used by President Barack Obama during his electoral campaign in 2008. His election campaign focused on the need for change in America, and he tried to capture this concept in this phrase: we can make change happen. The use of the pronoun 'we' is essential. In using it, Obama aligns himself with the public. It is important to know that 'we' can be used inclusively as well as exclusively. The inclusive 'we', as you would expect, includes the people being addressed. The exclusive 'we' can function in two ways. It may be used to refer to the self and some other people, not the addressees. For example, the leader of a nation may use 'we' to refer to herself and other important government officials: 'We're working hard to fix this economic problem.' It can also be used to include some people, but not everyone. Thus, when political parties address their members at conferences and rallies, they will refer to the party and its followers as 'we' while excluding other political parties and their followers, 'they'.

Obama's 'we' is an inclusive one, suggesting that he as the president will work for society as a whole. The message is that change can happen when America works together. The slogan 'Yes we can' traces back to César Chávez, a Mexican American labour leader and civil rights activist who came up with a similar expression in 1972: 'Si se puede' – Yes, it can be done. 'Si se puede' is also used by the United Farm Workers (UFW). By using an English translation of this slogan, Obama shows that 'we' does not only include the white middle class of America, but all of the nation's inhabitants. During the campaign, the slogan was important because it made people associate positive concepts, such as change and reconciliation, with the presidential candidate. The slogan was used to persuade people to vote for Obama.

The art of persuasion is called **rhetoric**. Rhetoric is a practical skill; a tool to persuade an audience, generally traced to ancient Greece. They came up with a five-step process for speech making: invention/idea, arrangement, style, memory and delivery. By following these steps the speaker would be able to deliver a believable and persuasive speech. The element we are going to focus on is style, or *elocutio*, in rhetorical terms. This step is concerned with how to word the argument, how to shape the text to become as persuasive as possible. It is important not to see style just as something added on to words; style is more than just ornamental, it is fundamental for communication and persuasion. It is important to find the right style for the message you are sending and the addressee to whom you are speaking. The way someone shapes and styles a message can have a strong influence on how we as hearers or readers understand the message. We are going to look at examples from a famous political speech, and look at how this speech makes use of rhetorical 'tricks' to appeal to the audience.

3.3.1 Analysing a political speech

On 20 January 2009, Barack Obama took his oath to become the 44th president of the United States of America. After becoming the president of the USA, Obama delivered his inaugural address: a speech which presented the main themes of his policy. What goal does Obama have in outlining his intentions as the new president? Part of it is informational, but it is also about emotion and connecting with the people of the USA. The inaugural address makes use of many rhetorical figures. These figures of speech are used as a tool to rally the American people, and make them believe in him as a president. During his election campaign, Obama made a number of promises to the people. While the position of president of the USA is in itself very powerful, politicians (even presidents) have to speak to their nations in a persuasive and inclusive manner. Naima Boussofara-Omar describes what is at stake in their political speeches:

> Politicians use language as the site at which they promote, protect and legitimate their power and voice of authority, and rationalize their visions

of political order and their representations of social harmony. Political speeches are a critical locus for translating those visions and representations of reality into words. Presidential political speeches are elaborately composed, scrupulously revised and edited – resulting in numerous drafts – in order to carry the voice of authority and power of the president while they are carefully crafted to be heard as the voice of the collectivity.

(2006: 326)

In his first speech as president, this authority and inclusivity has to be carefully managed. In particular, the new president needs to outline how the expectations he created during his election campaign will be met; as the leader of the nation, he also needs to persuade his opponents of his ideas. How does Obama manage this task? In the following, we will analyse this speech in terms of rhetorical figures and see what message Obama sends to the American people.

Obama begins by addressing the nation: 'My fellow citizens.' The phrase creates a feeling of inclusion for the hearer. While Bush chose to address the people as 'My fellow Americans', Obama chose to include all nationalities and ethnicities in his address and to reference a political individual: the citizen. Already in his introduction, Obama has established an agenda simply through his choice of address terms. Throughout the speech, Obama consistently uses the pronoun 'we' in an inclusive way. 'We' is the pronoun used most often in Obama's speech. This establishes his focus on unity and inclusion: 'We are a nation of Christians and Muslims, Jews and Hindus – and non-believers. We are shaped by every language and culture, drawn from every end of this Earth.' Other pronouns have different functions: 'they' or 'them' are often used to create an illusion of otherness, while 'you' can be used by the speaker to separate herself/himself from the listener.

3.3.2 Metaphor

Forty-four Americans have now taken the presidential oath. The words have been spoken during rising tides of prosperity and the still waters of peace. Yet, every so often the oath is taken amidst gathering clouds and raging storms. At these moments, America has carried on not simply because of the skill or vision of those in high office, but because we the People have remained faithful to the ideals of our forbearers, and true to our founding documents.

In this section Obama acknowledges the past leadership of the nation and thus places himself in a political and national tradition. This is key to establishing his authority in his presidential position.

The **metaphor** as a figure of speech is important in this section. Aristotle defines metaphor as 'giving the thing a name that belongs to something else' (*Poetics* 1457b: 6–9). Thus, metaphors are often used in poetry to create verbal images, to create pictures in our minds. Because the name of one thing is used for something else, connections are made between concepts that we might not have considered as related. While metaphor is most usually associated with poetry and the poetic function of language, Ricoeur reminds us that it also has a rhetorical function (1994: 12) and thus is a tool often used in politics. Obama states that 'the oath is taken amidst gathering clouds and raging storms'. He uses this metaphor to explain that presidential oaths have often been taken in times when the nation has had problems and conflicts. By using a metaphor he does not have to explicitly state what these issues are. Rather, he creates an association with the weather, where clouds gather and storms rage, things which are not initiated by people. Clouds and storms happen naturally, just as conflicts and problems can arise, he seems to say. Obama does not place blame on any individual for the happenings of the past.

It is important to remember that metaphors are part of our everyday language. I. A. Richards claims that 'Metaphor is the omnipresent principle of thought' (1936: 92). Sayings such as 'falling on deaf ears', 'in the same boat' and 'on a silver platter' all have a literal meaning but when we hear them we understand them in a metaphorical sense. Further, as Lakoff and Johnson argue (1980), talking about things in metaphorical terms can influence the way in which we think and behave (see section 2.4). We use these expressions daily, often without knowing that we are using a metaphor. At the same time, metaphors can be used as a tool to understand new and complex ideas by using familiar language.

3.3.3 Simile

A figure of speech which is similar to the metaphor is a **simile**. Whereas a metaphor uses a different concept to describe another, a simile establishes an association by saying that something 'is like' something else. A typical example is the saying 'smells like a rose', which is used to explain that something smells nice.

She is a good boss because she acts like a man.

Sentences like this have been heard when explaining why some female leaders do a good job. The simile creates a connection between the woman's leading abilities and her masculine behaviour. It stops short of saying that she *is* a man, however. This example shows how political language is present in everyday life. The woman is a good boss, but the explanation for this is that she 'acts like a man'. There is seemingly a gender difference when it comes to power and authority. Does a woman really have to behave in a masculine way to be a good leader?

As already stated, a metaphor creates an association between two seemingly unrelated concepts, and is used as a tool in poetry and politics, at the same time as it is used consistently in our everyday language. In terms of politics, it is important because it can make concepts seem either positive or negative, depending on what metaphor is used. In political language, metaphors are used to connect concepts in a way that is beneficial for the speaker.

3.3.4 Rule of three

> That we are in the midst of crisis is now well understood. Our nation is at war, against a far-reaching network of violence and hatred. Our economy is badly weakened, a consequence of greed and irresponsibility on the part of some, but also our collective failure to make hard choices and prepare the nation for a new age. Homes have been lost; jobs shed; businesses shuttered. Our health care is too costly; our schools fail too many; and each day brings further evidence that the ways we use energy strengthen our adversaries and threaten our planet.

Obama tries in this part of his speech to establish what problems lie in front of the nation; emphasising the human angle invites solidarity. The structure here is also rousing as 'the rule of three' is used throughout the paragraph: 'Homes have been lost; jobs shed; businesses shuttered.' As listeners, we are comfortable with three-part statements. We are familiar with the rule of three from writing, speeches and film. The rule of three is especially important in fairytales, where characters and actions always occur in series of three, such as 'goldilocks and the three bears' or 'the three little pigs'. It is seen as more satisfying that things happen in groups of three. This is also true for political language. The rule of three can make things easier to remember, and is often used when trying to make an important point. Particularly in speech, the rule of three provides a rhythm which is pleasing and often persuasive. Other structural features are important for political speeches in providing an appropriate register and rhythm.

3.3.5 Parallelism

> On this day, we gather because we have chosen hope over fear, unity of purpose over conflict and discord.
> On this day, we come to proclaim an end to the petty grievances and false promises, the recriminations and worn out dogmas, that for far too long have strangled our politics.

The two sentences that are placed next to each other here have very similar syntactic structure. They are a response to the problems outlined in the previous section. Obama now tries to give an answer to these issues, a promise that these challenges will be met. This is an important part of Obama's speech: creating faith in the public that problems will be solved. He seeks to persuade people by using **parallelism**. The two statements' similar structure means that we understand them in relation to each other. In addition to using parallelism between the two parts, each also makes use of contrastive pairs. Problems in America will be solved because 'on this day', *hope* has been chosen over *fear*, and *unity of purpose* has won over *conflict*. Contrastive pairs are often used in political discourse. While they may suggest balance, they also help to emphasise the positive, as well as suggesting that issues are easily resolved into two contrasting views.

3.3.6 Euphemism and dyseuphemism

Yet another way of representing events and ideas from a particular angle is the semantic tools of **euphemism** and **dyseuphemism**. Euphemisms are usual when there is a constraint on being explicit for fear of causing offence or distress. This is often related to areas which can be considered taboo, such as death and bodily functions. Thus euphemisms seek to background negative aspects of something and highlight positive aspects. Dyseuphemisms do precisely the opposite: they highlight negative aspects of something and background any positive association. We see both in the following extracts taken from a speech given by former American president George W. Bush:

> On September the 11th, enemies of freedom committed an *act of war* against our country.
>   Fellow citizens, *we'll meet violence with patient justice* – assured of the rightness of our cause, and confident of the victories to come.
>
> (22 September 2001)

In the first, 'act of war' is a particularly effective dyseuphemism for the attacks on September 11. Not only does it highlight the negative, but it also shifts events into a legal frame, as 'act of war' has a specific meaning in international law. This is crucial in establishing a legal right of aggressive response. While such a response might be labelled 'retaliation', in the second extract we see that it is called 'patient justice'. Thus we have a euphemism for violence which uses positive virtues rather than a language of revenge. 'Violence', as used in the second extract, can also be seen as a dyseuphemism, especially when compared with 'patient justice'. Remember that signs take their meaning from their relationships with other signs (see section 2.2.2). Thus while 'violence' might otherwise appear to be a rather neutral term, when it is examined in relation to the other choice that is made, its negative connotations become more apparent.

Euphemisms are rather more common than dyseuphemisms. However, both may require explanation if they are not conventional. For example, recently in the United States, an email from the political organistion 'The Tea Party Nation' included the following in relation to proposed legislation for regulation of financial institutions:

Today is the day that Harry Reid has scheduled a vote to try and *cram* the 'financial reform' bill *down our throats*. This bill is a terrible bill. It needs to be killed.[1]

It's quite difficult to know what this means without the full context. Liberal commentator Rachel Maddow explained the highlighted dyseuphemism as follows:

By which they mean bring it up for a debate using a majority vote. That's cramming it down your throat in tea party speak.

(26 April 2010)[2]

There is another dyseuphemism in the Tea Party excerpt. Where is it and what does it mean?

We have encountered the following tools for persuasion:

■ Pronouns
■ Metaphor
■ Simile
■ Rule of Three
■ Parallelism
■ Contrastive pairs
■ Euphemism
■ Dyseuphemism

Find a political speech or any kind of persuasive writing (it might even be an advertisement, see Activity 3.6). Make sure you understand what these tools are. Find examples of them and explain how they might help to persuade a listener/reader.

Activity 3.2

3.4 HIDDEN IN PLAIN SIGHT[3]

Politicians, like other people, use language to persuade us of their agenda. We are aware that politicians want to change our political views and we know that politicians are able to use language to do this. But when we accept a broad definition of politics, we realise that there are many political situations we may not have noticed before. We may not have noticed the hidden ideology in an online community or the struggle for speaking rights during a family meal. In these situations, the political agenda is much more hidden than in, say, a political debate. That everything is political means that all situations we are involved in are a result of politics but that usually we are not aware of this. We do not always consider that perhaps our thoughts, ideas and actions have been formed by others.

As Geoffrey Nunberg explains, labelling of people who are mentioned in news media reports isn't just about providing information about those people. While Nunberg is dealing specifically with labels relating to political affiliation, the point is probably true more generally, because it's about managing the image of the speaker – that is, the one doing the labelling. Thus, such labels are 'a way of reassuring us that the writer and publication are comfortably in the center, at a safe distance from the extremes on either side' (2002). Appearing to be neutral can be important when trying to persuade an audience of something. You can think of it as ideological camouflaging. There are other ways of making persuasive efforts appear natural. We will now take a close look at how linguistic techniques can assist in hiding things in plain sight.

3.4.1 How to do the hiding

Presuppositions and **implicature** are the terms used to describe assumptions which can be drawn from a text or what someone communicates, but does not make explicit. This means that someone can have an intended message but does not state this message openly. Using these techniques allows the speaker a 'get out clause' in that s/he can argue, 'I didn't actually *say* that.' We will define both terms and then examine a piece of writing to see if you can identify them. It is important to remember that both presupposition and implicature are part of normal everyday communication – that is, like any persuasive technique, there is nothing sinister about them. We tend only to talk about them, however, when we are concerned with power, ideology and persuasion.

A starting point for defining presupposition is that it's like an assumption, something that is taken for granted. But it is more specific than this as it is assumed only by the particular form of the sentence. An implicature, on the other hand, is a conventional conclusion we come to based on what is said; it depends on what we know about the world and the communicative situation (Grice 1975). That is, implicature isn't confined to the form of the sentence. If we take an example this will become clearer:

I forgot to ask my cousin for her umbrella.

You might think that this means that it's about to rain. This would be an implicature. I utter this sentence and my interlocutor tries to find the relevance of it – that is, why would I say it at all. On a sunny day, it wouldn't make immediate sense to talk about umbrellas, so you conclude that it must look like rain. Presupposition is rather more specific but can also be rather banal. The utterance presupposes that I have a cousin, and that she is a woman. It also presupposes that she has an umbrella. It helps to know that if you negate a sentence, the presuppositions still stand:

*I **didn't** forget to ask my cousin for her umbrella.*

This sentence still presupposes that I have a female cousin and that she has an umbrella. You might say that the implicature is still that it's going to rain. Without more information, that might be a reasonable conclusion. But suppose I tell you that the preceding conversation had concerned the fact that I had found an excellent umbrella repair shop that I was about to visit. Then, the implicature would probably be that my cousin has a broken umbrella that I was going to take care of. One useful way of telling the difference is that implicatures can be countered – the technical term is **defeased** – through an explicit denial:

> *I forgot to ask my cousin for her umbrella, but it doesn't look like it's going to rain.*

This sentence is acceptable in a way that the following is not, demonstrating that presupposition cannot be cancelled out:

> **I forgot to ask my cousin for her umbrella, but I don't have a cousin.*

These may seem to be trivial examples. But it's important to remember that not all presuppositions and implicatures have an ulterior motive, apart from the usual efficiency of human communication.

There are some clues that can help detect the presence of presuppositions. We've already seen examples of some of these. In the following, illustrations will be provided, as much as possible, from President Obama's inaugural address.[4]

- *Possessives*: 'To those leaders around the globe who seek to sow conflict, or blame *their society's ills* on the West, know that your people will judge you on what you can build, not what you destroy.' This presupposes that the society has ills. Likewise, The use of 'my' and 'her' in the umbrella example above signal that the 'I' has a cousin ('my') and that the cousin is a woman ('her').
- *Adjectives, especially comparative adjectives*: 'The time has come to reaffirm our enduring spirit; to choose our *better* history; to carry forward that precious gift, that *noble* idea passed on from generation to generation: the God-given promise that all are equal, all are free, and all deserve a chance to pursue their full measure of happiness.' This tells us there are better, and worse, histories which can be chosen; it also presupposes that the idea of freedom and equality is a noble one. Note that what is presupposed may well be something we believe to be true and positive.
- *Subordinate clauses*: 'And we will transform our schools and colleges and universities *to meet the demands of a new age.*' This presupposes that there is a new age which brings demands.
- *Questions (rather than statements)*: Doesn't 'each day bring further evidence that the ways we use energy strengthen our adversaries and threaten our planet?' (adapted from Obama's speech). The

presupposition here is that energy use strengthens adversaries and threatens the planet. The key point here is not so much that the question form is responsible for the presupposition as the person being asked has to accept the presupposition if they respond with a 'yes' or 'no'. The closed question form means that if the person doesn't respond with 'yes' or 'no', they risk appearing uncooperative. If they do respond in that way, they have no choice but to accept the presupposition.

3.4.2 Bringing it all together: an example

In November 2009, Stephen Gately, a singer in the famous Irish boyband Boyzone, died while on holiday with his male partner in Majorca, Spain. Though a post-mortem report revealed that Gately had died from a build-up of fluid on his lungs, UK media spent considerable time speculating on the cause of his death as it was reported that Gately died after a night out with his partner and another man. Jan Moir is a British journalist and columnist, writing for the UK tabloid[5] *Daily Mail*. After Gately's death, Moir wrote an article in the *Daily Mail* titled 'A strange, lonely and troubling death'. We are now going to have a closer look at the article, and try to analyse what political message the article sends out and how it uses presupposition and implicatures to do this.

> Something is terribly wrong with the way this incident has been shaped and spun into nothing more than an unfortunate mishap on a holiday weekend, like a broken teacup in the rented cottage. The sugar coating on this fatality is so saccharine-thick that it obscures whatever bitter truth lies beneath. Healthy and fit 33-year-old men do not just climb into their pyjamas and go to sleep on the sofa, never to wake up again. Whatever the cause of death is, it is not, by any yardstick, a natural one. Let us be absolutely clear about this. All that has been established so far is that Stephen Gately was not murdered.
>
> And I think if we are going to be honest, we would have to admit that the circumstances surrounding his death are more than a little sleazy. After a night of clubbing, Cowles and Gately took a young Bulgarian man back to their apartment. It is not disrespectful to assume that a game of canasta with 25-year-old Georgi Dochev was not what was on the cards. Cowles and Dochev went to the bedroom together while Stephen remained alone in the living room. What happened before they parted is known only to the two men still alive. What happened afterwards is anyone's guess.
>
> [...]
>
> It is important that the truth comes out about the exact circumstances of his strange and lonely death. As a gay rights champion, I am sure he would want to set an example to any impressionable young men who may want to emulate what they might see as his glamorous routine. For once again, under the carapace of glittering, hedonistic

celebrity, the ooze of a very different and more dangerous lifestyle has seeped out for all to see.

(Moir 2009a)

> Before we do a close analysis of this, see if you can 'read between the lines' and say something about the message of this article. What is the angle of telling? Which sentences seem particularly important to this angle of telling? Make a note of them and try to pinpoint the word or sentence structure that makes it important.

Let us now look at the article on a sentence level, by analysing the three first sentences. What do these three sentences tell us? At first glance they say something is wrong with the way the story has been reported and sugar coated in the media, as healthy, fit 33-year-old men do not die in their sleep. But what more do the sentences tell us? What presuppositions are present? First, it is presupposed that the story has been spun into 'an unfortunate mishap'. This makes it seem that other media have taken Gately's death too lightly, almost as though his death was just bad luck. Do you think it likely that a young celebrity's death was really reported as a 'mishap'? Saying that there has been 'sugar coating' tells us that a 'bitter truth' has been hidden. Does the writer really have foundation for making such a claim? Yes, Moir argues, because Gately was 'healthy and fit'. But is that not also an assumption? If Gately died from natural causes due to a heart condition, he could not have been as healthy and fit as she assumes.

The first sentence presupposes that there has been an 'incident'. This is important, because incidents are unhappy events. It also presupposes some bias in the presentation of the story (with 'shaped' and 'spun'). As mentioned above, you can test for presupposition by negating the sentence, as the presupposition still stands. If we take the following example, a negation of the original: 'Healthy and fit 33-year-old men *do* just climb into their pyjamas and go to sleep on the sofa, never to wake up again.' This still presupposes that Gately is healthy and fit.

Looking at Moir's article as a whole, we notice that she not only makes presuppositions, she makes other suggestions too. When we read the article, we might come to some conclusions about Gately's death. We may think that this is because of the article as a whole, but we can be more specific than this. Moir hides a message of infidelity and drug use between the lines. This is not said explicitly. Nevertheless, referring to the 'sleazy' circumstances around his death, the explicit assumption that 'a game of canasta' with the other man was 'not on the cards', and references to hedonism, all suggest that somehow Gately's sexuality was fatal. Remember that **implicature** is something implicit in what is actually said, but communicated nevertheless. Implicatures depend on shared knowledge about how we communicate; as readers, we are really asking ourselves, 'why did she say that?' and coming to reasonable conclusions based on the information and context available. Moir never directly writes that Gately died because of his sexuality, but it is clear we are expected to come to this conclusion.

Many readers found the assumptions hidden in Moir's article extreme. Thousands of people filed complaints, including Gately's record company. But, as noted, the interesting thing with using presupposition and implicature is that the addresser can put the responsibility for the interpretation on the addressee. Because it is the reader that does the interpretative work to get to these conclusions, the writer can deny that the interpretation the reader has made is correct. The writer can, for example, say that the reader's conclusions are wrong, that only the explicit content was intended. Jan Moir made use of exactly this argument in the aftermath of her article.

> Absolutely none of this had anything to do with his sexuality. If he had been a heterosexual member of a boy band, I would have written exactly the same article. It was reported that Cowles went to the bedroom with the Bulgarian, while Stephen remained on the sofa. I have never thought, or suggested, that what happened that night represented a so-called gay lifestyle; this is not how most gay people live. Rather, I thought it a louche lifestyle; one that raised questions about health and personal safety …
>
> As for Stephen's civil partnership, I am on the record as supporting same-sex marriages. The point of my observation that there was a 'happy ever after myth' surrounding such unions was that they can be just as problematic as heterosexual marriages. Indeed, I would stress that there was nothing in my article that could not be applied to a heterosexual couple as well as to a homosexual one.
>
> (Moir, 2009b)

Moir states that the assumptions made by her readers are not her responsibility. On one level, we cannot be sure of Moir's true intentions, but it is important to remember that implicatures work in a conventional way. This is evidenced by the large number of people that understood Moir's message as critical of gay men. While presupposition can't be cancelled out, implicatures rely on shared understandings of how language works. Nevertheless, refusing to accept the understandings other people arrive at gives the writer a 'get out clause'.

The message conveyed by any text, whether written or spoken, is not simply a sum of the specific techniques that we have outlined here. Just as implicature depends on shared knowledge and context, the message that a speaker or writer conveys depends on the context in which their choices are made, the setting in which the text is delivered and the kind of audience that receives it. As Boussofara-Omar comments:

> The salience or insignificance of particular words, through their focalization or de-emphasization, and the prevalence or irrelevance of

particular voices, through their emphasis or erasure, are themselves forms of power. By speaking in particular ways, speakers activate complex webs of associations that link a wide array of discourses and contexts, and by using language in the specific ways they do, speakers construct linguistic selves and create linguistic images of their selves.

(2006: 330)

Politicians certainly construct linguistic selves, but the difference between what they do and what we all do is one of degree rather than kind. We often say that a popular politician has 'political capital' – that is, that they have influence and a certain power to get things done. Those of us not elected to high public office still have certain kinds of symbolic or cultural capital available to us (see section 9.2). How we accrue such capital, and how we are able to use it, depends very much on the ideological context we find ourselves in.

3.5 IDEOLOGICAL CHOICE AS POLITICAL CHOICE

As we have already established, politics has to do with situations of power, governing and authority, be it national law making or where the family is going on holiday. In these situations, language is the tool with which these power relations are constructed and maintained. In the previous section we saw the semantic and syntactic choices people can make to gain political power. In addition, it is also possible to gain power through physical force. Dictators with armed forces do not need to use rhetorical skills to win power over a nation, and neither does a playground bully. They can use their physical ability to force people to give them power. But in a democracy, politicians want us to give them power willingly. For us to give them power, they need to persuade us of their argument – that their political agenda is the best one for us. If we *give* them power instead of them *taking* it by force, we are more likely to follow their governing. The same happens in our daily lives; we may buy certain products because an advertising campaign appeals to us, not because the company *forced* us to do so. But how is it that someone can persuade us to give them power? How is it that someone's political agenda makes sense to us? Part of it is the rhetorical skills that they have, but another significant element is the ideologies they draw upon.

Ideology can be explained as a set of ideas that are used to view the world. As we saw in Chapter 1, everyone has an ideology, which we can understand as a way of describing the set of beliefs and behaviours we think of as natural or common sense. In addition, a community is often bound together at an ideological level – a mutual world view. As we saw, when there is a dominant world view, we can describe it as the **hegemonic ideology**. Ideological power struggles can ensue if people don't agree with the hegemonic ideology in a society.

3.5.1 The politics of the everyday

It's worth thinking about how all sorts of language can have an ideological side. We don't need to be talking about international power struggles for utterances to have an ideological level. If we take an everyday use of language, such as **address forms**, we see that these can signal dominant ideologies and how these ideologies are subject to shifting over time. In modern-day Norwegian, many forms of address previously used to signal politeness and respect have been removed. For younger generations, using formal modes of address for second person ('you'), such as 'De' (singular) and 'Dem' (plural), seems old fashioned and stale. The reason for the removal of these words from everyday Norwegian is not that Norwegians have become ruder, but rather that the language has been shaped by the dominant ideology in society. For centuries, Norway was under the rule of Denmark and Sweden. The upper class of Norwegian society was largely dominated by these nations. When Norway became a sovereign state in 1905, it was important to establish Norway as its own country. Language became a way of establishing Norway's identity. Remember that what counts as a language is often political (see section 1.3.4); 'language' is not just defined in technical linguistics terms. In the twentieth century, Norway went through a democratic process with strong focus on equality. While both Denmark and Sweden had aristocrats, upper classes and a monarchy, Norway was primarily a working-class society. Socialism became the dominant ideology of the nation, and this influenced the language. The focus on equality, seeing every person as the same, made the formal modes of address redundant and out of step with the values of society. Today, teachers, businessmen, priests and customers are all addressed informally and often by first name. Terms similar to 'Mr', 'Madam' and 'Sir' are rarely, if ever, used in contemporary Norwegian society. The only people to be addressed by their formal title are the royal family, where 'your royal highness' is still in use.

To take a very different example, in Lhasa Tibetan there are various address terms arranged in a binary system. Here, I describe a form of address which is gestural rather than linguistic: showing the tongue. This 'is used mainly by the older generation in encounters with highly competent or well-respected individuals such as a well known medical doctor' (Feurer 1996: 48). Anecdotal information suggests that some young people are adopting it, suggesting a comeback. These younger users may also supplement showing of the tongue with 'a further sign of submission, scratching their hair with their right hand' (Feurer 1996: 48). Thus, where Norwegians will use the same term of address to most people they meet, where there are choices, you have to know something about the person to whom you are speaking in order to be able to address the person 'correctly'. (Notice that this knowledge is part of the communicative competence a speaker has to have.) In this way, we see that society's dominant ideology can influence language and that this ideology can change. But our world view can also be shaped by language (see section 2.3).

3.5.2 The entrepreneurial university

In the domain of higher education, there has been a significant ideological shift, especially in Australia and the UK, in part driven by adoption of a particular discourse. The 'entrepreneurial university' is used to describe a twenty-first century university model. The idea is that universities should now change their activity and organisation to focus on new processes and outcomes. The entrepreneurial university should engage in profit activity, restructure the organisation to facilitate market behaviour and focus on efficiency, dynamism and innovation. An ideology which focuses on commercial success has been established. In this model, the discourse of higher education has increasingly made use of business jargon. Indeed, universities are encouraged to see themselves as businesses rather than educational institutions.

The following words and phrases are found in documents produced by universities aligning with this entrepreneurial model (from Mautner 2005). Can you see any commonalities? What values do these terms indicate? What ideologies can be said to produce these terms?

- 'Strong', 'modern', 'dynamic', 'top', 'new', 'innovative', 'young', 'corporate', 'high quality'
- 'Highly, distinctively, active and competitive'
- 'Market driven in partnership with business'
- 'Meeting the durational needs of learners worldwide'
- 'Overflowing with talented students'
- 'World-class researchers and excellent teaching staff'

Activity 3.4

In 2005, Gerlinde Mautner conducted research on the concept of the entrepreneurial university. She states that 'There can be no doubt that in those kinds of sources [university documents], "entrepreneurial", is considered a good thing for a university to be, something to aspire to if you aren't, and to hold on to if you are' (2005: 105). Those sceptical about this change in ideology argue that '*the entrepreneurial research university might violate the soul of academe and that the university which insists on charting an entrepreneurial course runs the danger of turning into a business, valuing capital more than talent* ... if the university becomes business, then *it's no longer a university*' (Banja, 2000, cited in Mautner 2005: 106, italics in original). Arguments such as this depend on a particular view of the university as an institution, particularly in terms of its structure and purpose. Such a view, that universities are primarily about education and research, has been the dominant ideology in the past. However, as Mautner's work shows, this seems to be changing.

This new conception of the university as business influences not only the ways in which universities present themselves but also how they behave.

Mautner found that the marketing of higher education is very prominent in university websites, vice chancellors' speeches and mission statements. Given that governments have also gone a long way in adopting this business model for their own work and self-presentation, it is not surprising that competing views tend to be marginalised. This way of thinking about universities is not new for some countries, but where there was previously a publically funded system, it already appears to be the common sense, dominant view. It is worth noting that the university as business is a metaphorical association, in so far as we are encouraged to understand the university *as* a business. Once this ideology is common sense, however, and once it is naturalised, we no longer see the metaphor. The university *is* then a business. This view is so entrenched that humour can be generated from the idea that students 'buy' their degrees.

Activity 3.5

The following is an extract from an article in *The Onion*. What features of business are attributed here to the university?

According to documents collected as a part of the Justice Department's ongoing investigation, some University of Michigan undergraduates attended classes fewer than three times a week. During these classes, students were asked to do little more than listen to lectures delivered by their professors.

Comey said that, while it seems apparent that the universities under investigation were conducting a monetary transaction, millions of degree-buyers believed that they had not bought, but 'earned' their diplomas.

'The university is very careful to circumscribe the financial element of the transaction,' Comey said. 'The employees who conduct lectures are made to seem above the world of commerce. Students don't give their payments to the professors, nor to the departments from which they purchase their degrees. Rather, checks are mailed to the 'Office of the Bursar,' this 'bursar' being someone who's nearly impossible to track down.'

(www.theonion.com/content/node/30632)

3.5.3 New media

Ideologies are influential in all aspects of life. A new domain in which ideologies are apparent is in new media. We will consider these new media in terms of the change to mass media in the next chapter (see section 4.4.2). For the moment, it is worth thinking about the persuasive opportunities that such media allow. Moreover, it is important to remember that these modes of communication are open to many people, not just to government and large corporations. Challenges to hegemonic ideology can be made via these new modes. That is not to say that the internet is always a challenge to the dominant ideology. However, we examine it here as it provides a good example of how political action takes place in areas which we might not think of as political.

Digital technology connects people all over the world, and the internet has become a place for social engagement. Political discussions and ideological debate are frequent in online communities. Online relationships are formed in part according to these political views, a mutual view of what constitutes 'common sense'. New media is increasingly characterised by user-generated content; this is also true of what we normally conceive of as 'mass media' (see Chapter 4). Where traditional mass media may be subjected to censorship and other less obvious restrictions, new media has made it possible for 'everyone' to participate in the exchange of information and views. Digital communication technology thus creates new types of social networks and new ways of doing politics and new ways of using language. Sometimes this is multimodal – that is, written, spoken and visual all at once.

YouTube is a video-sharing website accessed by millions of users from all over the world every day. People upload videos, view videos and comment on them. The website is a place for social engagement of various kinds. In the following (see Figure 3.1), I examine some material from YouTube which is political, ideological and social.[6]

Stevie is a video-blogger (vlogger). He posts videos regularly, where he talks about his life, asks and answers questions and comments on issues which are important to him. His videos are made in response to other YouTube videos. Together with four other YouTube vloggers, he forms the 5awesomegays collaboration channel. 'Collaboration channel' is a term used

Figure 3.1 5awesomegays collaboration channel

to describe groups of people who come together (virtually) to make a YouTube channel through regularly and consistently posting video-blogs. These channels form an online community. The 5awesomegays channel becomes a place for social interaction, but it also becomes a place for political engagement. They conduct a conversation with each other, and with their 'virtual' audience.

As the channel name suggests, the members of this specific collaboration channel are all gay. This is not the only thing they have in common; in addition they are all white, young, male Americans. But it is their focus on sexuality which makes them stand out from other YouTube channels and with which they self-identify. The 5awesomegays members create an identity in part by developing a distinctive linguistic repertoire, using phrases such as 'stay cute' and a so-called 'camp'-language, to interact with each other and thus to create themselves as a social and linguistic community. One important characteristic of the community is their sexuality. They use their sexuality when making videos – as a resource for humour, to generate topics, as a basis for shared references and thus as a way to perform inclusion and alienation. They set themselves apart from other collaboration channels by playing with their sexuality, performing stereotypes to create humour, referring to gay culture and overtly discussing their sexuality. Sexuality, and a positive view of homosexuality, becomes part of the channel's ideology and thus of their political message. Notice that we can only think of this as a political message if we take a broad understanding of 'politics'.

Activity 3.6

We know that advertising is used to sell us a product and you've looked at advertisements already (Activity 1.4). It's worth looking at advertisements again because it's fun and also because thinking about the political ideologies they might communicate can be challenging. To put it in other words, advertisements don't only sell a product, but also an idea, a way of looking at life – an ideology.

Find an advertisement you think has a political ideology, or just choose an example and then try to figure out what the political ideology is. The following questions might help.

1. Why does the advertiser think that we as consumers should go out and buy this product? Be as specific as you can. What ideology does this rely on? What world view are we asked to accept?
2. Who is promoting the product: is it an expert, a celebrity or a 'normal' person? Why do you think the person was chosen? What kind of symbolic capital does the person have? What would be the effect of another spokesperson?
3. Is there anything political about this message? Remember that the political is associated with power.

Other people are drawn to this world view as audience members at different levels of engagement. In other words, the guys use language and the particular identities they construct to persuade people to watch their channel and to engage in their social network. Significantly, over time, they develop their own in-group communicative rules and norms. Moreover, without specifying a political agenda, they may well shape people's world view and can be understood as being part of a political debate regarding gay rights. This is a powerful mode of engagement as it is entertaining, enjoyable and informative. New media technology allows interaction with people we might not otherwise be able to speak with. It also allows us to connect with people who share our values and world views. Political language and ideologies are not always just about government policies, elections and legislation. If we understand politics as being about how society is organised, how people interact, the choices that are made in representations and the kinds of things that can be thought and said without adverse consequences, everything is political.

3.6 ANALYSING EVERYDAY CONVERSATIONS

Metaphors, pronouns, contrastive pairs and three-part statements are, as we have seen, important tools in political speeches. But as I established in the introduction, political language is not just a phenomenon that occurs in the world of politicians. Every day we engage in situations where we struggle for power. It is important to recognise the political aspects in these situations as well as being aware of the tools that are used by politicians to persuade us of their agenda. We have looked at how language can be used to influence ideas about the role of universities and the way language is used in new media such as the internet in order to move away from a restrictive understanding of the political. Hopefully you will have realised that the persuasive strategies that politicians use are exactly the same ones you might use to convince someone to do something. Thinking about our own everyday communication as political reminds us that every communicative event negotiates and constructs a particular relationship. Power is always a potentially important part of this negotiation.

The home life of a family is one arena where political debate takes place. 'Families are political bodies in that certain members review, judge, formulate codes of conduct, make decisions and impose sanctions that evaluate and impact the actions, conditions, thoughts and feelings of other members' (Ochs and Taylor 1992: 301). The different members of a family have authority over each other and can influence the way other members act and think. In their research, Ochs and Taylor looked at the family dinner as a political event. They looked at the way in which different family members talked to each other and exchanged stories, and questioned each other's behaviour, during a family meal.

Example 1

Mother: Oh:: You know what? you wanna tell Daddy what happened to
    you today?=

Father: Tell me everything that happened from the moment you went
    in -until:

Example 2

Mother: Jodie tell Daddy then what happened.

                                             (1992: 324)

Following these utterances, the child goes on to tell a story of the day's
events. These examples are similar to the conversations which happen in
many other families. During the family meal, the children of the family tell
more stories than the parents. But the stories they tell are very often initiated by the parents. The parents can control the conversation and positively
or negatively evaluate their reported behaviour and the way they tell their
stories. They have the power to decide topics and conversation direction.
You can probably think of many other occasions in your home life where
parents have authority and express this verbally.

Other forms of control exist and are obvious at a more local level.
'"Conversational dominance" is the phrase used to refer to strategies which
enable speakers to dominate their partners in talk' (Coates 1998: 161). The
way one party in a conversation can dominate the other is a clear example
of situations where the struggle for power is won. In a 1977 study, West and
Zimmerman found that men often dominate women in conversations:

Female: How's your paper coming?=

Male: Alright I guess (-) I haven't done much in the past two
           weeks.

(1.8)

Female: Yeah::: know how that can

Male: Hey, ya' got an extra cigarette?

(-)

Female: Oh sure ((hands him the pack)).
            Like **my** pa

Male: How 'bout a match?

(1.2)

Female: Ere ya go uh like **my** pa

Male: Thanks

(1.8)

Female: Sure (-) I was gonna tell you my

Male: Hey, I'd really like ta' talk
                            but I gotta run (-) see ya

(3.2)

Female: Yeah

                    (adapted from West and Zimmerman 1998: 172)

In this exchange the female is completely silenced. The male dominates the conversation and does not listen to a word of what she is saying (see section 5.6.2). West and Zimmerman found that the men in their data often used certain strategies, such as interruption, giving no response, providing a delayed response or simply remaining silent to dominate conversations with women (see Chapter 5). Do these findings sound right to you? The study by West and Zimmerman was carried out in 1977. Is the difference in conversational power still there today?

Next time you are with more than one member of your family (or a group of friends), make a note of the roles people play. For example, who asks questions? Does one member ask others for stories (perhaps by asking how their day was)? Do some people question behaviour of others? Do some talk more than others? Taking note of this kind of detail will allow you to make a 'political portrait' of your own family/friends. This is even something you might do using the classroom as your data site.

Activity 3.7

3.7 SUMMARY

Wherever there is power there is politics; wherever there is politics there Is power. In this chapter we started with what is traditionally understood as politics and then examined how other situations can also be understood as political. This was done to explore the different ways in which people use language to create and exert power. We saw that ideology is a crucial part of this. Moreover, the detail of language is essential in the construction, acceptance, maintenance and indeed critique of ideological positions. Politicians, parents, the media and individuals all have a political agenda of some kind or another in that we all have ideologies. We all have a certain view of the world that we accept as natural. As language producers, we all have the ability to shape our messages in particular ways and thus influence the minds of our addressees. The **rhetorical** tools that politicians use are exactly the same that other people use. Nevertheless, metaphors, presuppositions and so on are so much part of everyday language use that they can easily be hidden in plain sight. As audience members, it is important that we are aware of the bias that different media broadcasters can have. When listening to politicians or other people with authority, it is important that we are critical about what we hear and see.

FURTHER READING

Beard, A. (2000) *The Language of Politics*, London: Routledge
Boussofara-Omar, Naima (2006) 'Learning the "linguistic habitus" of a politician: a presidential authoritative voice in the making', *Journal of Language and Politics*, 5(3): 325–8.

Carter, R. et al (2001) *Working With Texts*, London: Routledge.

Fairclough, N. (2000) *New Labour: New Language?* London: Routledge.

Grice, H. P. (1975) 'Logic and Conversation', in P. Cole and J. L. Morgan (eds), *Syntax and Semantics, vol. 3: Speech Acts*, New York: Seminar Press, 46–58.

Herring, S. C. (2001) 'Computer-mediated discourse', in T. D. Schiffrin, and H. Hamilton (eds), *The Handbook of Discourse Analysis*, Oxford: Blackwell, 612–634.

Johnstone, B. (2008) *Discourse Analysis*, 2nd edn, Oxford: Blackwell.

Mautner, G. (2005) 'The entrepreneurial university – a discursive profile of higher education buzzwords', *Critical Discourse Studies*, 2 (2): 95–120.

Nunberg, Geoffrey (2002) 'Media: label whores', *The American Prospect,* 13 (8). Online: www.prospect.org/cs/articles?article=media_label_whores (accessed 20 July 2010).

Ochs, Elinor and Carolyn Taylor (1992) 'Family narrative as political activity', *Discourse & Society,* 3 (3): 301–340.

Orwell, G. (1988 [1946]) 'Politics and the English language', in *Inside the Whale and Other Essays*, Harmondsworth: Penguin.

Simon-Vandenbergen, A.-M. White, P. R. R. and Aijmer, K. (1999) 'Presupposition and "taking-for-granted" in mass communicated political argument: an illustration from British, Flemish and Swedish political colloquy', in Fetzer, A. and Lauerbach, G. (eds), *Political Discourse in the Media: Cross-Cultural Perspectives*, Pragmatics and Beyond New Series, Amsterdam: John Benjamins, 31–74.

Thornborrow, J. (2002) *Power Talk: Language and Interaction in Institutional Discourse*, Harlow: Longman.

NOTES

1   http://ragingdebate.com/economy/stop-doddgy-financial-reform (accessed 2 May 2010).

2   www.msnbc.msn.com/id/36799387/ns/msnbc_tv-rachel_maddow_show/ (accessed 2 May 2010).

3   The idea of being 'hidden in plain sight' comes from an Edgar Allen Poe short story, 'The Purloined Letter'.

4   The following has been adapted from the previous edition, Jones and Stilwell Peccei, pp 42–3.

5   A tabloid is a newspaper of small format giving the news in condensed form, usually with illustrated, often sensational material. See section 4.2.1.

6   www.youtube.com/user/5awesomegays#p/u/558/VLlbDdlFZ9U.

CHAPTER 4

Language and the media

Anthea Irwin

4.1 INTRODUCTION

Before discussing language in the media, it is necessary to define what we mean by 'the media', because the definition is not as simple as it might initially seem. The more 'obvious' aspects of media include television, radio and the press, which would traditionally have been called the 'mass media', referring to the fact that the same media message was reaching a mass of people. The media is currently in a state of flux, however, and the relationship between producer, message and audience has to be revisited. The development of online and digital communications has changed the role of the audience member so that we are much more active; we construct and consume the media. This is not to say that audiences previously just accepted what 'they' in the media said.

Nowadays, however, to take news as one example, audiences can choose what news they consume: some digital television channels offer a range of viewing options, extra 'mini screens' of information and so on; viewers can leave comments on news stories on the websites of TV channels and newspapers; and they can produce their own alternative news via blogs, social networking sites, YouTube and so on (see section 3.5.3). There is the possibility for traditional audience members to shift from being consumers to being producers and the name given to this is 'citizen producers', 'citizen journalists' or 'user-generated content'.

This chapter will begin by considering what is still a key site for exploring language, society and power: the traditional, yet changing, genres of press and broadcast news. We then take a more expansive view of the media by considering other kinds of programmes from television and online media. Thus, we consider the ways in which comedy and satire challenge current power relationships, at least in imagined worlds, and will end by considering the implications of new media for interpersonal and wider societal relationships, and the nature and profile of the language itself. All the areas we look at have something in common: it is *mediated* communication. There is something that stands between the speaker/author and audience. This may be simply the form of the media (newspaper, television etc), but each form has its own constraints and affordances: editors, advertisers and the technological possibilities can shape the message in various ways.

4.2 NEWS COVERAGE

Telling a news story is not a simple case of 'telling the truth'. Yes, journalists have strict guidelines to follow and they must avoid defaming individuals. But it is impossible to translate events fully into language, just as it is impossible to fully appreciate a piece of music or a piece of art via a description or review of it. As soon as language is used to represent something, it undergoes a change. To use an old, but still pertinent, example, one person's 'terrorist' is another person's 'freedom fighter'. The topics we examined in Chapter 2 are relevant here. Whenever language is used, representational choices are made. There is always an angle of telling.

Fowler (1991) draws our attention to the implications of word choice and of **transitivity**, or the verb processes employed, for how an event, and the news actors involved in it, are viewed, and therefore saying 'A shot B' is quite different from saying 'B was shot' and different again from saying 'There was a shooting'. We can analyse this in terms of the transitivity model explored earlier (see section 2.5). These choices alter the focus of a news story, making some people and events more visible and relevant than others, implications for representation in general, and where responsibility is seen to lie in particular.

Fairclough (1995b) talks about 'degrees of presence', the fact that different aspects of an event can be foregrounded, backgrounded or not mentioned at all, or simply presupposed – that is, taken for granted (see section 3.4). This can occur simply because of where in the newspaper a story is, which part of it is chosen for the headline focus, and where in the article different points appear. Van Dijk (1998) brings in a relational aspect when he observes a common relational pattern in news discourse that he labels the 'ideological square'. This consists of an 'us' group and a 'them' group with the 'good' and 'bad' acts of each being variously highlighted or mitigated. The four 'sides' of the square can be described as follows:

1. Emphasize our good properties / actions
2. Emphasize their bad properties / actions

3. Mitigate our bad properties / actions
4. Mitigate their good properties / actions

(van Dijk 1998: 33)

We often see this in reports of wars in which the reporting country is involved. Examining who is 'us' and 'good' in a story can give us an insight into the particular ideology of a news producer.

While we can analyse representational differences at the level of the sentence or clause, Michel Foucault reminds us that there are various competing 'discourses' or ways of speaking about any issue, and these compete to become 'dominant discourses', akin to the hegemonic ideologies we have already discussed (see section 1.4). We can think about these discourses as comprising recurring representations (for us, through language) of values, points of view and ideologies. When we group all these things together, it is useful to think about discourse as a representational lens. The metaphor of a lens is useful as we can think of representations in the media as akin to a version of the world viewed through a 'filter' of values.

For example, a person with strong conservative views will see the world and events, and represent them, in a particular way. At the time of writing, legislation increasing access to health care has just been passed in the USA. Those who think government should be as small as possible, a conservative view, understand this legislation as government interference with individual liberties. Conservatives see the legislation through their ideological lens. When they express their views, they draw attention to this government interference, labelling the move as 'socialist' or even 'communist'. Those on the other side of the political spectrum view the legislation as positive, as increasing equality and reducing individual hardship. Their representational lens can be understood as filtering out the issue of 'government interference' and foregrounding the benefits they see for individuals. The same event, the passing of a particular piece of legislation, is viewed and represented very differently by people with different values and ideologies. In this context, it might be helpful to recall the Sapir–Whorf hypothesis (see section 2.3). Ideologies can be understood as having a language attached; this is key to understanding the world and communicating this understanding to others.

Immigration and crime are two areas subject to this kind of representational filtering. The case study below looks at an event in an asylum detention centre which touches on both, so it is relevant to think first about more general discourses around asylum in particular and immigration more generally. A 'threatening' discourse of asylum can be exemplified as follows: 'These people are coming to our country and taking our jobs and our homes and leaving us in a worse situation than we were in before'; a rather different 'humanitarian' discourse of asylum can be exemplified with the words 'Of course we should welcome people who are having to flee war, persecution and poverty in their home country; we would hope that others would do the same for us.' The first of these is often associated with conservative politics and the second with a more liberal politics. Again, we are dealing with exactly the same event, immigration, but the two representations are so different, it is as though we are talking about two very different phenomena.

We have seen that labelling things and changing word order can have significant effects. If we move beyond the word and the clause, we find that there are other ways of representing events. One of these is by making choices about how to report the order of the events that occurred. The socio-linguist Alan Bell (1998), who has been a working journalist, points out that news narratives, unlike most informal oral narratives, are not chronological: news reports generally start not with what happened first, but what the authors consider to be most important. This is very clear when looking at newspaper headlines. The result of this, Bell argues, is that it is possible to suggest a number of relationships between the events in terms of what led to what, or even to leave out some events altogether. In reporting on a war, for example, who 'started' it is often subject to debate and different viewpoints. The party said to be responsible for the start of hostilities might not be the party that acted first. Remember that events are always happening; deciding which events are relevant to an ensuing war is not always obvious. Hostilities may start with gun fire or with an insult; which event is chosen as being responsible is very much an ideological and representational choice.

4.2.1 A case study of asylum in the news: unrest in detention

16 in asylum riot quiz

Figure 4.1 *The Evening Times* headline

Arrests after violence at detention centre

Figure 4.2 *The Herald* headline

£500,000 cost of riot at the asylum 'hotel'

Figure 4.3 *The Scottish Daily Express* headline

Explanatory note: In the UK, there are two main types of newspaper, tabloids and broadsheets. A tabloid is a newspaper of small format giving the news in condensed form, usually with illustrated, often sensational material. A broadsheet is a newspaper of larger format which gives the news in a more extended form; 'quality' is a similar term, which is becoming increasingly useful given some traditional 'broadsheets' have contracted their size and are sometimes referred to as 'compacts'. A 'middle market' newspaper sits somewhere between the two.

While even a summary of the events reported here will have its own angle of telling, it is useful to try to provide a basic background to the events reported on below, albeit without necessarily making cause and effect links between them; the ways in which the various newspapers do or do not do this forms part of the analysis. On 20 July 2004, a detainee at the Harmondsworth detention centre outside London committed suicide, there was some violence at the centre, and some detainees were moved to Dungavel detention centre in Lanarkshire, Scotland. Let's now look at how a sample of three papers reported this and consider the implications for representations of asylum seekers, police, government and others, and for wider societal relations between these groups. Throughout the analysis I have emphasised in italics what I believe to be key words.

The Evening Times (a 'tabloid' regional paper based in Glasgow) was the only paper in the sample to carry the story on Tuesday 20 July. The story appears at the top of page 6. The headline reads: '*Riot* after asylum seeker's *death*'. This is the only headline that includes any reference to the suicide and thus the only one which suggests any kind of link between that and the violence occurring. However, note that the word 'death' rather than 'suicide' is used. The paper may have taken the decision to use this label because the full facts of the case had not yet been released by the police. The chief inspector of prisons, Anne Owers, is quoted as saying that Harmondsworth detention centre was 'failing to provide a safe and stable environment' and that 'this was reflected in increasing levels of disorder, damage and escape attempts'. This implies that these problems could have caused the suicide.

The Evening Times continues the story on 21 July. It appears on page 4 in the 'Britain today' section with the headline '16 in asylum riot *quiz*' (Figure 4.1), signalling there are unanswered questions about the event and therefore problematising blame rather than attributing it. The lead sentence reads: 'Sixteen men are today being quizzed by police about *riots* that rocked a refugee centre.' Simple though it seems, to label the asylum seekers 'men' allows them more complex identities than usual; as they are more usually described as ungendered and unspecific 'asylum seekers'. Although the word 'riots' is an emotive one and perhaps questionable in the circum-stances, the syntactic construction 'riots that rocked a refugee centre' puts the abstract noun 'riot' in the position of agent rather than placing the asylum seekers there and, again, does not attribute blame.

The Herald (a 'broadsheet' regional paper based in Glasgow) carried the story on Wednesday 21 July on the bottom half of page 4. The headline (Figure 4.2) reads: 'Arrests after violence at detention centre'. The first reference to the death/suicide is in the following sentence: 'The tornado unit, a squad of prison officers with a *formidable* reputation for swiftly bringing control back into the hands of the authorities, was *deployed* early yesterday to *quell* the disorder which broke out within hours of the death.' The military discourse is striking here with the use of the words 'deployed' and 'quell', reinforcing the stereotype of the asylum 'problem' as a two-sided 'battle'. However, describing the reputation of the prison officers as 'formidable' may suggest heavy-handedness. While asylum, and asylum seekers, are represented as a problem, it could be argued that the military style of dealing with the 'problem' is criticised rather than seen as necessary.

The Scottish Daily Express (the Scottish edition of a UK middle market paper) also carried the story on 21 July, on page 3, taking up the whole page. The headline reads: '£500,000 cost of riot at the asylum "*hotel*"' (Figure 4.3). The focus is on cost and the article is rather decontextualised – that is, the full focus is on the 'riot' itself, and we are given very little background (context); the suicide, for example, is not mentioned until later. The use of the word 'hotel' in the headline, and later attributed to Mr Kehra, one of the centre's chaplains, arguably *recontextualises* the situation by suggesting the asylum seekers had no reason to 'riot' given their favourable conditions (staying in a 'hotel'), which redoubles the negative connotations applied to the detainees. It is *recontextualising* as it places events in a *new* frame by calling the facility a 'hotel'.

War metaphors are present in *The Express* article as in *The Herald* article, but in *The Express* article the blame lies squarely with the asylum seekers: 'Riot *forces* fought a 16 hour *battle* to *quell an uprising* by asylum seekers yesterday at the UK's leading detention centre.' The 'us and them' differentiation is further reinforced by the following sentence: 'Rapid-response "Tornado unit" prison officers were called in to *corner* 80 rioting inmates.' Using a word normally associated with the hunting of animals dehumanises the asylum seekers involved, thus further disempowering them.

Activity 4.1

Choose three newspaper articles covering the same event and compare and contrast them in terms of:

- word choice (Do the words have positive or negative connotations? Do they conjure up a common image?)
- sentence structure (Who/what is present in/absent from the sentence? Who is doing what to whom and how?)
- story structure (How does the headline relate to the news story as whole? Can you work out from reading the story what led to what? Draw a time line if that helps.)

4.3 MEDIA VOICES: ACCENT, DIALECT AND REGISTER

4.3.1 News media voices

In the material just analysed, the voices of the asylum seekers were not fully represented. When we listen to the news on radio or television, what voices do we hear? The answer, regardless of which country we are listening or watching in, is primarily voices speaking the standard variety of the official language with a recognisably middle-class **accent**. Why should this be the case? The people who speak with this kind of voice are in a distinct minority in any society, so wouldn't it make more sense to have the news read in the voice(s) of the majority? This poem by Tom Leonard deals with some of the issues from a particular UK perspective. You can listen to the poem,[1] and I have glossed it into Standard written English.

this is thi	This is the
six a clock	Six O'clock
news thi	News the
man said n	man said and
thi reason	the reason
a talk wia	I talk with a
BBC accent	BBC accent
iz coz yi	is because you
widny wahnt	wouldn't want
mi ti talk	me to talk
aboot thi	about the
trooth wia	truth with a
voice lik	voice like
wanna yoo	one of you
scruff. if	scruff. If
a toktaboot	I talked about
thi trooth	the truth
lik wanna yoo	like one of you
scruff yi	scruff you
widny thingk	wouldn't think
it wuz troo.	it was true.
jist wanna yoo	Just one of you
scruff tokn.	scruff talking.
thirza right	There's a right
way ti spell	way to spell
ana right way	and a right way
to tok it. this	to pronounce it. This
is me tokn yir	is me pronouncing the
right way a	right way of
spellin. This	spelling. This
is ma trooth.	is my truth.
yooz doant no	You don't know
thi trooth	the truth
yirsellz cawz	yourselves because
yi canny talk	you can't speak
right. this is	properly. This is
the six a clock	the Six O'clock
nyooz. belt up.	News. Shut up.

By writing in a way that represents the speech of a person with a broad Glaswegian **accent** and **dialect**, in this poem Tom Leonard suggests that the choices made regarding presentation of the news have a lot to do with power and with language attitudes (see Chapters 2 and 10). His use of 'thi man' in lines 3 and 4 contains echoes of the fact that we often refer to the media as 'they', something detached from and distant from us, and depersonalised. Leonard's poem suggests that the news only has authority when it is presented in a standard language, and that this continues because speakers from all backgrounds appear to concur on this. He goes as far as to say that 'trooth'/truth is contingent on the voice it is presented in ('yooz doant no the trooth yirsell cawz ye canny talk right'/'you don't know the truth yourselves because you can't speak properly).

A theoretical concept introduced by Michel Foucault is helpful here (1980). Foucault coined the term 'power/knowledge' because he believed the relationship between the two aspects was so close as to warrant a term that rendered them indivisible. The backslash mid-term suggests a fusion of power and knowledge – that is, that they are part of the same process or attribute. Recalling what de Saussure had to say about the nature of the

Activity 4.2

1. What was your reaction to Tom Leonard's poem? Do you think you would be less likely to believe news reported in a broad accent and/ or dialect? What does this suggest about your own attitudes to different language varieties? Is it possible to say which varieties you would find more persuasive?

2. Look at the cartoon in Figure 4.4. What does this suggest in terms of attitudes towards Glaswegian? What does this mean in terms of power?

Figure 4.4

sign may be useful here, that trying to separate the two 'parts' (the signifier and signified) would be like trying to cut one side of a piece of paper. In this way, we can think of power and knowledge in Foucault's term as being two sides of the same thing, the same piece of paper. While we might distinguish between the two for theoretical reasons, it is important to remember that cutting them into separate parts is impossible.

'Power/knowledge' suggests two things: that having knowledge gives you power; and, more importantly for our project here, that what the powerful have to say will be more likely to be taken as knowledge and, by extension, truth. The powerful are always those who speak and write in the 'right way': 'thirza right/ way ti spell/ ana right way/ to tok it' (there's a right way to spell and a right way to pronounce it). If there's a right way, there's also a wrong way (see Chapter 10).

4.3.2 Register

It is not just the voices we hear on the new that are an expected type, so too is the format. We expect to hear serious topics presented to us in a relatively formal way, although within these limits there are some variations. To analyse this technically it is necessary to consider the concept of **register**. Register might just seem to be a technical term that makes more complicated what is already part of language users' knowledge. As Agha notes, 'Speakers of any language can intuitively assign speech differences to a space of classifications of [different registers] and, correspondingly, can respond to others' speech in ways sensitive to such distinctions' (2004: 23). That doesn't mean that we have a command of all of them, or that we can precisely analyse register in order to make sense of these differences. But competence in particular registers can be crucial in gaining access to power as, 'An individual's register range − the variety of registers with which he or she is acquainted − equips a person with portable emblems of identity, sometimes permitting distinctive modes of access to particular zones of social life' (Agha 2004: 24). That is, competence in particular registers is a kind of **symbolic capital**. Here we focus on how we might analyse the register of texts that are reasonably well established. While register in conversation can be subject to negotiation and development, the forms used in the mass media are comparatively stable. This does not mean, however, that there are not changes over time. This relative stability also means that humour can be generated by exploiting aspects of register, as we see below.

Register has been defined as **linguistic variation** according to the context of use (Halliday 1978). This means that we expect to find language used in different ways according to the situation in which it occurs; for example, the discussion between students in a seminar or tutorial class is likely to be rather different from their discussion after class in the cafe or pub. We expect differences according to different types of media too; for example, we expect 'tabloid' newspaper coverage to be rather more informal and sensational than 'broadsheet' newspaper coverage. There are three aspects to register: **field**, **tenor** and **mode**. Field is the topic or subject matter, tenor is the style, level of formality etc, and mode is the channel of communication used; for example, speech, writing, visuals, or a mixture of these. In general terms, traditional expectations of news broadcasting are that the field will be serious subject matter, the tenor will be formal and the mode will be one newsreader sitting behind a desk and delivering the news via speech. What we think of as formal, however, is subject to change. The way in which the news is presented on television now is very different from how it was presented when broadcasting first started.

Activity 4.3

Watch a range of news broadcasts on the same day and comment on the field, tenor and mode employed in each. If they are on at the same time, you may be able to watch them on the internet. Can you observe patterns according to the remit of the television channel and/or its main audience? Describe them in terms of field, tenor and mode.

We all have some competence in detecting and deploying various registers. This is not always something that requires a conscious choice. Alan Bell's research (1984) on radio presenters in New Zealand shows that the same person, speaking to different audiences, will change even the fine detail of their language (see section 9.6.1). The choices that authors make will usually be influenced by the audience they are addressing. If the audience does not have the competence required to make sense of the register, the programme can hardly be successful. The following section deals with comedic manipulation of register, but this relies on the audience knowing the codes being used. There have been various instances of audiences misreading such manipulation, resulting in complaints about what was intended to be ironic or satirical, being perceived as offensive.[2]

4.3.3 'Playing with' register: hoaxes, satire and comedy

The same expectations of linguistic register apply to other media **genres**; there are conventions of appropriate language use for specific types of programme. Where these conventions are well established, 'playing with' them makes for intelligent hoax, satire and comedy: in a hoax, the form in which something is presented can outweigh the content; in satire and comedy the boundaries of the conventions are pushed, but not crossed, which results in a recognisable situation made somewhat strange, which in turn allows for satirical comment on the original situation.

A famous media hoax used a well-established media format (the documentary) to broadcast information that was false. A report of a 'spaghetti harvest', broadcast on BBC 1's documentary programme *Panorama* on 1 April 1957 (1 April being a traditional date for practical jokes), showed strands of pasta apparently growing on vines, while a male RP voice-over provided a serious commentary on traditional spaghetti farming in Italy. The hoax was very successful, and we can analyse its effect using register analysis. The field is the agricultural industry, indeed the scientific aspects of this industry, the tenor is formal due to the use of Standard English and **Received Pronunciation**, and the mode is news reporting complete with 'footage', all of which worked together to over-ride many of the audience's doubts about spaghetti growing on trees.

Comedy programmes can work creatively with register in ways that question not only the norms of (media) representation, but also the wider societal power relationships that these underpin. Take the following extract from 'Going for an English', one of the most famous sketches from the 1990s UK comedy sketch show *Goodness Gracious Me*, which was lauded for its pertinent comment on power relations between groups of different ethnicities.[3]

Nina:	Erm, could I just have the chicken curry please?
All:	Oh Nina!
Nina:	Oh, what?
Nitin:	Nina, come on, this is an English restaurant, yeah. You've got to have something English, no spicy stuff.
Nina:	Mmm, but Nitin, you know, I don't like anything too bland, yeah.
Nitin:	Yeah, have some a *little* bland, huh? Hey James [mispronounces waiter's name], what do you have that is not totally tasteless?
James:	Er, the steak and kidney pie is only a little bit dull.
Nitin:	Ah, there you go Nina, steak and kidney [pi:] huh?
Nina:	No, that blocks me right up. I won't go to the toilet for a week.
Sanjeev:	Nina, that's the point of going for an English.
Nina:	Well, Meera, what are you going to have?
Meera:	Well, I can't decide between the steak and kidley (sic) [pi:] and the Cod Mornay.
Nina:	Well, I'll tell you what: you have cod, I'll have the [pi:] and we can mix and match.
Meera:	OK. Actually, I think that's the way you're supposed to eat this sort of food.

Goodness Gracious Me was written and performed by a group of British Asian[4] comedians and gained accolades for exploring British Asian culture and its interactions with British culture on the one hand and Asian cultures on the other. One of their comic strategies is to take a recognisable social setting and make some pertinent changes to it to 'make strange' some of the content and relationships, thus highlighting sometimes taken for granted stereotyping.

We can use Norman Fairclough's (1992) work on **genre** to inform our analysis here. While there is a great deal of work on genre, Fairclough suggests that it is useful to think of genres in terms of the choices made in four different categories, which can be seen as a variation of more traditional discussions of register. Usually the choices made fit together in traditional patterns, and these reproduce recognisable genres of text – sometimes they 'jar' a bit, causing the audience to 'look again', and this is more likely to happen with comedy and satire. In the 'Going for an English' sketch, we recognise the situation but the people we see and the voices we hear 'jar' with the situation. We can analyse its effect in more detail by considering Fairclough's categories. The first of the four categories is **activity type** – that is, what is going on in the texts. This category is similar to field but has a more 'active' approach that looks at what participants are *doing*; examples are school class, interview, date and work meeting. The activity type in the sketch is going for a meal, but more specifically 'going for an English' in Bombay (now Mumbai) in India. It is a 'new' activity type, but recognisable because it draws **intertextually** on 'going for an Indian', something UK audiences recognise as a common after-pub activity. To say the activity type is intertextual is to notice that one text draws on or has echoes of another; we make sense of the new text with reference to the one that it refers to. Sometimes in UK culture 'going for a curry' means just that, but depending on who is involved in the activity type it can be bound up with much cliché and myth making about Indian people and food, making it ripe for comedic treatment.

The second category is **style**; for example, how formal or informal a text is – in this way, it is similar to tenor. In the sketch, the style is exactly as it would be in the most clichéd and myth-making version of 'going for a curry', as it is informal and somewhat disrespectful. The third category is **mode** – that is, the mode of communication, such as spoken, written, visual (similar to mode as used above). The mode in the sketch is spoken and gestural, as it is visual. Fairclough includes a key fourth category that could be seen to straddle both field and mode. This final category is **voice** – that is, who is speaking in the text. The voices in the sketch are Indian voices, but they mimic some of the stereotypical characteristics of English voices in the 'going for a curry' context; for example, the names of people and food are mispronounced. It is on the substitution of these for English voices and the substitution of 'going for an English' for 'going for an Indian' that the comedy hangs, and that explodes some of the myth making that goes on in the traditional 'version' of the activity. The viewers need to have some of this knowledge in order to make sense of the sketch. As the audience supplies some context, this can be understood as a form of participation; however, there are more obvious forms.

4.4 PUBLIC PARTICIPATION IN THE MEDIA

In the introduction to this chapter, I discussed the fact that there are increasing opportunities for diverse voices to be heard and read in 'the media' broadly defined. Below I will discuss the latest developments in this regard, **user-generated content** and **citizen journalism**. First, I will explore the area where diverse voices are heard by the widest audience, the place where they were originally heard and where increasing numbers of them are being heard all the time. I am referring to mainstream public participation programmes. These can be considered a new kind of media if we take a long view. The public have always been represented and sometimes participated in programmes. However, because of new technology, and perhaps fashions in broadcasting, we are seeing new kinds of audience participation. The main questions that need to be asked of these programmes are the following: do they provide an increasing diversity of voices and thus a more democratic media? Or does the way in which those voices are framed and positioned by programme structure, genre and dominant discourses simply reinforce existing power structures?

4.4.1 Public as participant

The discussion programme is a genre in which 'current' issues are discussed by participants – either members of the public with experience of or interest in the issues, or 'experts' with knowledge about them. This genre increasingly dominates the airwaves across the US and Europe, particularly during the mid-morning and early afternoon slots. Given this scheduling choice, there is much more likelihood that the viewers of these programmes, and therefore probably the people who apply to 'tell their story' on them, are relatively less empowered members of society – those who do not work outside the home and thus may be on lower incomes. This is an important aspect to bear in mind when considering the implications of these programmes for wider societal power structures.

The relevant aspect of intertextuality for discussion programmes is role-borrowing – that is, a programme using conventions from another genre. Thus, infomercials borrow from informative programmes, with extended talk and interviewing, while actually being an advertisement. Fairclough's analysis of genre is also helpful here as shifts away from the regular choices made in one or more of the genre categories (activity type, style, mode and voice) can lead to genre mixing, in which a discussion programme 'acts like' or 'mixes with' another genre.

Discussion programmes from the 1990s, such as *The Time, The Place* and *Kilroy* in the UK and *Donohue* and *Oprah* in the US, could be seen to be intertextual with education settings in terms of how they were structured (see Sinclair and Coulthard 1975 for analysis of classroom discourse). Each programme took a newsworthy issue and had an audience made up of members of the general public and some experts to discuss it. The following extract is from a discussion on *The Time, The Place* about weight management.[5]

Presenter: lady on the back row there we'll pursue that in a minute lady on the back row

Participant: I mean they tell you that (.) when you're in hospital (.) and (.) if you breast feed that it's gonna help you get your figure back to normal well I stopped breast feeding when (.) my baby was seven weeks she's eight months now and my bust size has stayed the same and I still can't lose the weight

Presenter: why's that Marge d'you think

Marge: (.) it's a fallacy (.) I don't know if this is your question {laughter} it's a it's a fallacy it's a fallacy that breast feeding (.) burns (.) up the fat (.) a lot of research has shown that it doesn't burn up the fat it also shows that when women are at home erm their lifestyles change at work you're mmm mmm or whatever and you haven't got access to food all the time added to which you've got the baby you're pressurised I remember saying to one of my ladies in my post natal exercise class (.) cause she was moaning about her weight what did you have for breakfast so she said half a packet of chocolate biscuits

Presenter: yeah not healthy

[*moves conversation on to another participant*]

The presenter selects the next speaker just as a teacher does in the classroom, and sometimes this even involves participants raising their hands. Obviously there are practicalities involved here, as we could not have every participant in a discussion programme audience speaking at once. Still, there are obvious power issues when the order and duration of contributions are controlled by one person. The order is not random either. The usual pattern is that represented by the transcription: a member of the general public are asked for their experience, they give it, the presenter sometimes 'reformulates' – that is, rewords what the member of the public has said (although not in this particular transcription) – the presenter then asks an 'expert' (who has their name displayed whereas members of the public do not) for their opinion on the experience. The presenter notably does *not* then go back to the member of the public to ask for their thoughts on the expert's comments on their situation, but more often than not acknowledges the 'correctness' of the expert's point by an utterance beginning with 'yeah', as in this transcription. This relates to Joanna Thornborrow's (2001) observation that, while 'experts' on public participation programmes are attributed a title and status by the presenter and thus have a ready-made context in which to perform their expertise, members of the public are attributed no such status and have to find a way to gain it for themselves. While everyone involved literally has a voice, there is a hierarchy of voices, with experts and the presenter at the top.

The American programme *Jerry Springer* follows a very different pattern to *Kilroy* and *The Time, The Place*. Rather than the whole audience discussing an issue pretty much on an equal footing (with the caveat of the member of the public vs expert issue raised above), the focus is on one individual or group of individuals who have had a particular experience and who are physically separated from the rest of the audience on a 'stage'. These individuals are spatially **foregrounded** as they are set apart from other people. The tone of the discussion is combative, with the people on the stage often shouting abuse at each other and members of the audience shouting abuse at those on stage. The fact that programme 'bouncers' are standing by indicates that this kind of interaction is expected. The design of the programme means that verbal and sometimes physical violence become the norm on the show. The intertextual element here is akin to the Victorian Freak Show or the public trial.

Other programmes, such as the British *Trisha* (later *Trisha Goddard*) and *Jeremy Kyle*, incorporate what could be described as a 'discourse of therapy', following the lead of some US discussion programmes, notably those presented by women, such as *Ricky Lake*. Key contributors are placed on a 'stage' as they are in Jerry Springer, but their position is more one of being 'on the couch' than 'in the stocks'. Their problems are discussed and solutions sought. The process and the potential outcome of this may seem rather more positive than in *Jerry Springer*, but it is still the case that participants are relatively passive, 'stage managed', and thus disempowered; they are there to be 'fixed' by more powerful individuals.

Discussion programmes that are primarily about experiences rather than opinions tend to include material that up until recently would have been too personal for public display and, in Goffman's (1959) terms, would have tended to appear 'backstage'. Goffman's term is useful here as the 'backstage' metaphor links nicely with television formats. It is of more general application, however, and refers to events that take place in the private sphere and in the company of one's closest family and friends. The display of what was formerly backstage behaviour is arguably part of a wider pattern in reality TV generally. This may be because many of us know our immediate neighbours much less well than we would have done thirty or forty years ago, and we interact with them much less often and in less detail than we might have done in the past. But millions of us tune in via Reality TV to watch and listen to the intimate details of the lives of people we have never met before, as the global phenomenon of *Big Brother* shows (see Frau-Meigs 2006). This suggests a substantial change in our society and raises the question: is reality TV filling a gap left by societal change, or is it causing that change? Or a bit of both? These are questions that require sociological research. You should also remember that it is possible that these shifts are attributable to changes in what audiences and production companies deem appropriate.

4.4.2 Public as producer

'User-generated content' and 'citizen journalism' are terms used to describe the phenomenon whereby people from outwith the professional journalism industry, who would traditionally have been consumers of media, are enabled by new technology to become producers of media. This takes several forms. For example, an individual may post completely single authored pieces on YouTube or personal blogs (see section 3.5.3). On first impressions, this would seem to be a highly democratic development allowing for a much greater diversity of voices to comment on affairs in the world. We should certainly stop short of seeing it as any kind of 'revolution' however, because even if the *potential* reach of these newly produced texts is considerable because they are posted online, the *actual* reach of many of them remains extremely limited compared with traditional news broadcasts and press coverage. This is a question that can only be answered by research into consumption habits of actual people.

A key consideration is that citizen journalism involves an *interaction* between user-generated content and the mass media which requires ongoing negotiation as it develops. Here I am referring to coverage of disasters and unexpected events made up of eye-witness photos and footage captured on the cameras and mobile phones of bystanders before professional journalists arrive on the scene. We have seen this with the 9/11 attacks, the tsunami, Hurricane Katrina and the attempted bombing of Glasgow airport to name just a few examples. The photos and footage are usually taken and incorporated into professionally produced broadcasts along with journalists' own recordings. This is significant in terms of whose voice is heard. While someone witnessing an earthquake might provide footage of the event, their understanding of what is happening and what this means may be entirely absent.

What happens when the citizen journalist is the only kind present? In Iran, for example, there is currently a ban on foreign journalists, so the citizen journalism coming out of that country is significant. At the same time, it may be a double-edged sword: it is positive in so far as coverage is possible at all, but there are also concerns about objectivity because the pictures and footage may be coming from a person with a specific viewpoint. At the very least, such contributions are likely to be from a young demographic and thus not fully representative of the population. We have already discussed above that complete objectivity is not achievable when events are 'mediated' with language and image choices, but journalistic standards can go some way to eliminating extreme bias. Even in the Iran situation, some degree of representativeness is possible because news providers may be sent multiple pictures or pieces of footage that cover the same event, and, while journalists cannot be 'on the streets', they can still do some degree of follow up, by comparing sources or even corresponding to citizen journalists. Indeed, Twitter has been a key tool in this regard; journalists will follow what is happening via multiple 'tweets', providing them with an up-to-the-minute feed of information that they can then follow up via various sources in order to confirm. This work is probably best done by professional journalists; citizen journalists probably won't completely usurp them.

Bill Thomson, a BBC technology journalist, is adamant that citizen journalism does not mean the end of professionalism or the profession. In a BBC online news story about the Iran situation and surrounding issues, he is quoted as saying:

> The role of the journalist is not just to be the person who gets the information, but the person who puts it in context and makes sense of it. When it comes to complex political situations, where people's lives are at risk, the mainstream news organisations come into their own because they have done this before. We know how to check something, we know how to get the balance right.
>
> (in Dave, 2009)

This gives us some idea of what media professionals think about user-generated content. A question we haven't addressed yet is what audiences think about user-generated content.

In relation to this topic, a team from Cardiff University's School of Journalism, Media and Cultural Studies, working in collaboration with the BBC, have produced research into audience attitudes to user-generated content that comes to some interesting conclusions (see Williams et al 2010; Wardle and Williams, 2010; Wahl-Jorgensen et al 2010). They find that audiences in general see user-generated content as a guarantee of authenticity, using words such as 'immediate', 'drama', human emotion', 'more real' and 'less packaged' when talking about it. It is notable that this is somewhat in conflict with the concern for impartiality mentioned above. That is, it is important *not* to assume material is authentic but to check sources thoroughly to ensure its trustworthiness, especially because the provenance of user-generated content immediately suggests authenticity.

The Cardiff research looks at both the user-generated *news* (providing eye-witness photos, footage and reports) and user-generated *views* (providing comments on news websites, texting into television news shows and so on). The results are strikingly different: whilst two-thirds of people think user-generated news is a good thing, they are much less positive about user-generated *views* and use words such as 'uninformed and inarticulate', 'publicity seekers' and 'extreme views' about the people who provide such views. Despite this difference, there seem to be many people who approve of user-generated views, as more audience members submit views than news.

With both news and views, there is a slight gender differentiation, with more men than women contributing or saying they would potentially contribute, and an unsurprising age differentiation, with 18–24 year olds more likely to contribute to online content. What is most striking is the differentiation along class lines: between three and four times as many ABs (people with professional and managerial occupations) as C2DEs (people with skilled and unskilled manual occupations and unemployed people) say they would consider contributing. Given that more than 90 per cent of UK households now have access to the internet, it would seem that the digital divide still exists, but it may now be more of a skills divide than a technology divide. Indeed, it may be possible that some people have the skills required, but are simply not interested in participating.

Most news outlets, whether newspapers or television channels, will have an online presence. For particular stories and topics, comments are often invited. Find some of these comments. How many of them could be considered user-generated news? Are you surprised at the opinions that people express? Look at a few stories dealing with different topics and events, and try to find similar stories on different sites. Is there a difference in the kind of things that people contribute? Is there a difference in the language they use (in terms of register)?

4.5 MOBILE AND ONLINE INTERACTION

User-generated news content, especially for online sources, is one kind of online interaction. The accessibility of internet and mobile forms of communication for those on the right side of the digital divide means that there are other vectors of interaction that need to be considered. As discussed in the introduction to this chapter, mobile and online communication has the somewhat paradoxical potential to simultaneously bring us closer together and move us further apart. By way of illustration, a recent advert for BT (British Telecom) in the UK (with the obvious caveat that its purpose is to sell landline telecommunication) captures well the **connotations** of mobile versus landline phone calls: a grown-up son calls his mother who asks 'are you in the pub?', 'are you in a cab?', 'out shopping?' to which his final reply is 'I'm at home, mum. I just fancied a chat', at which his mum's face lights up. The tag line is 'if a call is worth making, use your landline'. Of course the advertisement only makes sense in relation to an assumption that the caller is on his/her mobile phone.

With texting and emailing, the face-to-face or 'voice-to-voice' co-present element is missing; this is an ever-changing picture however, and instant messaging and Skype, for example, can provide a similar co-presence to that of a phone call. For now, though, my own experiences and anecdotal observations would suggest that texting and emailing can be used as an avoidance strategy when people do not want to talk in detail about difficult subjects; indeed, people often voice criticism of the avoidance involved in people ending a relationship or making an employee redundant via text message. A Google search for 'fired by text message' gave results from the UK, the US, France, Italy, Sweden and Israel in the first forty hits, suggesting that this is becoming a global phenomenon. Despite minor criticism and some generational differences in approach, use of mobile phones, email and online chat has increased over the past decade or so to the point that for many it is the norm. This has led to a new **mode** of communication and arguably a new **code** as well.

When we are texting, emailing and instant messaging, what are we doing in communication terms? Are we writing? Are we speaking? Or something else entirely? Perhaps the most obvious answer is that we are writing, because we physically type, or at least hit keys, when we do these things. But all the rules, norms, and even etiquette that accompany writing do not seem to apply in a straightforward way to these newer forms of communication.

4.5.1 Rules and standards in new modes

There are different types of rules to be considered. The popularity of texting, particularly among children and young people, has led to concerns over their ability to spell and punctuate. Teachers speak anecdotally about children writing '2' in place of 'to' in their homework, and anyone who spells out words fully and uses a semicolon for anything other than creating a 'wink' emoticon is viewed with some amusement. There have long been debates about the acceptance or otherwise of dialect in the classroom (see Milroy and Milroy 1999, particularly chapters 8 and 9), and perhaps the evolution of 'textspeak' forms part of a similar debate (see section 10.6.1). Should it be discouraged on the basis that it will detrimentally affect children and young people's use of Standard English, or should it be embraced for the levels of creativity it encourages, and because knowledge of more than one code can be viewed as an advantage? It has long been argued that children who are bilingual employ more attention to detail in both codes because they see the differences between the two or more codes they use, and that it makes them more culturally aware. Similar arguments have been applied to dialect and have led to calls for the education system to embrace non-standard dialects, provided children and young people are also allowed to become competent in using Standard English. Could the same argument be made for new technological codes such as textspeak?

It is not just rules of technical correctness that have to be considered. The creativity of textspeak has already been mentioned, and this is probably clearest in the large number of emoticons that exist. Many mobile phones now come with emoticons as standard, suggesting the latter have very much entered 'the code'. Emoticons started life, however, when individuals recognised that a colon and a right bracket could create a smiley face, a colon and a left bracket a sad face, a semicolon and a right bracket a wink and so on. These innovations were fulfilling a function. Email and text, mostly because of the rapidity of their usage, left behind many of the rules of written Standard English, and with this many of the politeness norms and affect signifiers. Email and text had not generally been used in place of written letters; they were used in place of phone calls or even personal visits. This may well be changing, especially given examples such as being fired by text message! Nevertheless, while there are rules and standards in terms of layout and style for written letters, similar conventions for email and text versions are not yet settled. The material in texts and emails, although 'typed', is arguably closer to spoken language than it is to written language. This of itself is not problematic. However, the interactive context of spoken language traditionally includes facial expression and tone of voice, or at least the latter even in phone communication. The development of stock abbreviations and emoticons has gone some way to ensure that interlocutors 'understand' each other, but there was a significant teething period as this was developing when probably the majority of us experienced misunderstandings via email or text, as the perpetrator or the victim. Indeed, there were even reports of workplace disciplinary action based purely on email misunderstandings. In some cases, such misunderstanding continues, especially when emoticons are not considered appropriate for inclusion, as may be the case in some work contexts. So we can see that the new rules that have come into being for this new code did not happen automatically; they are instead an excellent example of the users of a language or code developing its functionality according to the contexts in which they use it. Further, these rules are not uniform or even fully settled.

4.5.2 Creative texting

Such misunderstandings may be a reason to bemoan the use of email and texting. It is important to examine the advantages of these new modes before coming to a decision. What looks like a problem may in fact be something to be welcomed. For example, the concern about texting leading to literacy problems may be misplaced. David Crystal, in his 2008 book *Txting: the Gr8 Db8*, certainly fails to see the reason for adult antipathy to text messaging: he reminds us that regardless of the moral panic over texting and literacy, there is in fact evidence to suggest texting *improves* literacy. He exemplifies the creativity of texting, but points out that this is creativity within limits (2008: 9); young texters want to be different, but they are also well aware that they have to make themselves understood, so they intelligently develop a co-produced code. That is, the code is developed through interaction with other texters (see section 3.5.3). Crystal draws our attention to a competition run by *The Guardian* newspaper in the UK in 2007 in which the challenge was to write a poem within the confines of the 160 character constraint of the mobile phone screen. Below is the winning entry by Hetty Hughes (on the left) and the winner of the most creative use of SMS 'shorthand' by Julia Bird (on the right, 2008: 14–15).

Txtin is messin	14: a txt msg pom
mi headn'me englis	his is r bunsn brnr
try2rite essays, bl%	his hair lyk fe filings
they all come out textis.	W/ac/dc going thru.
Gran not plsd w/letters she getn	I sit by him in
Swears i wrote better kemistry	it splits my @oms
B4 comin2uni	wen he ☺s @ me.
& she's african	
Hughes	Bird

Crystal points out that while the winning poem gives the impression of being more conventional because it does not use emoticons such as ☺ and special typographical symbols such as @, it arguably deviates more from Standard written English than does the 'creative' poem: only ten of the twenty-seven words in the poem on the left are in Standard English whereas over half the words (eighteen) in the poem on the right are in Standard English; the poem on the left uses 'i' where the poem on the right uses 'I'; the poem on the left uses less standard punctuation than the poem on the right; the poem on the left has more elliptical grammar than the poem on the right. It is clear to see from this comparison that relationship between 'textspeak' and standard written language is more complex than it may at first appear, and close linguistic analysis allows us to reflect on that relationship.

> Carry out *The Guardian's* challenge by writing a poem within the confines of the 160 characters of the mobile phone screen, being as creative as you can with textspeak. Then analyse your poem using some of Crystal's pointers, and comment on the relative amount of creativity and standard usage it contains. Think about the reasons for the standard usage: would understanding be lost if you changed it? What does your poem tell you about texting as 'creativity within limits'? Does it change what you think of as a 'poem'?

Activity 4.5

4.6 SUMMARY

In conclusion, it seems to me that there are three key things to point out in relation to language and the media today. First, regardless of the fact that media has shifted more and more to being image led than language led, analysis of the language we find in the media is still of the utmost importance, though we always have to keep in mind its multi-modal nature. Second, whilst there have been shifts in language usage related to media and technological developments, we should not view these as a sea change but, rather, as an organic development that retains many of the aspects of traditional usage. Third and relatedly, the relationship(s) between language, the media, society and power are shifting, with relatively more choice of what to access, relatively more 'challenging' media material, and relatively more possibilities for audiences to produce as well as consume media messages. However, we should be careful not to celebrate some sort of victory for media democracy, but instead realise that the power relationships may now be more nuanced, but they are still there in the reach and framing of the new media voices.

FURTHER READING

Fowler, R. (1991) *Language in the News: Discourse and Ideology in the Press*, London: Routledge.

Hodge, R. and Kress, G. (1988) *Social Semiotics*, Cambridge: Polity Press.

Irwin, A. (2008) 'Race and ethnicity in the media', in N. Blain and D. Hutchison (eds), *The Media in Scotland*, Edinburgh: Edinburgh University Press, 199–212.

Mertz, E. (1998) 'Linguistic ideology and praxis in U.S. law school classrooms', in B. B. Schieffelin, K. A. Woolard, and P. V. Kroskrity (eds), *Language Ideologies: Practice and Theory*, Oxford: Oxford University Press, 149–162.

Miller, Laura (2004) 'Those naughty teenage girls: Japanese kogals, slang, and media assessments', *Journal of Linguistic Anthropology*, 14 (2): 225–247.

Thornborrow, J. (2001) 'Authenticating talk: building public identities in audience participation broadcasting', *Discourse Studies*, 3 (4): 459–479.

NOTES

1   http://leonarduk.com/tom/audio/6oclocklow.wav.
2   *Brass Eye*, a British programme which was a satirical comment on some reactions to paedophilia received so many complaints, individuals even started complaining they couldn't get through to complain. See Allison, Rebecca (2001) 'Callers deluge Channel 4 over Brass Eye paedophilia spoof', *The Guardian*, 27 July www.guardian.co.uk/media/2001/jul/27/channel4.broadcasting1 (accessed 20 April 2010).

The more international figure Borat has also been the subject of complaints from various figures. See Carvajal, Doreen (2005) 'Kazakh officials don't see spoof's humor', *New York Times*, 15 December http://www.nytimes.com/2005/12/14/world/asia/14iht-borat.html (accessed 20 April 2010).
3   BBC 2 1998–2001.
4   In the UK, 'Asian' generally refers to people from the Indian subcontinent – that is, Pakistan, Bangladesh and India.
5   Anglia Television, 1998.

CHAPTER 5

Language and gender

Pia Pichler and Siân Preece

5.1 INTRODUCTION

In this chapter, we look at the relationship between language and gender. We begin by exploring how language is used to represent gender and reproduce asymmetrical gender relations and gender stereotypes. We then examine everyday talk in relation to gender and consider some of the typical claims that are made about the ways in which men and women talk.

5.2 VIEWS OF GENDER

To develop your understanding of the relationship between language and gender, you need an idea of what language is (Chapters 1 and 2) and what gender is. When asked to define gender, students often say that gender is the same as biological sex. This is not surprising given that in everyday use very little, if any, distinction is made between these terms. This default position assumes that men and women are different and that this stems from innate characteristics. Put simply, male and female brains are said to be hard-wired differently and this determines masculinity and femininity to a greater or lesser degree.

This view of gender and gender relations has come under attack for many decades, particularly among social scientists. Feminist scholars often refer to Simone de Beauvoir's (1949) famous saying 'One is not born, but becomes a woman' to emphasise that there is a difference between sex and gender. A common explanation is that sex is biologically based whereas gender is a cultural construct. A classic example is the use of colours to create gender differentiation between boys and girls. In many cultures, pink is associated with girls and blue with boys.[1]

Whereas it was once argued that gender was a relatively fixed cultural identity that we learn once and for all in early childhood, many scholars have come to see gender as more fluid and as something we repeatedly construct or perform. This viewpoint is influenced by 'social constructionist' theories of identity (see section 5.7.4) and often related to Judith Butler's (1990: 33) notion of gender as 'performative', which she explains as 'the repeated stylization of the body, a set of repeated acts within a highly rigid regulatory frame that congeal over time to produce the appearance of substance, of a natural sort of being'. Gender only *seems* natural to us because we are constantly interacting with messages about gender in the world around us. We may reproduce, subvert or resist messages about gender norms by the way we dress, move, speak and behave and through our interests, work, friendships and sexuality. We use the resources at our disposal, including language, to stylise ourselves as particular kinds of gendered beings; this does not depend on our biological sex.

Whatever our viewpoint on gender, there is still gender inequality in the world in which we live despite the advances that women have made. In comparison to men, women are still underrepresented in high-status occupations, hold fewer and less senior positions in the workforce, earn less, own less, do more domestic labour and take more responsibility for caring for others. Women are also much more likely to be the victims, rather than the perpetrators, of violence.

Given that there is still an uneven distribution of power between men and women, in this chapter we will be looking at how language and linguistic practices reflect and reproduce asymmetrical gender relations.

5.3 SEXISM IN THE LANGUAGE SYSTEM

The word 'sexism' came into use during the 1960s and is generally associated with the activities of the Women's Liberation Movement in the United States. Sexism has a negative connotation and is used to refer to prejudice based on sex, particularly discrimination against women. The idea of sexism was taken up in language and gender by examining ways in which sexist language had become embedded into the language system. Underlying the study of sexist language is a concern with power and the desire to uncover asymmetrical gender relations. As we shall see, sexist language refers to the extent to which gender asymmetry has become hidden in the language system and to the ways in which language is used to represent and reproduce gender stereotypes.

5.3.1 Insult terms

One of the areas we can look at to investigate sexism in the language system is the language used for insulting people. We can ascertain the extent of sexist language by considering whether insult terms refer and apply equally to male and female appearance, behaviour and anatomy or whether there are more derogatory terms for women than men.

Activity 5.1

To examine whether there is a sexist bias in insult terms, make a list of insults that are used:

1.   Mainly for women.
2.   Mainly for men.
3.   For either men or women.

First do this activity in English and then in another language that you know if possible. Study your lists and notice which of these terms are related to

■   body parts
■   sexual behaviour
■   appearance
■   animals

Are there any other categories? Compare the terms in English that are used mainly for women with those that are used mainly for men. What do you notice about them? Can you comment on the strength of these terms? How obscene are they? How do they compare to another language that you know? What do you notice about the terms used for either men or women? Are there different insult terms to denote gender in relation to age, social class, sexuality, race, disability, etc? Decide whether your lists provide evidence of sexist language.

When making lists of insult terms in English, it is common to find that there are more derogatory words and expressions for women than for men, that insults for women generally appear harsher and less amusing and that the most taboo words relate to women's sexual organs, not men's.

5.3.2 Symmetry and asymmetry

Another way in which we can examine how sexism is embedded in the language system is through **symmetry** versus **asymmetry** in vocabulary or **lexis**. A good example of symmetry in English can be found in the lexis for horse. Horse is a **generic** term that refers to animals of either sex:

Example 1
Generic	horse
Female	mare
Male	stallion
Young	foal (either sex)
Young female	filly
Young male	colt

The terms for human beings follow a similar system, but are more asymmetrical in the way that they are used:

Example 2
Generic	person/ human
Female	woman
Male	man
Young	child
Young female	girl
Young male	boy

Speakers and writers often blur the distinction between 'man' and 'person' or 'human'. This is illustrated in example (3) below. These were the introductory lines to the original series of *Star Trek*,[2] the cult American TV series following the adventures of the Starship Enterprise:

Example 3
Space: The final frontier
These are the voyages of the Starship, Enterprise
Its 5-year mission − to explore strange new worlds
To seek out new life and new civilizations
To boldly go where no man has gone before

While there was concern about the use of the split infinitive (to boldly go) among those concerned about the use of Standard English (see Chapter 10), there was less concern about the use of 'man' to refer to both men and women. This is because 'man' has commonly been used as a generic term for 'person' in English.

The next example is in three parts.

Example 4a
[Lead headline *National Geographic* front cover, January 2010]
Merging Man and Machine: The Bionic Age

While the alliteration is certainly pleasing, whether this is a sexist use of 'man' and, in what kind of way, depends on the actual story inside. That is, 'man' might serve as a generic noun for 'people' here. It might also be the case that the story is only about males, and thus accurate, though perhaps still problematic.

Example 4b
[Table of contents entry for story]
The blind can see, a one armed-woman can fold her shirts

Example 4c
[Start of the story]
Photo of a woman and story about her 'bionic' arm.

Thus, the cover headline doesn't mention women; the contents page refers to women only in relation to 'folding shirts', but the first substantial story is about a woman's bionic arm. These are the first of many examples in our chapter revealing an androcentric view of language in which the male is seen as the norm and the female is marked. Many people now regard such usage as an example of sexist language.

5.3.3 Titles

Another way sexism is embedded in the language system is in people's titles. In Anglophone cultures, titles are used to differentiate men and women and to indicate women's marital status. This is not the case for men.

Example 5
woman   Miss/Mrs/Ms
man   Mr

'Mr' is the default title for men in English-speaking countries. A man would need to indicate that he had another title, such as 'Dr', or he would automatically be referred to as 'Mr'. The situation is more complex for an adult woman, who is frequently required to choose one of three titles: 'Miss', 'Mrs' or 'Ms', unless she can use a professional title, such as 'Dr' or 'Judge'. These titles reveal much more personal information about a woman than 'Mr' does about a man. By using 'Miss' or 'Mrs', a woman presents herself as unmarried or married. One reason that this is viewed as sexist is that 'Miss' and 'Mrs' suggest how sexually available a woman is from a man's point of view whereas 'Mr' gives women no such information. While 'Miss' and 'Mrs' may not give accurate information on a woman's marital status (married women may choose to use 'Miss' or 'Ms' instead of 'Mrs' and divorced or widowed women may use 'Mrs' or 'Ms' instead of 'Miss'), the continued use of 'Miss' and 'Mrs' indicates that in Anglophone cultures, heterosexual relationships within marriage are viewed as the norm. The assumption is that 'Miss' should become 'Mrs' at some point.

In some languages, the imbalance between male and female titles has been addressed by phasing out the use of terms equivalent to 'Miss' and using 'Mrs' for both married and unmarried women. For example, in German and Italian 'Fräulein' and 'Signorina' have been replaced by 'Frau' or 'Signora' in many contexts. In Anglophone cultures, on the other hand, 'Ms' was introduced to replace 'Miss' or 'Mrs'. This has not been entirely successful although there is some evidence that in the USA, Canada and Australia more women use 'Ms' than in the UK (Pauwels 2003). All three titles are still in everyday usage and have come to suggest particular identities, allowing others to make assumptions about a woman's political viewpoint; this is not the case for men. For example, if a woman uses 'Ms' in preference to 'Miss' or 'Mrs', some people may label her as a feminist. If an older woman uses 'Miss' in preference to 'Ms', she may be regarded as a spinster and also as an anti-feminist. If a woman uses 'Mrs' instead of 'Ms', she is likely to be viewed first and foremost as a wife and mother.

5.3.4 Unmarked and marked terms

We can find further examples of sexist language in English in the use of **unmarked** and **marked** terms for animate beings. The unmarked form is viewed as generic and refers to both the male and the female. For example, 'lion', is an unmarked form and refers generally to any lion, whether female or male. However, we can also differentiate gender by using the **umarked** form, 'lion', to refer to a male lion, and the **marked** form, 'lioness', to refer to a female lion. The female is **marked** in the language system by adding the suffix '–ess'. This suffix derives from French and illustrates how English makes use of other languages to differentiate gender. Other suffixes forming distinctly feminine nouns that have come into English from French are '-enne' and '-ette'. At one time suffixes were commonly used to mark gender for both professions and title of office and rank. For example:

Example 6

prince	princess
count	countess
waiter	waitress
actor	actress
host	hostess
comedian	comedienne
usher	usherette

Gender was differentiated by using the 'unmarked' term on the left to refer to the male and the 'marked' term on the right to refer to the female. As cultural attitudes to women in the workforce have changed, marked terms have become less commonly used in the workplace and it has become more usual for the unmarked form to be used regardless of sex. In the case of titles of rank, however, suffixes are still in common usage. 'Princes' are differentiated from 'princesses' in rank (a prince has precedence over a princess in terms of royal succession) and in gender. Suffixes are also still used to mark the feminine in new vocabulary entering the English language. One example in British English is the addition of '-ette' to 'lad' to form 'ladette' to refer to young women who behave in ways more commonly associated with adolescent males (with negative connotations of being loud, sassy, vulgar, out for a 'good time' and drunk). The US term 'tomboy' is similar to some extent. This also has clear associations with young male behaviour ('boy'); using a male term for a woman may also suggest that she is behaving in a gender inappropriate way. This illustrates how the language system is still based on the male-as-norm with the female being marked and measured against the male.

Interestingly, feminist campaigners in languages which mark the grammatical gender of nouns and adjectives have frequently adopted the strategy of 'gender-specification/feminisation', to make women equally visible as men, particularly in generic contexts (Pauwels 2003). A radical version of this in German would be to replace the generic masculine form, for example, 'Student', with a generic feminine, that is, 'Studentin'. A mitigated and much more common version of this strategy is the use of 'gender splitting' – that is, the representation of both feminine and masculine forms in generic contexts. An example would be 'StudentInnen', the German equivalent of 'the students', which (even graphemically) represents the masculine 'Student(en)' as well as the feminine 'Studentin(nen)'. Draw up a list with further examples of gender neutralisation, such as 'actor' or 'host' used for both men and women (see unmarked English terms on left of list 6 above), and of gender-specification/feminisation, as in the German example 'StudentInnen'.

5.3.5 Semantic derogation

Semantic derogation is the way in which words that refer to women have acquired belittling or sexual connotations; 'deroge' means 'to cause to seem inferior'. The following examples illustrate this process.

> Example 7
> gentleman or lord   lady

'Lady' is the counterpart for 'gentleman' in expressions such as 'Ladies and Gentlemen', which public speakers often use on formal occasions. 'Ladies' and 'Gents' is often written on the door of toilets in public places in the UK. However, 'gentlemen' is not used as the counterpart of 'ladies' in many contexts, particularly those related to work. The semantic derogation of 'lady' is evident in expressions such as dinner lady (UK) or lunch lady (US) (a female worker who serves meals to school children). The following news headline broadcast on ABC news illustrates this:

> **Cutting Calories in Lunch Lady Land**
> Baltimore's school lunch program is trying to offer healthier meals on a budget.
> (ABC News, 20 October 2009)

While referring to a woman as a 'lady' can be viewed as polite, in a work context, it is more likely to be understood as belittling or demeaning women or the work roles that women have traditionally done. It is highly unlikely that a woman's male counterpart at work would be routinely referred to as a 'gentleman'. Is it likely, for example, that this news item would have run with the headline 'Cutting Calories in Lunch Gentleman Land'?

Similar patterns are found in other fields, as the following example shows.

Example 8
    bachelor   spinster or old maid

All three terms in (8) refer to a person who has never married. 'Spinster' and 'old maid' are viewed as negative terms. It suggests that a woman is deficient in some way. This relates to cultural associations to do with a woman's appearance (she is not deemed to be physically attractive) and age (she is judged as 'old' or past 'her best'); these factors have made her an unattractive proposition for a man seeking a wife. The term 'bachelor', however, does not carry the same negative associations for unmarried men. A 'bachelor' is usually used to describe an unmarried man who lives independently from his parents and is neither married nor cohabiting with a partner. It is often paired with 'eligible', 'life' and 'pad' – an 'eligible bachelor', the 'bachelor life' and a 'bachelor pad' (an apartment for a single man) – to indicate glamour and financial success and a man who is a desirable mate for marriage. Consider this newspaper headline in a British newspaper:

Britain's top 50 most eligible bachelors
Prince Harry has been voted Britain's most eligible bachelor by a panel of judges which included the television presenter rumoured to be his girlfriend.

(*Daily Telegraph*, 14 June 2009)

It is unimaginable that a newspaper would print the headline 'Britain's top 50 most eligible spinsters' to present a list of glamorous and successful women who were unmarried. To avoid the stigma associated with 'spinster' and 'old maid', unmarried women who are judged to be glamorous and attractive by cultural norms are sometimes referred to as 'bachelor girls' (UK) or 'bachelorettes' (US). As we can see, these terms follow the pattern for marked forms in example (6) in which 'bachelor' is regarded as the male norm against which 'bachelor girl' and 'bachelorette' are judged.

These examples highlight how asymmetrical gender relations become embedded into the language system. In all cases, the term used to refer to the male is regarded as the norm while the term used to refer to the female is marked in opposition to the male, either by the use of a different word or a suffix. In some cases, a masculine term is also used generically to refer to both males and females. This usage either makes women invisible or means women will be evaluated in relation to cultural norms associated with masculinity and male behaviour. In these cases, language serves to demean and belittle women's status in relation to men, by representing women as 'belonging' in a relationship with men (marriage and family), or as having lower status in the workplace and public life, or as being treated as sexual objects for men's pleasure. If we agree with the arguments in Chapter 2, sexist language not only represents the male-as-norm against which women are measured, but also reproduces common perceptions about gender norms in society that contribute to many women having less power than men and less access to material resources.

5.4 HOW IS ENGLISH USED IN SEXIST WAYS?

We can also look at how language is used to represent gender in the **discourses** we encounter in our everyday lives. There are many different definitions of 'discourse' (see Mills 1997; Cameron 2001), but the one that we shall use here defines 'discourse' as language use shaped by and shaping ideologies or belief systems. Many scholars also refer to Foucault's (1989 [1972]: 54) definition of discourse, 'practices that systematically form the objects of which they speak', to examine how language is used to produce particular ways of viewing the world and to analyse which views are dominant. You can think about a discourse in this sense as how an ideology is realised by language – that is, a discourse is simply ideology in a linguistic form. From a discourse perspective, we can see how spoken and written language is used to represent gender and consider whether the representation is sexist. We can also look at how language is used as part of **multimodal** communication. In other words, we can see how language is combined with other forms of communication, such as photography, cartoons, gesture, moving images and music to produce cultural and ideological messages about gender.

The example in Figure 5.1 is adapted from a full-page advertisement aimed at young women for a well-known brand of razors. As is often the case, we were not given permission to reproduce the original advertisement, so we have provided Figure 5.1 to indicate the general layout of the original. We have had to modify the original text of the advertisement, but the text we provide captures the linguistic features we're interested in here. You will have to imagine the colour schemes and the detail of the graphics. As we shall see, the advert combines language with other forms of communication to produce a powerful message about gender:

> Example 9
> **Say Goodbye to Swimsuit Fears!**
> This summer it's all about bikinis, but does the thought of even trying one on make you shudder?
> It's bad enough to worry about your thighs and abs without thinking about your bikini line. Don't worry! We have launched the lazer razor – the first beauty tool to cut through all your summer anxiety. You can trim and groom, even in the shower!

Say goodbye to
SWIMSUIT fears

This summer it's all about bikinis, but does the thought of even trying one on make you shudder?

It's bad enough having to worry about your thighs and abs without thinking about your bikini line. Don't worry! We have launched the *lazer razor* – the first beauty tool to cut through all your summer anxiety. You can trim and groom, even in the shower!

Precision Steel
LAZER RAZOR
for women

SIDE TIE
This style is versatile as you can wear it high or low.
Groom like this: Put your suit on where you want to wear it and tidy up with lazer razor.

HIGH LEG
This style can suit everyone. It's feminine and sexy.
Groom like this: You need to groom carefully and often with the lazer razor.

BOY LEG
Perfect for the active girl! This style is fashionable and wearable. Go for a striking colour!
Groom like this: You'll only need a trim with the lazer razor.

His little secret.
Tony from Walsall tells us what men really think: 'I don't mind what she's wearing, as long as she's wearing it well. Girls are sexier when they're happy in their suit'

The Makeover Miracle

At last! A simple solution to your summer troubles. You can groom and shave with this girly gizmo. It does both! You'll never have to worry about beach time again.

At all good stores

Fantastic Competition

Go to our website and enter the code from your purchase to be in the running to win great prizes and treats.

Figure 5.1 Women's razor advertisement

The page features a young smiling woman in a bikini. Her head is bowed and her gaze is directed downwards. Over the top of this image, the page is laid out in two columns. In the left-hand column, the strap line 'Say Goodbye to Swimsuit Fears' is printed in white on a pink background. Under this, the column is divided into sections that feature cartoon images of different bikini briefs. The accompanying text comments on how women look in the briefs, links the style of the briefs to women's body shapes and gives 'grooming tips' on ensuring that no pubic hair is visible. The cartoons and the subheadings are in pink. At the bottom of the column is a photograph of a young man. His thoughts on the subject are laid out in a blue bubble entitled 'His little secret'. He represents men's views in direct speech 'I don't mind what she's wearing, as long as she's wearing it well. Girls are sexy when they're happy in their swimsuit.' In the right-hand column is a picture of the razor in blue on a pink background. The razor is described both as 'the makeover miracle' and a 'girly gizmo'.

This advertisement illustrates how language in combination with other **modalities** constructs a **discourse** on gender. Language is used to make overt references to gender ('men', 'women', 'girls', 'girly', 'bikinis', 'bikini line'). Young women are informed that a very small bikini is fashionable and that they need to make sure that no pubic hair is visible. They are given advice on how to identify their own bodyshape from a list and to use the associated advice when choosing a bikini style and 'how to groom' (ie remove) pubic hair with a razor. Female pubic hair is presented as an embarrassment, rather than a normal feature of the adult female body. Young women are encouraged to avoid social stigma by removing pubic hair with a 'makeover miracle' (the razor). Language is also used to create gender differentiation by giving the information in the context of 'what men want'. Language is used in both a sexist way (by pairing 'men' with 'girls', not 'women') and a heterosexist way (by representing heterosexual relationships as the norm). The advert tells us that 'men' want 'girls' who are prepared to make themselves 'sexier' by wearing as little as possible and by removing pubic hair. The advert presents this as a way of increasing female confidence when men are around. A particular discourse is represented through the use of language in combination with colour, cartoons, photographs and page layout. This discourse encourages young women to make themselves sexually attractive to men by removing their pubic hair. As pubic hair is a symbol of womanhood, a resistant way of reading of this advert is to argue that its removal sexually objectifies women by making them appear like girls for men's pleasure.

Collect some examples of magazine or TV advertisements for male and female products. How is language used in a multimodal way to represent gender in these advertisements? In what ways do the advertisements construct discourses on gender?

Why do you think we weren't allowed to reproduce the original advertisement?

Activity 5.3

5.5 THE TALK OF WOMEN AND MEN

Whereas the previous section examined how women and men are spoken about, we now turn our attention to the way that women and men are said to speak. It is a good idea to remember that these two questions are linked. For example, women are more frequently associated with terms such as 'chatter-box' in English, 'Klatsche' in German, and 'chiacchiericcio' in Italian. The frequent association of such terms with women not only suggests that there are gender differences in speech style, but frequently also implies that women's way of talking is inferior to men's, for example, that women talk too much. Interestingly, even early linguistic work on language and gender contains many examples of negative stereotypes about women's language. Thus, for example, the Danish linguist Otto Jespersen (1922) claimed that women's use of vocabulary is more restricted than men's, that their language use is less grammatical, and that they jump from topic to topic. Even the pioneer of language and gender studies, American linguist Robin Lakoff (1975), felt that women use more **hedges** such as 'well' and 'you know', and that they produce statements which sound like questions. However, Lakoff's famous work served her feminist aim to highlight that what she felt was tenta-tive and unassertive 'women's language' reflected and perpetuated women's lack of access to power. This issue of power imbalance rarely survives in current popular debates about language and gender differences.

Many language and gender studies have investigated and frequently also challenged these stereotypes about gendered language use. However, gender stereotypes should not be dismissed in scholarly debate entirely, as they reveal interesting **ideologies** about how women and men *ought* to speak. These ideologies shape dominant discourses which are accepted as 'common sense' by many members of socio-cultural groups, and therefore serve as points of orientation for speakers in their actual language use (see Cameron 2003).

The following section will provide a rather complex answer to the question of whether women and men speak differently. To really answer questions about difference, we need to be precise about the level of language being investigated. For example, **variationist** sociolinguistic research investigates the relationship between specific phonological, syntactic and morphological features of language as well as examining social 'variables' such as social class (see Chapter 8) or gender. In relation to the former, researchers have found interesting differences between women and men with regard to their pronunciation and grammar. One of the classic findings of variationist studies (Trudgill 1974; Eisikovits 1989) has been that women tend to use more standard forms of pronunciation and grammar than men. However, several other studies suggest that gender may not be the only factor researchers have to consider. It can be the type of 'networks' (Milroy 1980) and '**Communities of Practice**' (Eckert and McConnell-Ginet 1992, 1995) that women and men are part of, together with the norms and practices of these social groups, which influence grammar and pronunciation (see section 8.5). You can find interesting discussions of this quantitative work on phonology, morphology and syntax in Coates (2004) and Meyerhoff (2006). The remainder of this chapter, on the other hand, is dedicated to the conversational style and discourses used by women and men in their talk.

5.6 CONDUCTING CONVERSATIONS

Popular opinion and academic work frequently describe women's way of speaking as 'collaborative' or 'supportive' and men's as 'dominant' or 'competitive'. However, not all studies confirm this gender dichotomy (see section 5.6.4). The following section provides an overview of four conversational strategies, which have been investigated by language and gender scholars interested in the conversational practices of women and men, both in mixed and in same-sex groups. There are many other conversational strategies which you could explore in the talk of men and women, including choice and development of topics, use of questions, levels of directness, politeness features such as compliments, use of swearing and taboo language, humour and teasing (see Coates 2004 for a wider list of features). We begin by looking at the amount of talk women and men produce in different conversational situations.

5.6.1 Verbosity

Research on number and lengths of **turns** taken by women and men challenges the stereotype of the talkative woman in many respects. Several studies report that men talk more than women, whether in academic faculty meetings (Eakins and Eakins 1979), in academic electronic discussion groups (Herring et al 1992) or in classroom interaction where boys are encouraged by teachers to talk more (Swann 1989). The studies mentioned here are based on 'institutional settings', so the question arises: do women still struggle to have their voices heard in public settings? Spender (1980) and Herring et al (1992) suggest that there are societal expectations for women to speak less than men, so that even if women only speak as much as men, they are perceived as being too verbose. This goes some way to explaining the persistence of the stereotype.

However, there is evidence that the situation may be reversed in private settings. DeFrancisco's (1991) study of married couples at home found that in this domestic space, women talk more than men. Women worked at starting conversations, by introducing topics, for example. Despite these efforts, women were less successful in getting their topics accepted than those raised by their husbands. This shows that it is important for analysts not only to count turns or words, but also to ask *why* one speaker talks more than another, and what effect this has on the other person. If you carry out a study in which you find a noticeable imbalance in speaker verbosity, this might be a sign of speaker dominance, especially if the speaker interrupts others, thus stopping them from speaking. An imbalance in talk might also be because one speaker talks more in order to keep the conversation going; for example, by asking questions in order to encourage the other speaker to participate.

5.6.2 Turn taking and interruptions

There is a considerable amount of evidence to confirm the existence of gender differences with respect to **turn-taking** practices. The classic studies of Zimmerman and West (1975) and West and Zimmerman (1977) found that men interrupt women systematically in mixed-sex interaction, whether these are between friends/partners or previously unacquainted persons. Such **interruption** exerts interactional dominance. Eakins and Eakins (1979) confirm these findings in their data from university meetings, but an overview of research on interruptions by James and Clarke (1993) concludes that the majority of studies do not confirm this big gender difference in interruptions. How can this be explained?

First, some scholars point out that gender is not the only factor that needs to be taken into consideration, that the status of the speaker also plays a role. Thus a man who interrupts his wife might not interrupt his female boss. Even more importantly, to unravel these apparently conflicting studies, we need to know what an 'interruption' is. On one hand, **interruptions** need to be differentiated from **overlaps** – that is, very short instances of simultaneous speech, occurring very close to what could be the end of a turn or utterance. The following two examples capture this difference. They are taken from the talk of one friendship group of 16-year-old British private school girls.

> Example 10[3]
> Nicky: I was watching Kilroy* and there was this guy
> Roberta:
>
> Nicky: who says like he sleeps with [five other]
> Roberta: {amused}   [can we learn] from Kilroy
>   *TV chat show
>
> > (Pichler 2009: 218)

> Example 11
> Elizabeth: she said she (-) first had sex when she was like
> Jane:
>
> Elizabeth: twel[ve]
> Jane: [she] **did** and she kissed me on the lips once
> > (Pichler 2009: 230–231)

The first example here is an interruption, as Nicky is not near the end of her turn; in fact, Roberta stops Nicky from completing her utterance. In the second example, though, Elizabeth's turn does look as if it is over. Jane has not stopped Elizabeth speaking, she has just started her turn as Elizabeth is finishing hers. This second kind of simultaneous speech is not felt to be impolite.

Thus, there are many instances of simultaneous speech which are meant to be supportive, rather than disruptive. For example, when **minimal responses**, such as 'mhm', are produced whilst somebody is speaking, or when a 'listener' completes an utterance at the same time as the speaker, this could be a sign of active listenership, rather than an attempt to 'grab the floor'. We therefore use 'simultaneous speech' as an umbrella term for all kinds of talk at the same time, reserving 'interruption' for those instances which are meant to be disruptive, aiming to grab the floor from the current speaker. Confusingly some research uses the term 'interruption' for all instances of simultaneous speech (collaborative as well as disruptive). As a result, it may then be necessary to specify that despite a lack of gender difference in overall use of 'interruptions' – that is, simultaneous speech – women produce many more supportive 'interruptions' – that is, instances of simultaneous speech – than men (James and Clarke 1993; Menz and Al-Roubaie 2008).

It is also important to note that speakers themselves at times feel interrupted, even if the intention of the person producing the simultaneous speech may have been to support them (Talbot 1992). An interesting contribution to the topic in this respect comes from Edelsky (1993) and Coates (1996), who found that there are two different types of 'floor': one where speakers prefer to speak one-at-a-time (Sacks et al 1974), and one where speakers are very comfortable with producing (supportive) simultaneous speech. Coates (1996, 2002) shows that women friends, in contrast to men, very much enjoy the jointly developed floor, having no problem with understanding utterances produced simultaneously.

Record some people talking (with their permission) and transcribe 1–3 minutes of their talk. When you listen to the recording and work through your transcript, watch out for simultaneous speech. Who speaks at the same time as someone else? Does the simultaneous speech lead to one speaker giving up their turn? Does the behaviour seem to be gendered to you? If so, why and in what way?

Activity 5.4

5.6.3 Back channel support and minimal responses

There are many language and gender studies which suggest that women give more **back channel support** in conversations than men (Fishman 1980; DeFrancisco 1991; Preisler 1986). This support frequently comes in the form of so-called **minimal responses** such as 'mhm', 'yeah', right', which can at times be inserted in between utterances of the current speaker, but frequently are produced whilst the other person is speaking (see section

5.6.2). The following is an example of such minimal support, taken from the talk of a group of 17–18-year-old male British students with Nigel, an ethnographer, who is interviewing them.

Example 12
Phil: I I'll tell he was drunk I'll tell you what I know [because]
Aaron:
Nigel: [hm mm]

Phil: I am never drunk because I'm dead smug [erm:::]
Aaron: [he's never]
Nigel:

Aaron: drunk it's true
                                                          (adapted from Wetherell 1998: 395)

The function of this minimal response and other, perhaps non-verbal back-channel support such as nodding or smiling, is frequently to signal to the speaker that the listeners are still paying attention and to encourage the speaker to continue talking. Note also the simultaneous talk between Aaron and Phil, which is not an interruption but an overlapping, slightly longer, supportive utterance. Of course, as with all other conversational features introduced here, it has to be noted that not all instances of minimal responses function in the same way. If a listener says 'yeah' they could also be agreeing with what has been said, rather than just signalling that they are listening. Or, minimal responses could also be the exact opposite of being supportive, especially when there is a delay before they are produced. These delayed minimal responses may suggest to the speakers that their audience is not paying close attention. Zimmerman and West (1975: 121) give the following example of an uncooperative minimal response, produced by (male) speaker A with a delay of five seconds after (female) speaker B has competed her turn. Both the five second and the three second pause, as well as B's following utterance show that she would have expected A to show more interest in what she has said.

Example 13
B: this thing with uh Sandy´n Karen n´Paul is really bugging
A:

B: me   well it´s really complicating things you know
A: (5) um (3)

B: (.) between Sandy´n Karen n´ I
                                                          (adapted from Zimmerman and West 1975: 121)

Some scholars argue that there are gender differences not only with respect to the quantity of minimal responses used by speakers, but also their function. **Difference theorists** (see section 5.7.3), such as Maltz and Borker (1982) or Tannen (1990), suggest that for women a minimal response tends to signal active listenership whereas for men it actually signals agreement with the proposition being made. DeFrancisco's (1991) study of heterosexual couples shows that men use minimal responses much more in a non-supportive way, signalling inattentive, uncooperative behaviour, by delaying them, for example. However, Reid-Thomas (1993 in Cameron 2001: 118) finds no such gender difference in the use and interpretation of minimal responses in her own data, suggesting that minimal responses serve different functions, depending on the context in which they are used.

5.6.4 Hedges

There is a widespread belief that women use more **hedges** such as 'well', 'you know', 'kind of',' I think', 'like' and **epistemic modal** forms such as 'should', 'would', 'could', 'may' and 'might' and other mitigating forms such as 'perhaps', 'maybe'. All these forms are said to function as **mitigation**, either by reducing the force of an utterance or by expressing the speaker's attitude (lack of certainty) towards their utterance. The belief that women's language is tentative has not only featured in Robin Lakoff's (1975) pioneering work on language and gender, but is still wide-spread in popular discourse, even fuelling assertiveness training courses and self-help books targeting women. Several empirical studies have found a gender difference with respect to hedges, indeed some confirm that women's overall use is higher than men's (Fishman 1980; Preisler 1986), but the findings of most empirical studies are rather more complex, pointing to the multifunctionality of these forms.

'You know' can have a very positive interactional function, allowing speakers to signal their sensitivity to the feelings of others (Coates 1996), or aiming to get another speaker's attention (Fishman 1980; Holmes 1984, 1987). This latter function is exemplified in the following example from a group of 16-year-old girls discussing contraception, where one states '*you know* boys think condoms are passion killers'. Of course, 'you know' can signal uncertainty, as in the following example of private school girls complaining about their socially unaware fellow students, 'some people just don't think that other people perceive you as sort of (.) *you know* over-privileged'. However, it can express certainty as in the following argument between two teenage girls 'I get good grades in English *you know*' (all examples from Pichler 2009). Intonation can also play a very important role in determining the function of hedges and other conversational features.

Studies investigating gender differences with respect to the different functions of 'you know' and other hedges found that women use 'you know' more frequently to express confidence than men (Holmes 1986, 1987). Men outdo women in their use of the hedge 'sort of/kind of' in both its positive and its negative politeness function (Holmes 1987). Men's use also exceeds women's use for 'I think' in its tentative function, as in, 'it'd be about two o'clock *I think*', whereas women outdo men in their use of 'I think' in its deliberate function, '*I think* that's absolutely right' (examples from Holmes 1987: 61).

These studies highlight that forms such as 'you know', just like all the other features discussed in this section, can fulfil different functions in conversation. To properly assess gender differences, we need to look at the form *and* function of the feature under consideration.

5.7 POSSIBLE EXPLANATIONS

A range of different explanations have been offered by language and gender scholars to understand the relationship between language and gender that has been explored in the empirical studies mentioned above. While these are presented in a more or less chronological order, as will become clear, it is not the case that the explanations become outmoded if a new one is introduced. That is to say, there isn't a single explanation for the differences one might find. Other factors need to be considered before an appropriate explanation can be offered.

5.7.1 Deficit

In her pioneering work on 'women's language', which was briefly introduced above, Robin Lakoff argues that 'women's language' is marked by a lack of assertiveness, caused by a self-image which reflects women's lack of access to social power. As indicated above, Lakoff's description of women's language as tentative (as well as her reliance on introspection rather than empirical data) has been critiqued by subsequent research. Lakoff's aim is a feminist one, allowing women more access to power; however, her sugges-tion that women would benefit from acquiring more 'neutral' or male language implies that it is 'women's language' which is in some ways deficient. This implication has been highlighted critically by many other language and gender scholars. However, the notion of women's language as deficient has not disappeared altogether. It is contained in many dominant discourses about women's language. In European contexts these discourses have, for example, fuelled the belief that women need assertiveness training courses. In China, Jie Yang's (2007) study shows that even domestic violence against women is justified by a discourse which presents women as deserving victims of male anger due to their allegedly deviant linguistic style, labelled as 'deficient mouth'.

5.7.2 Dominance

Without perceiving 'women's language' as lacking, the 'dominance' theory also argues that spoken language reflects and perpetuates social gender inequality. West and Zimmerman's research in the 1970s is most famously associated with the dominance theory. Their work provides a very close analysis of mixed-sex interaction, focusing on interruptions and overlaps, likening women's speaking rights to those of children (1977). Similarly, Fishman's (1980) and DeFrancisco's (1991) study of heterosexual couples suggest that men are more dominant than women in mixed-sex interaction, with Fishman arguing that women end up doing all the 'interactional shitwork' to keep the conversation going.

You may think that that this is no longer a concern. However, there are still considerable material differences between women and men, with recent Equal Opportunities Commission (UK) statistics indicating that men have more power than women, not just in a physical sense, but also in the realms of politics, finance, economics and the workplace (see Baxter 2008). Moreover, recent linguistic studies also provide supporting evidence for the dominance theory, including studies of institutional contexts such as US academic electronic discussion groups (Herring et al 1992), as well as more personal contexts such as mixed-sex interaction between Japanese university students (Itakura and Tsui 2004). In situations where power is at stake, where women are found to have different (speaking) rights than men, where they are inter-rupted more, have to fight harder to hold on to their turn or to be heard, the 'dominance theory' continues to offer a very valuable explanation.

5.7.3 Difference

The difference approach has been both embraced and criticised by feminist linguists. On the one hand, it allowed researchers to reassess features of women's talk as cooperative and supportive instead of as produced by male dominance. This led to a celebration of women's ways of conducting conver-sations (Coates 1996, 2004) and to a wealth of research on all-women and, later, on all-male interaction (Coates 2002; Eder 1993; Kuiper 1991). However, in spite of the possibilities the difference paradigm opened up, especially for same-sex research, some versions of it have also been accused of being counterproductive to the feminist cause, mostly because they ignore questions of gendered power imbalance.

The difference theory sees gender differences caused by norms and practices associated with what is described as two different women's and men's subcultures, likening mixed-sex interaction to talk between speakers of different languages or national/ethnic/cultural backgrounds. Anthropologists Maltz and Borker's (1982) review of previous psychological and sociolinguistic research comes to the conclusion that boys and girls are socialised into different behaviours, with boys' groups being organised in a much more hierarchical way than girls'. The resulting communicative patterns, of boys' assertion of conversational dominance, and girls' use of talk to achieve intimacy and friendship are, according to Maltz and Borker, carried over into adulthood, where they can cause miscommunication between women and men.

This notion of 'miscommunication' has influenced popular debate about language and gender considerably. Best-selling books such as Deborah Tannen's (1990) *You Just Don't Understand*, or John Gray's (1993) *Men are from Mars, Women are from Venus* have contributed greatly to the public's preference for this extreme version of the difference theory over the dominance approach. It is certainly less face-threatening for women and men to see themselves as 'different' rather than as 'oppressed'/'oppressors', as that would be to admit a power imbalance. In fact, the lack of critical focus on issues of power and inequality with respect to gender are reasons for the intense critique that the difference approach has received from many scholars (Troemel-Ploetz 1991; Uchida 1992; Cameron 1998, 2007).

5.7.4 Social constructionist

Although both dominance and difference theories remain relevant to scholarly and public discussion, language and gender studies has been dominated by another explanation since the late 1990s. According to this theory, women and men speak the way they do because they are 'constructing' themselves as feminine and masculine in their talk. This approach is variously named as 'social constructionist' (eg Holmes 2007), 'postmodern' (eg Cameron 2005), 'performative' (Butler 1990), and 'dynamic' (Coates 2004). The approach presents a more flexible model of gender, opposing the gender dichotomy that is implicit (and at times explicit) in many of the other models (see Cameron 2005 for a critical overview of terminology). This theory emphasises the multiplicity and **heterogeneity** of femininities and masculinities, arguing that not all men and women speak in the same way, as there are many other factors which influence how individuals speak in a specific situation. Gender is seen in relation to 'identity' (see Chapter 9) and as interacting with many other factors, such as regional, cultural and social background of the speaker, ethnicity, nationality, religion, age, sexual orientation and sexual identity (Pichler 2009; Preece 2009; Eckert and McConnell-Ginet 1992; Bucholz and Hall 2004). But, according to this approach, none of these factors absolutely determine how we speak. Instead, individual speakers can present themselves, or 'construct their (gender) identities', differently according to the situation they find themselves in. For example, if you speak to your university tutor or to your manager at work, rather than to a friend or family member, you will most likely adopt a different style of speaking which will allow you to construct a different (gender) identity. Even within the same situation – for example, at work –speakers can switch from one speaking style and discourse to another. Janet Holmes's (2009) research of workplaces in New Zealand shows that men draw on different interactional styles to accomplish different types of masculinity and leadership, constructing themselves at times as 'hero', and other times as 'father', or even as a 'good bloke'. As the verbs 'constructing', 'accomplishing', or 'doing' gender suggest, this approach gives a more active role to speakers (see Chapter 9).

In addition to turn-taking and conversational features such as interruptions, hedges and minimal responses, researchers aligning themselves with a social constructionist approach to language and gender have been paying particular attention to the analysis of different types of **discourses** (see section 5.4). When we voice specific discourses, we present ourselves/our 'identities' in particular ways, depending on the ideologies invoked by these discourses. For example, Deborah Cameron (1997) focuses on a group of young men who use conversational features associated with 'gossip'. However, as Cameron argues, this does not mean that the young men are adopting a feminine conversational style. In fact, the heterosexist discourses that these young men voice when they speak about women and other men (labelled as 'gay' when they deviate from the group's norm of masculinity) show that they are still constructing their gender identities as 'red-blooded heterosexual males' (Cameron 1997: 62).

Even though speakers may not be fully conscious of their identity performances, they are nevertheless influenced by dominant norms, practices and discourses which circulate in society or, more specifically, in the friend-ship, sports, family, activity-based, social and other groups or 'Communities of Practice' (Eckert and McConnell-Ginet 1992, 1995) that speakers belong to (see section 8.5). These constraints are not only responsible for people's ability to identify certain interactional and social practices as 'feminine' or 'masculine', but they also act as incentives for many individuals or groups to behave according to the norms. Not abiding by norms may mean that their behaviour is labelled as deviant; for example, as 'effeminate' in the case of men, or as 'laddish' or even 'masculine' in the case of young women.

The social constructionist approach has been highly influential in recent decades of language and gender research. However, it has at times been critiqued for focusing too much on local contexts and people's agency, rather than issues of power (in the form of material, structural or ideological constraints) which many scholars still believe to be central to our under-standing of gender inequality and many other aspects of the relationship between gender, language and identity.

The turn to social constructionism has gone hand in hand with a debate about how to approach the analysis of language and gender. The main question asked in this debate is: how can analysts claim that gender is relevant to a specific stretch of talk? Is it really sufficient to claim that when women talk they 'construct' femininities, and when men talk they construct 'masculinities'? Or do we need speakers to display that gender is relevant to their specific conversation in some way; for example by explicitly referring to gendered terms? Discuss these questions on the basis of the extract of spontaneous talk which you recorded and transcribed for Activity 5.4.

Activity 5.5

5.8 SUMMARY

In this chapter we have looked at the ways in which language represents gender and how language is used by men and women. While it is tempting to make generalisations about what women and men do with language, attention has to be paid to both the form and the function of the linguistic strategies that are used by speakers and to other socio-cultural factors which may be relevant to a specific situation. It is only possible to understand how gender is constructed by looking at this fine detail. Further, making sense of this variation, in terms of causes, is a complex area. The different accounts of why there might be difference need to take account of power relationships as well as gender roles. The discourses that we use to talk about women and men, including talking about their language use, often relate to these explanatory models. As ever, to properly understand the relationship of power, gender and society, different levels of analysis and various kinds of details need to be taken into account.

FURTHER READING

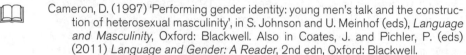

Cameron, D. (1997) 'Performing gender identity: young men's talk and the construction of heterosexual masculinity', in S. Johnson and U. Meinhof (eds), *Language and Masculinity*, Oxford: Blackwell. Also in Coates, J. and Pichler, P. (eds) (2011) *Language and Gender: A Reader*, 2nd edn, Oxford: Blackwell.

Cameron, D. (2007) *The Myth of Mars and Venus*, Oxford: Oxford University Press.

Cameron, D. (ed) (1998) *The Feminist Critique of Language: A Reader*, 2nd edn, London: Routledge.

Cameron, D. and Kulick, D. (2003) *Language and Sexuality*, Cambridge: Cambridge University Press.

Cameron, D. and Kulick, D. (2006) *The Language and Sexuality Reader*, London: Routledge.

Coates, J. (2004) *Women, Men and Language*, 3rd edn, London: Longman.

Coates, J. and Pichler, P. (eds) (2011) *Language and Gender: A Reader*, 2nd edn, Oxford: Blackwell.

Eckert, P. and McConnell-Ginet, S. (2003) *Language and Gender*, Cambridge: Cambridge University Press.

Hall, K. and Bucholtz, M. (eds) (1995). *Gender Articulated: Language and the Socially Constructed Self*, London: Routledge.

Holmes, J. and Meyerhoff, M. (2003) (eds) *The Handbook of Language and Gender*, Oxford: Blackwell.

McClure, L. J. (1999) 'Wimpy Boys and Macho Girls: Gender Equity at the Crossroads', *The English Journal*, 88(3): 78–82.

Meyerhoff, M. (2006) *Introducing Sociolinguistics*, London: Routledge, 201–237.

Mills, S. (2008) *Language and Sexism*, Cambridge: Cambridge University Press.

Pauwels, A. (2003) 'Linguistic sexism and feminist linguistic activism', in J. Holmes and M. Meyerhoff (eds), *The Handbook of Language and Gender*, Oxford: Blackwell: 550–570.

Talbot, M. (1992) '"I wish you'd stop interrupting me!" Interruptions and asymmetries in speaker-rights in "equal encounters"', *Journal of Pragmatics*, 18: 451–466.

NOTES

1   Note that this was not always the case. That is, it used to be the case that blue was the colour for girls and pink for boys (McClure, 1999: 81).
2   Note that this was changed, *ca* 1987, to 'where no one has gone before'.
3   All extracts of talk are represented in the stave system which is based on a musical score, representing all speakers taking part in the conversation even when they are not talking. The stave system clearly captures who speaks first (starting on the left) and who speaks at the same time as somebody else (indicated by vertically aligned utterances within one stave).

CHAPTER 6

Language and ethnicity

Satori Soden and Annabelle Mooney

6.1 INTRODUCTION

In this chapter, we trace the development of the use of ethnicity as related to language variation. As with the other variables of class, age and so on, ethnicity used to be seen as more or less fixed and easily determined. That is, a person's ethnicity has at times been treated as an unproblematic part of their essential nature: stable, determined and unchanging. It is true that some research shows a correlation between particular linguistic variables and ethnicity. However, we will see that it's not always quite so straightforward. How individuals articulate their ethnicity and how it is understood may vary because of the communicative context they're in, the people they're interacting with as well as other parts of their identity.

6.2 WHAT DO WE MEAN BY 'ETHNICITY'?

Before we examine the various ways in which ethnicity may be expressed and communicated, it's useful to have a sense of what the term 'ethnicity' includes. John Edwards (1994: 125) asks whether it is about common bonds, perhaps a common language, the same race or religion. Are some of those bonds more important in defining ethnicity than others? To get you thinking about what the term 'ethnicity' means, let's look at a quote from Edwards's book, *Multilingualism* which attempts a definition of ethnic identity:

> Ethnic identity is allegiance to a group – large or small, socially dominant or subordinate – with which one has ancestral links. There is no neces- sity for continuation, over generations, of the same socialization or cultural patterns, but some sense of a group boundary must persist. This can be sustained by shared objective characteristics (language, religion etc.), or by more subjective contributions to a sense of 'groupness' or by some combination of both. Symbolic or subjective assessments must relate, at however distant a remove, to an observably real past.
>
> (1994: 128)

Edwards discusses the term 'ethnicity' quite extensively and offers a variety of ways in which it may be used or thought of. However, people often use the term without clarifying exactly how they are using it. Looking at his definition, it's easy to see why. The central feature appears to be 'some sense of a group boundary' and an 'observably real past'. If we reflect on this, we can see that this may apply to families who have a strong group identity which they trace back through genealogies, and sustain through any number of in-group behaviours. In terms of how people use the term ethnicity, we need something more.

Activity 6.1

What is your ethnicity? How would you define it? How do you distinguish between your ethnicity and that of other people? Look at the quotation by Edwards and compare the features he mentions with the ones you have come up with.

In general, though not always, 'ethnicity' is ascribed to minority groups. In fact, minority is one of the most familiar **collocations** for 'ethnic'. Nevertheless, just as we all have an **accent**, we all have an ethnicity. But in the same manner as with accents, some are considered unremarkable while some are remarked upon. Dominant groups, whether in terms of number or status, within any given society don't usually define themselves as 'ethnic' groups, just as they do not usually see themselves as having an 'accent'. What happens as a result is that we only use the terms 'ethnic' and 'ethnicity' to describe minority groups and so the **connotations** (associations) of the terms become linked to these groups. The etymology allows us to think through some of this othering. As Edwards (1994: 125) points out, 'ethnos' is a Greek word which means 'nation', where this signifies a group commonly descended from the same place, in the past it had also become linked with outsiders or uncivilised people. This may, of course, be a reason that it is often used pejoratively today. When we say a word has undergone **pejoration**, we mean that the word has become devalued over time, and has come to have a lower meaning than its base, or literal definition. In short, that which we describe in terms of 'ethnicity' is very often the other: a 'them' to an 'us'.

Edwards also includes the idea of group boundaries, while pointing out that those boundaries may change. For example, first generation immigrants may be very different to third and fourth generation immigrants, but, if they still recognise themselves as a group separate from other groups, boundaries of some sort still exist. Finally, Edwards distinguishes between objective and subjective definitions. When he discusses objective definitions, he is referring to linguistic, racial, geographical, religious and ancestral criteria. Ethnicity is a verifiable fact according to these categorisations, even though the verifiability may be difficult! But this does not of itself explain the continuity of ethnicity across generations and changing social contexts. Here, he is making the point that an ethnic group can also define itself as such because it considers itself to be united by common bonds, including heritage: it is more a subjective belief in a common descent. So ethnicity is also a matter of belief, of shared values. We will see later, that claims to ethnic identities may also need to be ratified by others.

Ethnicity can also be defined, then, by people who believe themselves to be part of the same group. And we can say that the language a person speaks is often the most important marker of ethnicity. It is often a key factor in constituting ethnicity. For example, in Northern Ireland, Protestants and Catholics are not defined by language, as they speak the same language. So for those groups, religion is the most salient marker of ethnicity. However if we take the case of Wales and the Welsh language, we see that there may be a number of things that warrant claims to a particular ethnicity. Only 20 per cent of those who live in Wales speak Welsh, but who can argue that the person who speaks no Welsh, whose family has lived there for generations, is any less 'Welsh' than someone who speaks Welsh exclusively?

Edwards reminds us that 'ethnic' is a label only usually applied to minority groups. As mentioned, power relations within societies mean that dominant groups do not very often define themselves as ethnic groups. As Talbot et al (2003) point out in the UK, for example, people don't refer to the Women's Institute[1] as an 'ethnic group', or call fish and chips 'ethnic food' or refer to a bowler hat as 'traditional ethnic headgear'. Would we use the term 'ethnic riot' to refer to a white, middle-class disturbance in a predominantly white area? It's unlikely, because in UK society, 'white' and 'middle class' are considered to be 'neutral', 'unmarked' and the 'normal' state of being, in other words, not that which the label 'ethnic' is applied to.

6.3 ETHNICITY, THE NATION STATE AND MULTILINGUALISM

One of the most important 'boundaries' in the modern world is that of the nation state. While we don't deal exhaustively with multilingualism and language policy here (see section 10.2), it is worth noting the relationship between nation, language and ethnicity. While the three are often thought to be in a stable relationship, things are far more complex than a one-to-one relationship. When thinking about definitions of ethnicity you might have mentioned the country of which you are a citizen. One of us, for example, was born and brought up in Australia. Though she is 'white' and eventually of British descent, what does this mean in terms of ethnicity? Is 'white Australian' an ethnicity? Because this is not an uncommon identity to have in Australia is not always marked. Further, because it is the dominant group in Australia, it is not generally problematic in terms of definition – that is, because it is the 'norm' it is not generally a category which is debated and discussed. Nevertheless, it is certainly the case that Australia is home to people of various ethnicities (see section 6.4).

Race and ethnicity have a history of being associated with particular nation states. Language too is often important to the identity of the state (see Chapter 10). Jonny Dymond, in relation to Europe and language, writes:

> It is too easy to forget how important language is. Language matters because nations matter; both nations and languages contain stories and inspire loyalties. And that means more than folk dances and festivals.
>
> There are those who argue that it was what took place in the aftermath of the two great bloodlettings of the last century that enabled Europeans to live together in some degree of harmony. First, after the Great War, when the Russian, Ottoman and Austro-Hungarian empires dissolved into micro-nations of the Wilsonian settlement. Then, after the Second World War, when millions of 'others' – primarily but not exclusively German-speakers – were expelled from ancestral homes.
>
> Only after these two upheavals, runs the argument, did any kind of ethno-linguistic homogeneity come about; and only because of that homogeneity could the post-communist states of Europe be confident enough eventually to pool their sovereignty. The modern nation-state, secured by some kind of ethnic and linguistic purity, is, for good or ill, still the primary focus of popular loyalty. So those who long for a single European language to replace the armies of interpreters and translators in the EU are in for a long, long wait. Language still matters, dividing and unifying Europe at the same time.

(2010: 38)

This seems to suggest that modern nations are ethnically and linguistically homogenous. It may be that some people think that nation states *should* be this way, but it is not usually the case. Thus, when people propose language legislation or complain about 'deterioration' of an official language, this may be a covert way of raising issues around ethnicity and race. There is a potential clash here: while it is impossible to make people change their race, it is arguably possible to make people change their language.[2] Whether or not ethnicity can be changed depends very much on which boundaries define it.

If a racial definition is used, ethnicity is pretty much impossible to alter (see section 6.4). If ethnicity is linked to other definitions, such as a shared language, change becomes possible, though not necessarily desirable.

Find out about the official languages of nation states (or states); then try to find out which languages are spoken in the nation, and by how many people. Do they match up?

Activity 6.2

6.3.1 How many languages?

Taken as a whole, countries such as the USA or UK are predominantly monolingual countries – this means that a high percentage of the population speak only one language and in fact it is unusual to speak more than one. In the US, English serves as the *de facto* official language at the national level (see Chapter 10). The picture at the state level is much more varied. Certainly monolingualism is not the norm in many local areas, but if we look at these nations as wholes, the default position is that people are monolingual. Or at least this appears to be the case; different varieties of English challenge this assumption (see section 6.4). But in other countries, or continents such as Africa, speaking more than one language is a fact of life, something you have to do in order to communicate with the people you come into contact with, so most people are **bilingual** or multilingual. But even in countries where most people speak only one language, such as the UK and the US, many other languages are still spoken.

What exactly do we mean when we use terms such as 'bilingual' and 'multilingual'? Bilingualism can mean two or more languages within a society but as Mesthrie et al (2009: 37) point out, many writers use multilingualism to mean the same thing. So it is often a case of working out whether 'multi' means two or 'bi' means more than two, but usually it is clear in the context. There is a further issue of fluency that needs to be considered. If a bilingual is someone who speaks two (or more) languages, at what level of competence do they need to be able to speak it in order to be called 'bilingual'? Does knowing a few words in an additional language constitute bilingualism? And if it doesn't, what does? It may require being able to 'function' in that language in everyday life, or perhaps one needs to be 'fluent' in a language variety before you can be called a bilingual. The answers to these questions will vary, depending on who is using the term and in what context. A person might only know a few lexical items or formulaic greetings; on the other hand, they may be able to use very specialised registers and styles (see Wardhaugh 2006: 96). We can also differentiate between societal and individual bilingualism. As Romaine (2000: 33) remarks, Canada is officially a bilingual country (French and English) but there will be many Canadians who will not be bilingual, or who will learn either English or French as a second language (**L2**), whereas in countries such as India, most people know two or more languages.

There are varying attitudes towards multilingualism. At an elite level, at the higher end of the social scale, to be able to speak several languages is viewed very positively, and is of high social value (see Wardhaugh 2006: 96). If a person is multilingual because of education or social mobility (living in various 'prestige' countries, for example), this may provide them with a great deal of **cultural capital**. But on another level, multilingualism is not always viewed positively. In the US, the dramatic growth of Spanish for example, in places such as Florida and New York, has been perceived as a threat to English, even though the reality is that English is a dominant language. There is the perception that immigrants don't want to learn English, although, as Talbot et al (2003: 262) remark, this seems unlikely, given the cultural capital and opportunities that being able to speak/use English can bring. Some Americans are not comfortable with bilingual immigrants, but it's often the case that immigrants want to be able to speak English *and* retain their home languages.

Activity 6.3

A recent article in the *New York Times* dealt with the link between politics, culture and language:

'The end of French political power has brought the end of French' Mr Zemmour said. 'Now even the French elite have given up. They don't care anymore. They all speak English. And the working class, I'm not just talking about immigrants, they don't care about preserving the integrity of the language either'.

Mr Zemmour is a notorious rabble-rouser. In his view France, because of immigration and other outside influences, has lost touch with its heroic Roman roots, it national 'gloire', its historic culture, at the heart of which is the French language. Plenty of people think he's an extremist, but he's not alone. The other day Nicolas Sarkozy, the French president, sounded a bit like Mr Zemmour, complaining about the 'snobisme' of French diplomats who 'are happy to speak English,' rather than French, which is 'under siege.'

'Defending our language, defending the values it represents – that is a battle for cultural diversity in the world,' Mr Sarkozy argued.
(Kimmelman 2010: AR 1)

What boundaries are suggested here? What is the link between language, culture and ethnicity? Do you find the argument convincing?

The article goes on to argue that French as a language may not in fact be in decline. One has to go outside the nation state of France to see this, however. 'More than 60 percent of [those who speak French] are African' (Kimmelman 2010: AR 1). France's colonial history means that French has spread around the world. The same is true of English and other colonial languages. If language is linked to culture, what does this mean for French culture or English culture? Does it even make sense to speak in these terms?

Talbot et al (2003: 262) suggest that it is issues of race and ethnicity which underlie the worries that English is under threat. They draw on Padilla's point (1999: 117) that language and ethnicity are problematic when ethnic groups such as Hispanics start to campaign for better treatment in education, employment and housing. Once they start to challenge the status quo and the dominant group, this is the real threat, not the threat to a language (ie English). Moreover, studies suggest that ethnolinguistic groups, such as Hispanics follow the course of what we call language shift and become bilingual or monolingual in the dominant language – that is, English within one or two generations (www.apa.org).

6.3.2 Only one English?

In Chapter 1, we looked at definitions of 'language' and considered the possibility that what counts as a language is not just a technical question, but also one of politics and power. As Eades's work on Australian Aboriginal English below (see section 6.5.1) demonstrates, the fact that two varieties have the same name 'English' does not mean they are the same; they may be systematically different in fundamental ways. One of the clearest examples of this is William Labov's 'The logic of non-standard English' (1969). In this work, he argued that **AAVE** (African American Vernacular English) is not a substandard form of English 'proper' but, rather, a language with its own system, rules, grammar and logic. Labov analysed the speech of two informants: Charles, a Standard English speaker and Larry, a speaker of AAVE. He concluded that Larry was a highly skilled speaker whose speech demonstrated that he had greater abstract reasoning skills than Charles. Non-standard varieties, such as AAVE, are often spoken by ethnic minorities. The parallels in power are clear: the dominant ethnicity's language is also dominant. As a consequence, the minority and their language are granted, at best, second place. Such attitudes towards languages are closely connected to attitudes about its speakers. As we'll see in the next section, being part of a powerless minority can be very dangerous.

Labov's particular target was the application of the idea that AAVE is 'substandard' to educational practices. Education, like language, is central to the acquisition of **cultural capital**. While people seem happy to accept that foreign languages can differ in fundamental ways from English, variation in English seems impossible for some to tolerate. This attitude appears to be connected to the belief that there is a single correct form of English:

All linguists agree that nonstandard dialects are highly structured systems; they do not see these dialects as accumulations of errors caused by the failure of their speakers to master standard English. When linguists hear black children saying 'He crazy' or 'Her my friend' they do not hear a 'primitive language'.

(Labov 1972b)

Unfortunately, many people do hear a 'primitive language' and then suppose that it must be a 'primitive person' who is speaking.

6.4 ETHNICITY AND RACISM

As we've already noted, ethnicity is often associated with a minority group, whether this is a minority in terms of number or in terms of power. Distinctions between in-group and out-group may be made in terms of ethnicity. Moreover, this ethnicity may be claimed or attributed. The presence of a power differential and the distinction between different people means that the outside status of some groups may be reflected in racist terms and discourses. Even though individuals can expend a great deal of effort in establishing authentic ethnicities, these are not positively valued by all. In this section, we want to deal briefly with racism and racist discourse. Thus, it is important to make a distinction between race and ethnicity; the former is physical and the latter is socio-cultural. You can think of these two terms as being in the same relationship as sex and gender are (see Chapter 5). Nevertheless, 'racism' has remained the way of describing prejudice against the ethnic other.

Teun van Dijk has worked extensively on racist discourse and defines it as follows: 'Racist discourse is a form of discriminatory social practice that manifests itself in text, talk and communication' (2004: 351). Framing this discourse as a 'social practice' reminds us that speaking (and writing) are actions, that in using racist discourses we are *doing* something. Van Dijk argues that there are two forms '(1) racist discourse *directed at* ethnically different Others; (2) racist discourse *about* ethnically different Others' (2004: 351). One of the most obvious ways that racist discourse manifests is in particular pejorative words. What these are and about whom they are used, varies from place to place. Other manifestations can be seen in strategies of silencing in conversation through topic setting, impeding the right to speak, or simply looking bored (2004: 352).

Van Dijk elaborates on topic choice with respect to racist discourse and, while acknowledging that these are 'potentially infinite', identifies three topic classes when speaking about the Other: (1) *difference*, (2) *deviance* and (3) *threat* (2004: 352–353). In other work, van Dijk (1999) observes how people went to great lengths to deny that they were racist by presenting themselves positively, either as individuals in conversations or as groups, for example in newspaper reports. A common way of doing this is through an explicit denial: 'I'm not a racist, but…' and then speaking about an ethnic group in negative terms. Here is one of van Dijk's (1999: 550) examples from the British press about immigration:

> Our traditions of fairness and tolerance are being exploited by every terrorist, crook, screwball and scrounger who wants a free ride at our expense … Then there are the criminals who sneak in as political refugees or as family members visiting a distant relative.
>
> (*Daily Mail*, 28 November 1985)

Here, ethnicity is not mentioned; rather, immigrants are represented as 'terrorists', 'crooks' and so on. The 'argument' then, is not one about ethnicity, but about illegality and exploitation.

The way people speak about minority groups can be especially revealing. In a conversation with Satori about the government and immigration (it was the day after an election in the UK), a friend of hers, who rents houses to tenants, made the following comment:

> I've got a house full of Romanians at the moment and they look after the place, keep it very clean. It's really opened my eyes. Whenever I've let the house to English people they've trashed it and it's left in a terrible mess.

However, later on, he remarked that:

> They [the Government] just let everybody in, murderers, rapists and then it's too late. They don't control it like they do in other countries.
>
> (unpublished data, 2010)

Here, the speaker is making distinctions based on his negative perceptions about East Europeans, who are a large immigrant group in the UK. Despite his loyalty to English people (his own ethnic group), the Romanians have behaved 'better': they have exceeded his expectations ('It's really opened my eyes'). While his comments might be viewed as 'positive' towards the Romanians, his later comments nevertheless show an underlying suspicion of the Other.

Terms that were originally racist can be reclaimed as a positive marker of identity for use by the in-group. Whether such terms are available to those outside the group usually depends on how long the term has been reclaimed, how offensive it was before, and the precise relationship of the outsider using the term with the group. One such term is 'wog' and its use in Australia to refer to migrants (and their children) from Italy, Greece, the Mediterranean generally, including the Lebanon and the Middle East. While it was once a derogatory term, it has since been reclaimed and 'used to claim a common migration experience and background' (Kiesling 2005: 4). As a marker of identity, 'wog' began to be used to positively affiliate with a particular ethnic identity. This was so much the case, that the group even parodied their own language, their ethnolect, and other cultural behaviours, in productions for television and theatre, such as *Wogs out of Work*.[3]

Activity 6.4

Look closely at newspaper reports and listen to the way people speak about the 'Other' and see if you can identify examples in each of van Dijk's three topic categories.

Activity 6.5

Can you think of other previously pejorative terms that have been reclaimed? You might know some that aren't connected to ethnic identities, but to some other facet of identity. Do your colleagues agree that they have been reclaimed? Can everyone use these terms or are they restricted for the use of certain people?

6.5 ETHNOLECT

We've already seen that proficiency in a language can be an important way of establishing ethnicity. Here, we see that like age, class and gender, it is possible to find some correlations between ethnicity and specific linguistic variables. While we need to be careful about how we define ethnicity and how we interpret these correlations, it's worth remembering that ethnicity is a long-standing sociolinguistic variable. Here, we're going to look at Scott Kiesling's work on 'wogspeak', where a number of features need to be considered together.

Migration to Australia has occurred in various waves from different places since colonisation by the British in the eighteenth century. In the mid-twentieth century, significant numbers of Italian and Greek workers arrived in Australia with further waves of migration since. The children and grandchildren of migrants from the Mediterranean may now self-identify as 'wogs'. We'll continue using Kiesling's term for their ethnolect, New Australian English (NAusE). Kiesling's data comes from interview data where the interviewer was a Greek Australian student in Sydney. He examined a number of morphological and phonemic variables, notably the backness and openness of vowels and the influence on vowels of HRT (High Rising Terminal). HRT is used to describe the way a speaker's intonation will go up (rise) at the end of word or utterance. It is similar to the intonation pattern for questions, but tends not to be quite so high in pitch. Specifically he examined (er), such as at the end of 'better', to see if it was more open. 'Open' refers to a feature of vowels where the tongue is low in the mouth. Likewise, 'backness' refers to vowels where the tongue is placed at the back of the mouth. This had been suggested as a feature of NAusE. This appears to be confirmed in Kiesling's data, though there is variation between groups and individuals as Figures 6.1 and 6.2 show.

Note that while there is a great deal of variation among individuals, we can make some generalisations if we cluster the individual results into groups. Thus Kiesling summarises as follows:

> Greek-Australian speakers, when using HRT on (er), exhibit a dramatically longer average length [on the vowel] than all other groups.
>
> Lebanese-Australian speakers are also significantly different from Anglos but exhibit much more variability than Greek-Australians.
>
> (Kiesling 2005: 20)

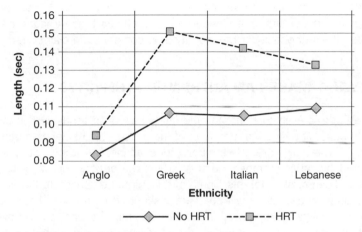

Figure 6.1 F2 by ethnicity, gender and age category

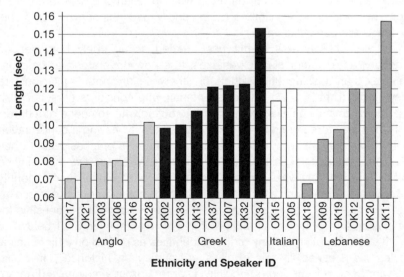

Figure 6.2 Length by ethnicity and HRT

The first means that when high-rising terminals occur with the sound (er), the length of this sound is longest for Greek-Australian speakers. Note that Kiesling points out that we shouldn't see the features he examined in isolation. The change in vowel openness that he identifies has to be understood '*together* with length and HRT' and that together, these create the style identified by speakers in Australia as 'wogspeak' (2005: 20; our emphasis).

It takes more than one feature to form the variety. Moreover, Kiesling points out that the interviewer who gathered his data has to be taken into account in understanding what is happening. He notes that interviewees will take various stances towards the interviewer based on whether their experiences as migrants are similar to hers or not. Kiesling argues that we should not see the material as 'distorted' because of this. Taking into account the context of communication is vital in understanding the varieties speakers use. Identity is not fixed; rather, it is emergent and negotiated in the context of specific encounters (see Chapter 9). Sometimes these encounters will question the authenticity of the identity a person seeks to claim.

6.6 WHAT MAKES AN AUTHENTIC ETHNICITY?

As we'll see later in this chapter, identities based on ethnicity sometimes have to be ratified by other members of the group. I might claim an ethnicity based on where my parents were born, for example. But whether this will be accepted by other members of this group will depend on what kind of evidence I can provide for this. Some of this might be constituted by linguistic variables, and as such will be evident simply from the way I speak. For example, a certain proficiency in a language may be enough to have an ethnic identity accepted. However, there might be other identity markers that need to be addressed in different ways, or even shown with different signs, by wearing certain clothes, having bodily markings or even being able to dance in a particular way.

While ethnicity was in the past treated as a largely homogenous category, as for other classic variables, it is now understood to be more complex than this. Identities, ethnic or otherwise, are not singular nor are they stable. That is, a working-class woman who considers herself Welsh has variety of stances available to her. Interacting with someone of a different class may foreground her working-class identity; having a conversation with a man may mean that her identity as woman is emphasised. Further, these identities intersect; what it means to be a Welsh for a woman may be rather different from what it means for a man. We tend to talk about identity categories such as ethnicity as though they are homogenous but, in reality, it is much messier than this. This messiness is at least partly responsible for a focus on turn by turn construction of identity (see section 6.6.1 below).

It's also tempting to think of these identities as ranked on a hierarchical scale. This is especially true of class, but particularly historically, it is also relevant to any discussion of ethnicity. Different groups may have different things they value; ideological differences may result in a way of speaking being prestigious in one community, but not in another. Labov's concept of 'covert prestige' helps us orient to this (1972a). 'Overt prestige' is garnered by speaking in a way which is valued according to hegemonic norms. Thus, speaking the standard variety of a language confers overt prestige. As we all know, such a language variety will be useless in other speech communities if you want to be taken seriously – other norms apply. The concept of 'covert prestige' acknowledges that some speech communities, usually ones that don't have a great deal of power in relation to other dominant groups, value very different kinds of speaking, often involving non-standard varieties (such as AAVE).

There is yet another factor that has to be taken into consideration; who is involved in the interaction. If two people from the same speech community, with the same values, are interacting, their understanding of what counts as prestigious will be more or less compatible. But what happens when these values clash? Before any judgements can be made about who has more cultural capital, or prestige, some ground rules need to be set. This won't be done in an explicit metalinguistic way, there won't be a conversation before the interaction where the participants decide whose variety is 'trumps'. Rather, interlocutors will try to frame the interaction such that their cultural capital has relevance. This is precisely what we see in the next section.

6.6.1 Different discourses of authenticity

In this section, we focus on research by Petra Scott Schenk which examines how individuals claim a Mexican ethnicity through their discourse. Schenk takes up a theme which is current in contemporary sociolinguistic research – that is, what is authenticity? She notes that authenticity, in this case in respect of ethnicity claims, is not predetermined. Rather, individuals appeal to ideological constructs of that ethnicity in order to formulate defensible claims to authenticity. We will look later at the interactional aspects of such claims; however, here we want to draw attention to the kinds of things that might be used to ground an ethnic identity. While this is just one context, with particular speakers, it draws attention to the kinds of things that may be relevant for definitions of ethnicity. Crucially, Schenk argues that 'positioning oneself as authentic often depends on positioning the other as inauthentic' (2007: 198). She also notes that power is crucial here, even if it is a local power structure, as 'the authentically positioned participant has the authority to delegitimize the authenticity of the other participant' (2007: 198).

Schenk's research examined Spanish-English code-switching – that is, moving from one language to another in the same encounter. We'll look more closely at code-switching later in the chapter (see section 6.8). Her data was collected in California from three students at a university, all bilingual. Schenk writes, 'In these data, Spanish linguistic proficiency, place of birth, and purity of bloodline are evoked as ideological tests for authenticity' (2007: 199). Not all of the informants were born in Mexico, and they don't all have Mexican-born parents. Finally, none of them are fluent in Spanish to the point of producing error-free speech. Schenk argues that all of these individuals are 'on the margin of the group' (2007: 199) that could claim Mexican ethnicity according to the three tests just mentioned. That they all know this means that claims to authentic ethnicity are important but also problematic. This kind of non-central membership is far from unusual. What it means, though, is that rather than ethnicity being a binary category (where you either belong or you don't; you're part of 'us' or 'them'), we find 'internal hierarchies of ideology and power that cannot be completely separated from the ideologies of the external dominant culture' (2007: 200). Thus, potential members of this group are positioned both by authentic/core members of the ethnic group and by values of the exterior majority.

The relationship of these in-group tests for membership to out-group norms is clearly demonstrated in the case of purity of bloodline. Even though Colonial American institutions valued 'European blood' over anything else, mixed bloodlines meant impurity and a lower place on the hierarchy of power. Indeed, Spanish was seen as 'white' and Mexican as 'mixed'. While the informants here have a concept of 'pure' Mexican bloodlines (as opposed to the colonial view of their ethnicity as mixed and impure), there has nevertheless been an incorporation of the broader ideological position in relation to blood and its purity. We can see appeals to purity and birthplace in the following exchange from Schenk [Lalo is a man and Bela a woman]:

11	Bela:	Este,	*Okay,*
12	Bela:	mira mira,	*look look,*
13	Bela:	[no empieces]	*don't you start.*
14	Lalo:	[hhh, {laughter}]	[hhh, laughter]
15	Bela:	T´u ni siquiera eres original	*You're not original either.*
16	Lalo:	M´as original quet u {smiling}.	More original than you {smiling}
17	Lalo:	Both of my	Both of my
18	Lalo:	[parents are-]	[parents are-]
19	Bela:	[Mas origi]nal?	*[More origi]nal?*
20	Lalo:	(.) are Aztec BLOOD	(.) are Aztec BLOOD
21	Bela:	Ay cal[mate] {smiling} [Tu]?	*Oh calm down. {smiling}. You?*
22	Lalo:	[hhh {laughter}]	{laughter}hhh.
23	Bela:	donde nacis[te] [En don-]	*where were you born. Wher-*
24	Lalo:	[Soy][PURO]	*I'm PURE*
25	Lalo:	Yo soy PURO.	*I am PURE*
26	Bela:	Cual [PURO:]	*What (are you talking about) PURE.*
27	Lalo:	[Soy nacido]-	*I was born-*
28	Lalo:	Soy nacido aqu´i pero,	*I was born here but,*
29	Lalo:	soy PURO	*I'm pure.*

{ 30	Bela:	Ay [sı mira mira] {mocking}.	*Oh yeah look look.* {mocking}
{ 31	Lalo:	[Please man]	Please man
32	Bela:	Donde nacieron tus papas	*Where were your folks born.*
33	Lalo:	Z:acatecas Jalisco,	Z:acatecas Jalisco
34	Lalo:	that's like the HEART.	that's like the HEART
{ 35	Bela:	[Zaca]tecas Jali:sco .hhh {laughter}	
{ 36	Lalo:	[Ye]-	
37	Lalo:	Yeah,	
38		my mom's from Zacatecas,	
39		my dad's from--	
40		(-) from Los Altos .	
41		(.)That's the HEART fool.	
42		That's where the REAL Mexicans come from.	
43	Bela:	Ay mira y tu ?	*Oh look and you?*
{ 44	Bela:	(.)De donde [saliste] .	*Where are you from.*
{ 45	Lalo:	[Psh that's-]	*Psh that's*
46	Lalo:	that's my land fool. ((quietly))	
47		(-) I came from my mother's WOMB.	

(adapted from Schenk 2007: 206–277)

We can see that both acknowledge that they're not 'original' and so the fight begins to establish who is 'more original' (line 16 ff). Lalo links this to his 'Aztec blood' as 'the Aztecs, as precolonial and hence pure-blooded Mexicans, ideologically represent the archetype of Mexicanness for many Mexican American people' (Schenk 2007: 208). It is somewhat strange that when Lalo provides evidence for his 'more original' position, he switches to English. It may be that he considers his lineage such strong evidence for his ethnicity that any performance in Spanish becomes redundant. Indeed, Schenk points out that the Spanish he does use here is not idiomatic. Thus, his switch to English may be to background his problematic position in relation to the requirement for Spanish fluency. Nevertheless, competence in a language is common as a discourse to claim ethnicity as well as a resource to display it.

6.7 LANGUAGE AS A MARKER OF ETHNICITY

As we've seen, speaking a language can be used to evidence an ethnicity. There are various ways this can be done. Here, we consider a case study one of us undertook in 2004. Satori interviewed a woman, who we refer to as Gwen. She was a woman who had been born and brought up in London. However, both she and her parents were Welsh and they had brought her up with Welsh as her first language. A person's first or native language is referred to as their **L1**. The language(s) a person learns subsequently is referred to as an **L2** or second language. The Welsh language was a very important symbol to Gwen of her ethnic identity and she made a great deal of effort to preserve and maintain her language skills. Living in London, surrounded by English speakers for most of her life, she took the decision to study at a Welsh university, specifically to consolidate her Welsh language skills. Gwen had gone to a great deal of effort to ensure that her daughter also had good Welsh language skills by sending her to a Welsh medium school in London, even though this was some distance from where they lived. In her interview with Satori, she had this to say:

> G: Welsh has been a language on the brink of dying out, and there has been a conscious revival, the conscious revival is there because you feel you've got something worthwhile keeping and there's so much tied in with the language, culture ... which most Welsh people do feel are very precious and worthwhile ... I think the Welsh have a very deep-seated sense of culture, it's very much a culture of the people
>
> S: and you think the language is part of that do you?
>
> G: oh yes ... culture is dependent on the language to a great deal to my mind ... you do feel rather proud that, arguably, Welsh is the oldest living language in Europe. You want to uphold it and encourage people to learn it.

A bit later on in the interview she said:

> G: I live my Welshness as I see fit ... [speaking Welsh] is the be-all and the end-all of being Welsh for me

And:

> G: ...I say to a lot of people, if it wasn't for the Welsh language, you wouldn't have an identity you could call Welsh ... there's more to being Welsh than just shouting for a Rugby team.
>
> (unpublished data, 2004)

So we can see that Gwen prioritised the maintenance of her Welsh language skills, despite her geographical location (London) and the fact that she is surrounded by English and English speakers. This is because, for her, the Welsh language is essential to her ethnic identity.

This feeling of connection to Welsh is true of people who live even further away from Wales. Research conducted in the United States on people who claimed a Welsh identity found 'the higher informants' competence in Welsh, the more intense affiliations to Wales they reported' (Coupland et al 2006: 363). We could argue that language proficiency is a clear and expedient indicator of belonging, of having verifiable and demonstrable roots. At the same time, it takes considerable effort to acquire such competence for L2 speakers. Clearly linguistic competence isn't the only way of claiming an ethnicity. There are other forms of cultural capital which can be developed and exploited.

Wray et al argue that it is possible to 'turf' an identity – that is, create connections even though there is no historical personal link to the ethnic community:

> Turfing entails the deliberate attempt to revitalise a historically 'rooted' community by encouraging outsiders to adopt aspects of its cultural identity. We use the metaphor of turfing because the outward manifestations of the culture are not, as with the original rooted community, an expression of a pre-existing identity. Rather, they are put into place *before* the affective identity arises, in the hope that 'roots will grow down', anchoring the new community members permanently into the adopted identity.
>
> (2003: 49)

The research subjects, American college students participating in a Welsh choir, are thus able to 'turf' an identity, in part by enacting salient practices: singing and specifically singing in Welsh at their college in the US and also during trips to Wales. We can understand the way an increasing number of people seek to trace their family history, especially those from former colonies, as a means of establishing a claim to an ethnic identity. It should be noted that the creation and maintenance of such identities is labour intensive. Individuals generally perceive some kind of cultural capital resulting from this labour.

6.7.1 Understanding misunderstanding

When obviously different languages are present, it's easy to see how misunderstanding can occur. However, when two people appear to be using the same language, for example English, the fact of misunderstanding can be obscured. For example, HRT might only be used by an English speech community for interrogatives. Indeed, the HRT is often associated with uncertainty and tentativeness, which may result in a whole ethnic group being perceived as unconfident. But as we've seen with Keisling's work above, HRT can also be a feature (combined with others) of an ethnolect. John Gumperz's seminal work in the 1970s focused on how speakers from different ethnic backgrounds misunderstood one another in this way. These were not misunderstandings that occurred because those from the minority ethnic background (his work concentrated on Asian and West Indian groups) could not speak English very well; on the contrary, misunderstandings often occurred when fluent speakers of English interacted with one another. It was just that their Englishes didn't have the same communicative norms.

Gumperz made the point that because of the differing discourse and contextualisation cues, such as intonation patterns used by different ethnic groups, comprehension difficulties occur. These different conventions are the ways groups have of signalling different attitudes in speech. Tone of voice and pitch alters the meanings associated with these cues. When we talk to people, we depend on the *way* they talk as well as what they say to understand and interact appropriately.

An example Gumperz (1997: 395) refers to concerns relations in a staff cafeteria at a British airport where Asian women, who had just been employed, were perceived as uncooperative by both their boss and the cargo handlers they served meals to in the cafeteria. Although there was little verbal interaction between the two groups, it transpired that the intonation and manner of the Asian women was interpreted negatively. When the cargo handlers were asked if they wanted gravy with their meat, the white British assistants would offer 'Gravy?' with a rising intonation, which is usual for questions. By contrast, when gravy was offered to them by the Asian women, they would use falling intonation, as if 'Gravy' were a statement, rather than a question. Once the problem had been identified, and explained to those involved in mixed sessions, the workers were able to better understand one another.

We find the same kind of conclusion in Diana Eades's work, though in a very different institutional context. Eades has looked at the way indigenous Australians are treated in the legal system and how their the conventions of Aboriginal English (AE) put indigenous people at a real disadvantage in a legal system which relies on and enforces Anglo conventions of communication. Eades points out some of the particular areas of misunderstanding including silence, gratuitous concurrence (see below), syntactic form of questions and interruption. For speakers of AE, silence is 'important and positively valued' (2003: 202). It signals, for example, the importance of the topic under discussion and as such can be understood as a sign of respect and attention. The rules of the courtroom, however, construe silence from a witness or suspect as evidence of deception or lack of co-operation. Neither is advantageous for the silent speaker in this arena.

Gratuitous concurrence describes how speakers of AE may answer 'yes' to closed questions, 'regardless of either their understanding of the question or their belief about the truth or falsity of the proposition being questioned' (Eades 2003: 203). In any context, this will be difficult. In a legal context, it can be very damaging and lead to serious injustice. There are other aspects of questioning conventions that differ for speakers of AE. Eades notes that it is not unusual for a declarative with rising intonation to be understood as a question that invites more than simply a 'yes/no' response. It is treated as 'an invitation to explain' (2000: 172). Given the restricted speaking rights of the courtroom, any extended speech may also be construed negatively in the legal context. Finally, and linked to these features, is the way in which AE speakers are interrupted and silenced in the court. Eades finds that such interruptions are often made by the judge. In the following lines, we can see how the judge's interruptions are linked to the witness trying to provide a detailed response to what is, for non-AE speakers, a closed question:

31. J: Have you spoken to them since?
{ 32. W: Oh [(xxxxx)
{ 33. J: [Since this event?=
34. W: =at court I did yeah– last=
35. J: =Have you indicated to them what you're telling me that you feel it was unwarranted and that you're sorry for it?
36. W: Yeah– yeah it's=
37. J: =You've said that to them?
38. W: Yeah– yeah.
39. J: You tell me that truly?
40. W: Yeah (1.2) I said it when I got charged that that was – you know – my stupidness

(adapted from Eades 2000: 174)

In this appeal against a sentence, the judge clearly wants a 'yes' response to the various questions asked. When the witness tries to say more, the judge interrupts. Had the witness been allowed to speak at line 32, his remorse may have been more readily apparent. These misunderstandings occur because of different communicative conventions in what look like the same language. When obviously different languages are involved in the same communicative context, it is at least easier to anticipate misunderstandings.

6.8 CODE-SWITCHING AND CROSSING

We saw in the example with Lalo and Bela above that moving from one language to the other in a single conversation can be unproblematic. This code-switching demonstrates membership of a particular language community on the part of the speaker, and acknowledges the hearer's membership of the same. We use the term **code-switching** to refer to the use of two or more codes within a conversation or even within the same utterance. There are a variety of reasons why a speaker may switch codes, whether consciously or unconsciously. It may relate to the topic or it may occur if another person joins the conversation who can only speak a particular code or variety. A switch may, therefore, also indicate solidarity and inclusion or, conversely, distance and exclusion (see Milroy and Gordon 2003: 209).

Crossing, 'language-crossing' or 'code-crossing', on the other hand, describes the practice of using language varieties that are associated with, or belong to, ethnic groups that the speaker doesn't belong to. As we have seen, competence in a language, or the 'right' to use it to claim membership of a group, may have to be ratified. Language use was one of the important features for claiming Mexican ethnicity above, for example. The sociolinguist Ben Rampton looks closely at crossing showing that it involves 'borrowing' a variety and perhaps a sense of trespassing on language territory that one can't authentically claim. Rampton's preliminary definition is that crossing 'refers to the use of language which isn't generally thought to "belong" to the speaker' (1997: 2).

Rampton thus differentiates crossing from code-switching as crossing involves a 'disjunction between speaker and code that cannot be readily be accommodated as a normal part of ordinary social reality' (Rampton 1995: 278). Thus, 'crossing either occasioned, or was occasioned by, moments and activities in which the constraints of ordinary social order were relaxed and normal social relations couldn't be taken for granted' (1997: 2). But why would a person want to use a variety that doesn't belong to them, and, moreover, how do they get access to that variety? According to Carmen Fought (2006: 196), research on crossing is vital in understanding language and ethnicity because, as she says, it can reveal processes of ethnic identity construction which would otherwise remain hidden.

Rampton's research study involved two years of **ethnographic** field-work with teenagers in a South Midlands town in England. He recorded conversations, interviewed participants and also asked them to comment on the data he'd recorded. He analysed instances of crossing into Panjabi, conversations involving stylised Asian English and those where Creole features were evident. He found that there were three different contexts where crossing occurred: when the teenagers interacted with adults; when they were with their peers; and also events such as listening to bhangra[4] music which was very influential amongst the young people in the neigh-bourhood (1997: 293). He concluded that crossing performed a variety of functions; for example, it was indicative of a resistance to adult norms, challenging expectations about ethnicity, and indicating identities other than ethnic identities. Significantly, crossing appeared to be connected to 'liminal-ity' and the 'liminoid' (1997: 7). Liminal spaces fall betwixt and between the spaces which are recognised and ratified in some way. Because of this, 'crossing never actually claimed that the speaker was "really" black or Asian' in the way that code-switching does, and it also suggests that in 'normal' spaces, 'the boundaries round ethnicity were relatively fixed' (1997: 7).

Clearly, crossing like this can only occur if the variety used is relevant and available. The key is **social networks** or contacts and, as you might expect, adolescents with social networks involving those from other ethnic backgrounds have more opportunities to cross and to learn the forms and linguistic features necessary to cross. As Fought (2006: 205) summarises, there are a number of ways that this might happen. A person's social network might include people from different ethnic backgrounds. On the other hand, an individual might know only one person and they may learn the features of a particular code from that person. It's also possible that the media has a part to play, especially because of the access it provides to music and other audio material, and the internet is probably very influential (see Stuart-Smith 2006). All these are key components of what constitutes 'youth culture'.

The following is an extract from Rampton's data (1997: 6). Bold in this extract indicates crossing into a Stylized Asian English (SAE).

> 'Participants and setting: At the start of the school year, Mohan [15 years, male, Indian descent, wearing radio-microphone], Jagdish [15, male, Indian descent] and Sukhbir [15, male, Indian descent] are in the bicycle sheds looking at bicycles at the start of the new academic year. Some new pupils run past them.'

1. Sukh: STOP RUNNING AROUND YOU GAYS (.)
2. Sukh: *{laughter}*
3. Moh: **EH (.) THIS IS NOT MIDD(LE SCHOOL)** no more (1.0)
4. **this is a re spective** (2.0) **(school)**
5. Moh: school (.) yes (.) took the words out my mouth (4.5)

Given the context, why does this crossing occur and why might SAE be used?

Let's bear in mind that in lines 3 and 4 we find the kind of directive that a teacher might give a student. Speaking in a variety associated with migrants is probably not going to be associated with authority and prestige. Rather, we can understand this crossing as a way of Mohan 'speaking down' to the students, thus turning the direction into something of an insult.

Activity 6.6

6.9 SUMMARY

Language can be used to demonstrate or claim an ethnicity. However, as we've seen, this is not always straightforward. It might be the case that this claim risks being challenged by someone else considered to be more authentic, or a claim may be apparent rather than genuine, as in the case of crossing. While this involves regimes of power, using a particular ethnolect may make a person vulnerable to other power structures, in the form of racist discourse, for example. What counts in terms of claims to ethnic identity depends on linguistic features, interactional negotiation and language ideologies. Even though the claim and attribution of ethnic difference is widespread, the way it works out locally depends on context.

FURTHER READING

Allport, G. (1954) 'The language of prejudice', in *The Nature of Prejudice,* Boston: Beacon Press.
van Dijk, T. (2004) 'Racist Discourse', in E. Cashmere (ed.), *Routledge Encyclopaedia of Race and Ethnic Studies*, London: Routledge, 351–355.

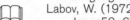 Eades, D. (1996) 'Legal recognition in cultural differences in communication: the case of Robyn Kina', *Language & Communication,* 16 (3): 215–227.

Eades, D. (2008) 'Telling and retelling your story in court: questions, assumptions and intercultural implications', *Current Issues in Criminal Justice,* 20 (2): 209–230.

Gumperz, J. J. (1997) 'Interethnic communication', in N. Coupland and A. Jaworski (eds), *Sociolinguistics a Reader and Coursebook,* Basingstoke: Palgrave, 395–407.

Gumperz, J. J. (2003) 'Cross cultural communication', in R. Harris and B. Rampton (eds), *The Language, Ethnicity and Race Reader,* London: Routledge, 267–275.

Hall, S. (2001) 'The spectacle of the "other"', in M. Wetherell, S. Taylor and S. J. Yates (eds), *Discourse Theory and Practice: A Reader,* London: Sage, 325–343.

Labov, W. (1969) 'The logic of nonstandard English', *Georgetown Monographs on Language and Linguistics,* 22, 1969.

Labov, W. (1972c) 'Academic ignorance and black intelligence', *The Atlantic,* 72, June: 59–67.

Mertz, E. (1982) 'Language and mind: a 'Whorfian' folk theory in US language law', *Duke University Working Papers in Sociolinguistics,* 93: 1–21.

Shenk, P. S. (2007) '"I'm Mexican, remember?" Constructing ethnic identities via authentication discourse', *Journal of Sociolinguistics,* 11 (2): 194–220.

Warren, J. (1999) 'Wogspeak: transformations of Australian English', *Journal of Australian Studies,* 23 (62): 85–94.

NOTES

1   The Women's Institute is a long-standing voluntary organisation, with local branches, in the UK. Established in 1915, they are often referred to as the WI. See www.thewi.org.uk/Index.aspx.

2   Of course, restrictive immigration regimes are often put in place exactly because of an apparent importance of racial/ethnic profile of a state.

3   This was a popular stage show that toured in Australia in the 1990s.

4   A kind of Panjabi music.

CHAPTER 7

Language and age

Jean Stilwell Peccei

7.1 INTRODUCTION: AGE AS A FACTOR IN LANGUAGE VARIATION

How would you describe yourself? Usually, quite a few possibilities come to mind. For example, I am a woman, an American who has lived in England for forty years, a 63-year-old 'baby boomer', a grandmother, and a retired university lecturer (just to name a few of my 'identities'). And, just as I have a variety of identities, I also have a variety of ways of speaking. Although in all cases I am speaking English, the language I use when talking informally to friends of my own generation can be quite different from the one I used in lectures to my students in London, or the one I used when talking with my grandmother in California. The way I talk to my husband is not the same way I talk to my grown sons. And the way I talk to my sons now is quite different from the way I talked to them when they were toddlers.

As Hudson (1980) has pointed out, we make a very subtle use of the language variability that is available to us. It allows us as speakers to locate ourselves in a multi-dimensional society and as hearers to locate others in that society as well. Age, like gender, profession, social class and geographic or ethnic origin, has often been studied as one of the factors that locate us in society and cause language variation.

Activity 7.1

One of the ways that I described myself was by my age and generation: a 63-year-old 'baby boomer' (the generation born between 1946 and 1964), and one of the factors that I felt would influence the way I talk in a given situation was the age of my conversational partner. To see how the ages of the speakers can give conversations a characteristic flavour, look at the three conversations below. Which one involves two teenage girls, which one involves an adult and a toddler, and which one involves an elderly person and a younger adult?

1   a: what – what are these pictures doing here?
     b: careful of them, darling. Gangan [grandmother] painted them.
     a: me like a little one best.
     b: do you?
     a: which one do you like first? a big one or a little one?
     b: I like that white one.
                                                (Fletcher 1988: 545)

2   a: it's your cheque, love. (2) yeah.
     b: (4) how much for?
     a: God! (2) shall I just read what it says to you? (3) dear sir or madam you are entitled to supplementary benefit of a hundred-and-fifty pounds for the articles listed overleaf.
     b: oh
     a: for a cooker. [stove in American English] so you've got a hundred-and fifty pounds for a new cooker. er from Social. Social Security because you're on supplementary benefit all right? (...) so you've got a hundred-and-fifty pounds. and that is to get a cooker with my love, all right? (1.5) aren't you lucky? eh? –didn't we do well?
     (adapted from unpublished data collected by Karen Atkinson)

3   a: Anna's so weird
     b: pardon{laughter}
     a: Anna. sometimes kind of hyper hyper
     b: and sometimes kind of lowper lowper
     a: no and {laughter} sometimes kind of 'We should care for the –animals of this world', you know
                                                (Coates 1996)

Apart from the topics of these conversations, you probably used certain features of the language to give you clues about the ages of the speakers. In extract 1, A is three years old and B is her mother. We notice that the toddler has a serviceable but somewhat 'imperfect command' of her native language and that her mother appears to be using a slightly simpler and clearer form of the language than you would expect to be used with another adult. We also notice the mother's use of a 'pet name', 'darling' when speaking to the child and a 'baby-talk' word for 'grandmother'. In extract 2, A is a home help and B is her elderly client. You perhaps noticed that the conversation contains long pauses between the **turns**, making it seem that B is having a hard time 'taking in' what is being said to her and then making a response. Did you notice that A seems to have assumed this since she sometimes does not wait for B's answer to a question, repeats what she says several times and 'translates' the contents of the letter for B? Interestingly, like the mother speaking to her child in extract 1, the home help uses 'pet names' with her client: 'love' and 'my love'. In extract 3, A and B are both fifteen years old. In contrast to extract 2, we notice that their conversation seems quite fluent. Each speaker comes in quite rapidly after the previous speaker's turn has ended. In contrast to extract 1, the structure of their sentences appears quite 'adult'. There are no sentences such as 'me like a little one best'. What might also give the game away is some of the vocabulary used by the girls: 'weird' and 'hyper hyper'.

Our everyday experience yields many examples of vocabulary used by teenagers and young adults which often appear to need 'translations' for older age groups. Some of the most obvious examples come from internet and text messaging, such as 'lulz'. From the abbreviation LOL for 'laughing out loud', it is now also used as a **noun** meaning 'laughter' or 'amusement'. Others arise more locally. Several years ago my 20-year-old British students added a new meaning for 'pants' (as in underwear) to my vocabulary. They said it was roughly equivalent to 'terrible' as in 'That was a pants exam.' This is probably not something similar students would say now, which demonstrates the constant change in what is considered 'cool'.

> Make a collection of current slang words used by children and teenagers. Some areas which might be worth exploring for children are: body parts, words for 'good' and 'bad', names for toys. For teenagers, investigate the same as well as terms for being drunk and vomiting. Ask people of different ages if they can give you a definition for those words. Do people of different age groups have differing perceptions of what those words mean and how they are used?

Activity 7.2

Age-related differences in vocabulary are often the ones most easily noticed by people, but there are other slightly less obvious linguistic differences between age groups as well. For example, sociolinguist Labov (1972a) found that older New Yorkers were less likely to pronounce the /r/ in words such as 'fourth' and 'floor' than were younger speakers, while Chambers and Trudgill (1980) found that in Norwich, England the pronunciation of the **vowel** in words such as 'bell' and 'tell' varied according to the age of the speaker (see section 8.4.2). Suzuki (2002) has proposed that Japanese young people's interest in American and European popular culture as well as their greater use of the internet and text-messaging (as compared to older Japanese) has resulted not only in an increase of foreign loan words entering Japanese but also in potentially permanent changes to the writing system, with a decrease in the use of Chinese characters and greater use of the Western alphabet.[1]

Before the 1990s, most studies on age as a sociolinguistic variable were done by taking 'snapshots' of language use by different age groups at various points in time (**synchronic** research). However, in the last twenty-five years there has been a growing body of research (summarised in Sankoff 2006) which actually focuses on language changes in individuals over the course of their lives (**diachronic** research). What emerges is a complex picture. One pattern of change, which Sankoff terms 'age-grading', involves linguistic patterns which remain fairly stable over time as markers of a particular age group in that **speech community**, such as the use of the **glottal stop** [?] by teenagers in Glasgow. These tend to be replaced as individuals enter a different age group, for example when teenagers become adults and enter the job market. A second pattern, which Sankoff terms 'lifespan change', involves changes over the course of an individual's life reflecting progressive and often rapid changes in the language itself. For example, listen to recordings of Queen Elizabeth when she first came to the throne in 1952 and those of her speaking now. You will hear a marked difference in her pronunciation, especially of the vowels, a difference which reflects a general change in the British **RP accent** over the last fifty years. Sankoff proposes that for many older speakers, exposure to young adults (who are often in the vanguard of linguistic change) may lead to them adopting the changes to avoid sounding 'old-fashioned', or just plain old. Indeed, detailed phonetic analysis of the Queen's language demonstrates that her vowels moved "towards one that is characteristic of speakers who are younger and/or lower in the social hierarchy" (Harrington et al 2000: 927).

Activity 7.3

Think of the last three new words or phrases you have encountered, or perhaps new pronunciations for certain words. For example, my students insist that the correct past tense form for texting on a phone is 'text' rather than 'texted'. Are there any that you started using right away? Are there any that you did not adopt as part of your everyday talk? Are there any that you would restrict to use with a specific age group? What factors do you think influenced your choices? Do you think I now use 'pants' in its new meaning in my everyday talk? What factors led you to that conclusion?

So far, we have touched on some of the ways in which the ages of speakers (and their conversational partners) will cause variations in the particular form of the language being used. However, there is another aspect to the language and age issue. Language is a fundamental human activity through which we communicate our particular representation of the world. It is primarily through language that cultural values and beliefs are transmitted from one member of a society to another and from one generation to the next. Thus, we can often see the way a particular culture views the world, and the kinds of distinctions that are held to be important reflected in the structure of a language (see section 2.3). Age distinctions are frequently reflected in the world's languages. For example, in Italian, as in many languages, the use of certain **pronouns** is partly governed by the ages of the speaker and the hearer. All children are normally addressed by the informal second person pronoun 'tu', while this pronoun is only used for adults who are relatives or close acquaintances (see section 9.4). Comanche, an **Amerindian** language spoken in the southern plains region of the US, had a special version with its own pronunciation patterns and vocabulary which was used with children under five years old (see Casagrande 1948). Closer to home, look at the opening sentences in these three newspaper articles:

4   Senior citizen Tom Ackles risked his own life to save a drowning dog – a beloved neighborhood pet that had fallen through the ice on a frozen lake. The 66-year-old retired college janitor got a frantic call from a neighbor that a large dog was drowning in a nearby lake.

(*National Enquirer*, 24 February 1998)

5   Lifeguards had to intervene to separate two brawling pensioners during an early morning swimming session. … Their dispute spilled out on to the pool side with both men clambering out of the water and squaring up to each other.

(*The Daily Telegraph*, 14 November 1997)

6   Film of grandmother attacking garage owner becomes internet hit. A pensioner has been cautioned for assault after footage of her beating a neighbor with a newspaper became an internet sensation.

(*The Daily Telegraph*, 24 October 2009)

Did you notice that at the very beginning of each article special terms which refer to their age group are used to describe the subjects: 'senior citizen' in the American extract and 'pensioner' in the British extracts? We can talk about these as being **marked**. In extract 6 'grandmother' also seems to function as a codeword for 'old woman'. You may also have noticed that much of the newsworthiness of the stories came from the fact that the subjects' behaviour was somewhat at variance with the cultural expectations of older people. Would a minor fight between two people at a local swimming pool normally make it into the pages of a national newspaper? We will return to this issue in section 7.2 where we will look more closely at how different age groups are represented in English.

In the rest of this chapter we will be concentrating on language issues at the two extreme ends of the lifespan, children under five, and the 'elderly', who we will provisionally define as people over 65. Two factors make these groups particularly useful for exploring the relationship between language, society and power. First, children and the elderly have a high degree of cultural salience in most societies. That is, they are clearly differentiated from the rest of society not only by their special social, economic and legal status but also by the language which is used to describe and categorise them. Second, there are aspects of the communicative abilities of these two groups which can sometimes be quite different from that of the 'middle segment' of the lifespan. By looking at these factors, we can explore the relationship between the way we talk to children and the elderly, the way they talk, and the more general attitudes of our society towards the status of its youngest and oldest members.

7.2 HOW CAN A LANGUAGE REFLECT THE STATUS OF CHILDREN AND OLDER PEOPLE?

In this section we will be looking at the importance of age as a cultural category and the way that our language might reflect a special status for the young and the old.

7.2.1 Age as an important cultural category

How often have you filled in a form where you were asked for your date of birth? It would be hard to imagine a culture which did not use age as a social category and as a means for determining duties, rights and privileges. Your age can determine when you can leave school, marry, drink alcohol, vote, draw a pension, or get into the movies at half price. To see just how important age labels can be, unscramble the words in (a)–(d) below, and put them into the order which seems most 'natural' to you.

(a) intelligent woman the old   (c) dishonest man young the
(b) singer the teenage attractive   (d) middle-aged the nurse kind

Most people produce the following:

(a) the intelligent old woman   (c) the dishonest young man
(b) the attractive teenage singer   (d) the kind middle-aged nurse

In every case, the age description is placed closer to the 'the person' than the other description. There is a very strong tendency in English to place the adjective expressing the most 'defining' characteristic closest to the noun.

What might seem to be a 'natural' word order for these phrases is really a reflection of which of the two characteristics we consider to be more important for classifying people. Even though intelligence, honesty, physical attractiveness and kindness are all important to us, they somehow seem to be secondary to a person's age. As Turner (1973) has pointed out, a word order such as 'the old intelligent woman' can seem a bit odd not because it violates any rule of grammar, but because it does not reflect our habitual way of thinking.

Collect a series of news articles about people of different ages. Take a look to see how many explicitly age-related terms appear. As we saw in extracts 4, 5 and 6, the subjects' relatively advanced age seemed particularly newsworthy. Do you notice any other age groups receiving this kind of treatment in your collection? If so, in what kinds of situations?

Activity 7.4

7.2.2 Labelling age groups

Even with today's life expectancy, the under-5s and over-65s account for only about a quarter of the lifespan, yet they seem to have a disproportionately large number of specialised age group labels. Write down all the labels you can think of which can be used for people under 5; between 20 and 60; and over 65, for example 'baby', 'woman', 'person' (for now, omit any derogatory expressions).

Below are some of the most common terms.

Under 5	20–60	Over 65
person	person	person
child	adult	adult
youngster	grown-up	grown-up
girl	mature person	mature person
boy	woman	woman
minor	man	man
newborn	lady	lady
kid/kiddy	gentleman	gentleman
tot		aged (as in the aged)
neonate		oldster
infant		elderly person
baby		elder
toddler		senior citizen
		retired person
		pensioner
		OAP (old age pensioner)

Did you notice that even though all the expressions used to label the 20–60 group could have been used just as accurately for the people over 65, it might not have occurred to you to use them? The first words that come to mind are often those which specifically single out the over-65s as having a special status, such as 'elderly person', 'senior citizen', 'pensioner'. If you did use some of the same terms that you listed for the 20–60 group, you may have added 'old' or 'elderly'. Explicit age marking also occurs with expressions for the very young, although for this group, size is also used as an age marker: 'little/young child', 'tiny/young tot'.

7.2.3 Talking about age groups: underlying evaluations of early childhood and old age

Have you ever noticed that some **adjectives** seem to 'belong' to a particular age group? Words such as 'wise', 'dignified', 'cantankerous', 'sprightly', 'frail' for the elderly and 'bouncing', 'cute', 'bratty', 'misbehaved' for young children are a few examples. On the other hand, have you also noticed that there seem to be several adjectives, both positive and negative, such as 'little', 'dear', 'sweet', 'fussy', 'cranky', 'stubborn', 'foolish' that are used very frequently to describe both these groups? Expressions such as 'second childhood' for old age make this cultural equation between children and the elderly quite explicit.

Childhood and old age are often viewed as particularly problematic and vulnerable life stages, requiring special attention from the rest of society. There are the terms 'pediatrician' and 'geriatrician' for doctors who specialise in treating children and the elderly, but no special term for doctors who concentrate on 20 to 60 year olds. We have *Save the Children* and *Help the Aged*, but a charity called *Save the Adults* or *Help the Grown-Ups* sounds quite odd and would be unlikely to collect many donations. Aid to Dependent Children and Medicare in the US and Child Benefit and Old Age Pension in the UK are just a few examples of economic resources that governments target specifically to these age groups. We also find special legal institutions designed to protect them. Children are in the care of their parents or guardians and are extremely limited by law in the choices they can make. You may even have left 'person' off the list of terms for the under-5s. The legal term 'minor' makes direct reference to this aspect of childhood.

Franklin (1995: 9) has pointed out that the term 'child' was originally used to describe anyone of low status, regardless of their age, and continues to express 'more about power relationships than chronology, although the two are intimately intertwined'. The cultural image of childhood as one of dependency and incompetence can also be seen in these experiences of the elderly:

> Elderly woman, Morocco: I have no liberty. It is simply that my – children have taken me in their charge.

(Tout 1993: 25)

> Woman who cares for her elderly mother, USA: I 'listen' to her requests but do what I think best.
>
> (Coupland and Nussbaum 1993: 233)

> Virginia Magrath, a retired nurse, waits with her husband, John, who suffers from Alzheimer's and must undergo surgery to remove a blood clot in his brain. She says the doctors ignore her, despite her medical training, speaking to her daughters instead. 'When you're old, people treat you like you're invisible'.
>
> (MSNBC, *Aging in America*, June 2001)

While, the over-65s, as a group, have far more legal independence than children, there is one restriction which can have quite far-reaching consequences for their status in society. The physical limitations that sometimes accompany the ageing process as well as retirement norms mean that the majority of people over 65 are no longer 'earning a living'. Some of the labels for the over-65s make specific reference to this aspect of their identity: 'retired person', 'pensioner' and 'OAP'. Lack of financial independence can be particularly problematic for the elderly. While it is assumed that children will one day become 'productive' members of society, people over 65 are often seen (and see themselves) as no longer capable of contributing to the general prosperity of their families or of the wider society, a potential 'burden' rather than an 'investment':

> Elderly man, Morocco: Nobody bothers with me. When I had means they were all here, but now that I have nothing, nobody knows me.
>
> (Tout 1993: 24)

> Nurse at a day hospital for the elderly, UK: All they've got to give is their memories. And that's why you find old people are always going on about the past ... because that's all they've got to give to say thank you.
>
> (Coupland and Nussbaum 1993: 68)

Another factor which has been proposed as contributing to ageism, at least in Western societies, is the fear of death. As death is feared, old age, the final stage before death is also feared. Butler (1969: 243) has suggested that: 'Ageism reflects a deep seated uneasiness on the part of the young and middle-aged – a personal revulsion to and distaste for growing old, disease, disability; and a fear of powerlessness, "uselessness", and death.' English has many **metaphors** which equate old age with death and decay, as much now as when Shakespeare wrote *Sonnet 73* in which the speaker reflects on his own aging and eventual death:

> That time of year thou mayst in me behold
> When yellow leaves, or none, or few, do hang

Upon those boughs which shake against the cold,
Bare ruined choirs, where late the sweet birds sang.
In me thou see'st the twilight of such day
As after sunset fadeth in the west;
Which by and by black night doth take away,
Death's second self, that seals up all in rest.
In me thou see'st the glowing of such fire,
That on the ashes of his youth doth lie,
As the deathbed whereon it must expire,
Consumed with that which it was nourished by.

(William Shakespeare, Sonnet 73)

You will have also noticed the equation of death with night in the sonnet and old age with twilight and sunset. The use of 'sunset years' as a **euphemism** for old age is still extremely common (type the phrase into a Google News search), but has been turned on its head by a large American chain of retirement communities, *Sunrise Senior Living*. Similarly, a counteraction of the equation of winter and barrenness with old age can be found in the number of retirement homes with the word 'Spring' in their names.

Cruikshank (2003: 26) has pointed out that increased longevity has made the over-85s the fastest growing age group in industrialised societies and in turn has led to new metaphors for the elderly as an 'alien horde' or a 'natural disaster' threatening the welfare of other age groups. She cites examples such as these:

Just as societies gird for the greatest onslaught of people ever to cross the threshold of old age.

(Boston Globe, 23 May 1997)

A demographic iceberg threatens to sink the great powers.

(advertisement in the New York Times for Peter G. Robinson's 1999 book, Gray Dawn: How the Coming Age Wave Will Transform American and the World)

The trend continues. Typing 'time bomb' or 'tsunami' + 'elderly' into Google will call up a myriad of examples. A recent example of the 'alien horde' metaphor can be seen in the *BBC Magazine* of 19 November 2009:

There's the ageing population, leaving about three of us to look after and pay the pensions of teeming millions in walking frames.

(Blastand, 2010)

In an interview in *The Sunday Times* of 24 January 2010, Martin Amis used both the 'alien hordes' and 'natural disaster' metaphors:

How is society going to support this silver tsunami? There'll be a population of demented very old people, like an invasion of terrible immigrants, stinking out the restaurants and cafes and shops.

(Chittenden 2010)

The number of negative, demeaning or insulting terms in the language which are exclusive to particular groups can also indicate a low, or at least problematic, status. The loss of status resulting from physical and economic dependence can be seen in a **thesaurus**. There are virtually no insulting or demeaning terms that are exclusive to the middle of the lifespan, but there are several for children, often accompanied by 'young' or 'little'. Examples are 'brat', 'punk', 'whelp', 'whippersnapper'. When we look at demeaning or insulting terms for older people, the choice is, unfortunately, vast. The terms 'fogey', 'hag', 'biddy', 'fossil', 'geezer', 'codger', 'crone', 'duffer', 'bag', 'wrinklies' are just a few examples. Most of these words can be made even more derogatory when preceded by 'old'. Perhaps because of this, many people over 65 reject the label 'old' entirely as a way of describing their age group, finding that it focuses too much on the negative aspects of ageing. In an American study described in Coupland et al (1991), the researchers found that the expressions 'senior citizen' and 'retired person' had positive connotations of 'active', 'strong', 'progressive' and 'happy', while, 'aged', 'elderly' and 'old person' were much more negatively evaluated. Three age groups carried out the rating task (17–44; 45–64; 65+) and all three groups tended to agree on the evaluations. However, more recent research using focus groups of people over 65 by Wooden (2002) suggests that older Americans harbour 'a profound anger at being labelled anything' and particularly dislike being labelled as 'retired'.

This raises some interesting questions about the complex relationship between language and thought – a subject which was the focus of Chapter 2. Our language might reflect underlying attitudes to children and the elderly, but does it also shape them? If so, would getting rid of ageist language also get rid of ageist attitudes? Would the use of more positive words and metaphors change our negative perceptions of old age? Or might it be the case that new socio-economic circumstances will lead to changed attitudes towards older people and then to a change in the way we talk about them?

Ask ten people to write down the first four words that come to mind for three different ages: 3, 23 and 83. Compare the age groups in terms of the proportion of words that refer to:

- positive and negative qualities
- physical qualities
- mental/emotional qualities
- legal or socio-economic status
- age itself, such as youthful, elderly, etc.

Activity 7.5

In 2006 American 'baby boomers' were turning 60 at a rate of 8000 per day, and by the middle of this century old people will outnumber young people for the first time in history, making this generation a powerful voting bloc. Post-war prosperity, smaller families, and increased career opportunities for women mean that when they retire, this generation will have considerably more economic power than their predecessors. By the turn of the twenty-first century, the advertising and marketing industries were re-thinking their strategies to adapt to the new economic reality (Kleyman, 2001). Indeed, the spending power of older people is recognised in the new coinage, 'the grey dollar'.

Medical advances allowing many more people to have a healthy and active old age could also change our perceptions of what it is to be 'old'. Williams et al (2007) analysed the changes in an advertising campaign in Britain for *Olivio* margarine between 1996 and 2003 and found an increasing tendency to depict older people as active and adventurous individuals who did not conform to the cultural stereotypes of their age groups.

7.3 TALKING TO YOUNG CHILDREN AND THE ELDERLY

In this section we turn from looking at the way the very young and the very old are talked about to looking at the way these groups are talked to.

7.3.1 Language characteristics of the under-5s and over-65s

Very young children's language takes its characteristic 'style' from the fact they are apprentice speakers. During the first five years of life, children are still in the process of acquiring the grammar of their native language and a 'working' vocabulary. Young children's speech also has a characteristic 'sound'. First, the pitch of their voice is quite high relative to that of adults. Second, their early pronunciations of words can be quite different from the adult versions.

Unlike young children, the over-65s are experienced language users. However, many people believe that old age inevitably results in a decline of communicative ability. Although there is evidence to suggest that older people may require slightly longer processing time to produce and understand complex sentences, numerous studies have shown that the normal ageing process in itself does not result in a significant loss of verbal skill unless serious illnesses, such as a stroke or Alzheimer's disease, intervene. In some types of discourse, such as complex storytelling, elderly speakers generally outperform younger speakers. However, hearing often becomes less acute as people get older, and this can lead to a reduced understanding of rapid or whispered speech, or of speech in a noisy environment. The 'elderly' voice, like a young child's, is instantly recognisable. The normal ageing of the vocal cords and muscles controlling breathing and facial movement results in slower speech and a voice which has a higher pitch and weaker volume and resonance than that of younger adults.

Of course, the way a person sounds is quite separate from what that person is actually saying. However, the problem for elderly speakers is that people do not always make that distinction. Just as different accents can lead hearers to make all sorts of stereotyped and often inaccurate judgments about everything from the honesty to the education level of the speaker, the sound of an elderly person's voice can immediately link the hearer into a whole set of beliefs about old age which may or may not be true of that particular person. Sataloff (2005) reports a small but increasing number of older Americans opting for cosmetic 'voice-lifts' – surgical and medical procedures to rejuvenate the vocal chords. His comment in a 2004 interview that 'there are people who pay $15,000 for a face lift and as soon as they open their mouth, they sound like they're 75' was reported by the Associated Press (Loviglio 2004) and sparked considerable debate in both the UK and US media.

You and I 'speak'. Children 'babble' and 'chatter'. Old people 'drone' and 'witter'. Or do they? The talk of people in other 'low status' groups is often devalued or described in negative terms. See if this might hold true for young children and the elderly by examining descriptions of their talk in literature, the media and in your own conversations. Then expand your research to look at descriptions of adolescents' language, particularly in the media. Penelope Eckert (2004: 361) notes that young people are often criticised as 'sloppy, imprecise, faddish, profane and overly flamboyant' speakers and even seen as a 'threat' to their native language. You might find a tool that allows you to pattern search the internet useful: http://webascorpus.org/.

Activity 7.6

7.3.2 Child Directed Language

Child Directed Language (CDL), sometimes called 'Baby Talk' or 'Motherese', is a special style used in speech to young children and has been extensively studied over the past thirty years. It has several characteristics, some of which were illustrated in extract 1:

- calling the child by name, often using a 'pet' name or term of endearment
- shorter, grammatically simpler sentences
- more repetition
- more use of questions and question tags ('That's nice, *isn't it?*')
- use of 'baby-talk' words
- expanding on and/or finishing a child's utterance.

CDL also has a characteristic 'sound':

- higher pitch
- slower speed
- more pauses, particularly between phrases
- clearer, more 'distinct' pronunciation
- exaggerated intonation (some words in the sentence heavily empha-sised, and a very prominent rising tone used for questions).

Observational studies of parents' conversations with their children have also highlighted several common features in the way in which the interaction proceeds (see section 3.6). Young children are usually perceived to be incompetent turn-takers with older speakers having expectations that their contributions will be irrelevant or delayed. The younger the child, the more likely their attempts to initiate a new topic will be ignored by older speakers and the more likely they are to be interrupted or overlapped (two speakers talking simultaneously). There is a relatively high proportion of 'directive' and 'instructive' talk from adults, either by blunt commands: be careful, don't do that, or by 'talking over' (talking about people in their presence and referring to them as 'we' or 'she'/'he'). Here is an example:

> C = Child, T.; M = Mother. C wants to turn on the lawn sprinklers. A researcher is present.
> C: Mommy.
> M: T. has a little problem with patience. We're working on patience. What is patience, T.?
> C: Nothing.
> M: Come on.
> {   C: [I want to turn them_._._.
>   M: [What is_._._.
> C: on now.
> M: patience? Can you remember?
>
> (Ervin-Tripp 1979: 402)

7.3.3 Similarities between Child Directed Language and 'Elder Directed' Language

In section 7.1 we noted that there seemed to be several parallels between the speech style used by the home help to her elderly client and that of the mother talking to her child. Coupland et al (1991) review several studies which confirm the similarity between CDL and the speech style which is often used with the elderly, particularly by their caregivers. These similarities involve both the content of the talk – simpler sentences, more questions and repetitions, use of pet names, etc – and the sound of the talk – slower, louder, higher pitch, exaggerated intonation, etc. As the next extract illus-trates, there can also be similarities in the ways speakers interact with young children and the elderly, interrupting and overlapping them, treating the person's contribution as irrelevant to the conversation, and using directive language, especially 'talking over'.

HH = home help; CL = elderly client; D = Relative of CL.
HH: How are you today?
CL: Oh I (xx) I've
{ CL: [got a (xx)
{ D: [She's a bit down today because we're leaving
HH: I guessed that's what it would be today

Later discussing cakes which have been left for CL who is still present.

D: They're in there and I'm hoping. They're in the fridge you see.
        I'm hoping she will go in there and take them and eat them.
HH: That's right yeah don't waste.
        (adapted from unpublished data collected by Karen Atkinson)

7.3.4 Why might these similarities occur?

One of the original explanations for the use of CDL was that parents used it as a language-teaching tool. Indeed, there are some aspects of CDL which could potentially be of help to novice speakers. The problem is that variations in the amount of CDL which children receive do not seem to significantly affect their progress in acquiring their native language, and as Ochs (1983) points out, not all cultures use this type of talk with young children. Clancy (1986) observed that Japanese mothers' speech to their children focused primarily on teaching politeness and communicative style, rather than on grammar and vocabulary. So, if CDL is not primarily a teaching tool of the language itself, why is it used in some cultures?

   One proposal is that one of its primary uses is to ensure understanding in someone who is not believed to be a fully competent language user. This might account for the considerable similarities between CDL and the language used with the elderly. Its use could therefore be closely connected to cultural expectations and stereotypes about people in these groups. **Matched guise experiments** have shown that speakers with an 'elderly' voice tend to be rated as vulnerable, forgetful and incompetent more often than speakers with younger voices. The low expectations of the elderly resulting from cultural stereotyping of old age as an inevitable decline in physical and mental capacity is illustrated in the following extract between a home help (HH) and her elderly client (CL):

CL: Well I don't know your name anyway
HH: Ann.
CL: Ann_._._.

{ CL: [mmm
{ HH: [Right.
  CL: I don't need to know your surname do I?
  HH: (2) Well you can know it. It's Campbell, but I don't think you'll
        remember it, will you. *{laughter}*
  CL: (2) What do you mean I won't remember it? I'm not dim.
        {sounding annoyed}

(adapted from unpublished data collected by Karen Atkinson)

Another proposed explanation for the use of CDL is that it asserts the power of the caregiver in relation to the child, establishing the caregiver's right to command compliance. When young children are taught the socially appropriate way to 'ask', the message is often that adults can make demands of children but children must make polite requests of adults.

  mother: I beg your pardon?
  child: What?
  mother: Are you ordering me to do it?
  child: Mmm, I don't know, Momma.
  mother: Can't you say 'Mommy, would you please make me
         some?'

(Becker 1988: 178)

The emphasis on unequal power relations between adult and child fits in with our observations about conversational interaction between children and the elderly on the one hand and their caregivers on the other, where the more powerful speaker tends to use interruption, overlapping and 'talking over' (see section 5.6.2). While the use of questions and question tags by caregivers can help elicit conversation, it also allows them to 'direct' the responses of their conversational partners. **Tag questions** can be especially controlling because they explicitly seek agreement with the speaker.

Atkinson and Coupland (1988) have suggested that using CDL with the elderly can reflect not only a cultural equation between these two groups which is potentially demeaning to elderly people but also a deliberate strategy to constrain and marginalise them, particularly in institutional settings.

However, there is another dimension to the use of CDL which is seemingly in contradiction to this proposal. That is, some aspects of CDL might reflect an attitude of affection and nurturance towards the recipient and a willingness to accommodate to their needs. This is an example of the **phatic** use of language, a particularly important function to consider for interactions with children and the elderly. Cromer (1991) has pointed out that affectionate talk to lovers and pets is also characterised by higher pitch, exaggerated intonation, pet names and baby-talk words. And, while no one is likely to appreciate being interrupted or talked over, a negative reaction by the elderly to pet names and repetition accompanied by slower, louder and simpler speech cannot be taken for granted. Coupland et al (1991) review of studies involving elderly people's evaluations of this style of talk has shown that some found it patronising or demeaning and negatively evaluated caregivers who used it. Others, particularly those who were very frail or suffering from deafness or short-term memory loss found it nurturing and 'encouraging' and a help in understanding and participating in the conversation. The American Speech-Language-Hearing Association estimates that in nursing homes, 60 to 90 per cent of residents have some degree of communication disability which can often be helped by caregivers using a simplified speech style and allowing extra time for responding.

7.4 CONCLUSION

At the beginning of this chapter, I asked you to identify the approximate ages of the speakers in three conversations. We will end with the same sort of task.

1

A: what have you been eating?
B: eating
A: you haven't been eating that spinach have you
B: {laughter} spin
A: you know what Pop_._._.happens to Popeye when he eats his _   spinach
(adapted from unpublished data collected by Karen Atkinson)

2

I'm CUTE and SMART and have a GREAT sense of humor. Look like an animated Q-Tip with curves in ALL the right places. Not overweight, clinging, needy, whiney, or psycho. And if I was ever fed ugly-pills, they DID NOT work!
(www.match.com)

3

Dominic, I'm putting some people in the bus. Now drive off. Down to the end ... Drive off down to the village, darling ... Now are you going to do that?
(Harris and Coltheart 1986: 79)

4

I remember love – the beauty, the ecstasy!
Then – how it hurt!
Forgetting helped time dissolve the hurt and pain
of defeated expectation.
(Thorsheim and Roberts 1990: 123)

Extract 1 is a conversation between a home help, A, and her elderly client, B. Extract 2 was written by a 70-year-old subscriber to an internet singles site. The speaker in extract 3 is four years old and is explaining how to play a game to her two-year-old brother. Extract 4 was written by an 80-year-old retirement home resident in the US. If you were surprised by the ages of some of the speakers in these extracts, it simply shows that there is a very complex relationship between physical, mental and social factors in determining a person's use of language and how others perceive and react to that language.

7.5 SUMMARY

In this chapter we have seen that age is an important cultural category, an identity marker, and a factor in producing language variation within a speech community. The way we talk about young children and the elderly reflects their special status in our society – a status which is partly determined by the amount of social and economic power which these groups possess. There are parallels between talk addressed to young children and talk to the elderly. These parallels cannot be explained entirely by physical and mental immaturity in the case of young children or by physical and mental decline in the case of the elderly. The status of young children and the elderly in our society, and culturally determined beliefs and stereotypes about their communicative abilities, can play a significant role in producing these parallels.

As a final thought, the following excerpt is from a somewhat tongue-in-cheek review of a television documentary about au pairs. Analyse the language, looking particularly at any references to children's socio-economic status, the 'characteristic' attributes of young children which have been highlighted, and the degree to which the piece reflects cultural attitudes towards childhood (or turns them on their head).

> Say what you like about Paul Newman, I regard him as the acceptable face of capitalism. His physiognomy may be prominently displayed on the side of every jar of his high-priced spaghetti sauces, but that's okay by me because he gives 100 per cent of his profits to a children's charity. Lloyd Grossman, who also sticks his face on his pasta sauce bottles, ensures that his profits go to an equally deserving cause (Lloyd's bank), and I'm planning to follow suit by marketing Vic's own brand of olive oil, made from freshly pressed olives. No, on second thoughts, I think I'll market Vic's baby oil instead, made from freshly-pressed babies. Mmmm, great on salads.
>
> I doubt if anyone who watched last night's Cutting Edge would need much persuading to operate the baby crusher. We all know that children are little, noisy, stupid people who don't pay rent but, worse still, here were dozens of precocious and over-indulged American brats, all fed on rocket fuel and all screeching 'mommy' through voice boxes

seemingly powered by the windchest of a Harrison & Harrison cathe-
dral organ.

(Victor Lewis-Smith, 'Days of Whine, Not Roses', *Evening Standard*,
4 March 1998)

FURTHER READING

Calasanti, T. and King, N. (2007) '"Beware of the estrogen assault": Ideals of old
    manhood in anti-aging advertisements', *Journal of Aging Studies*, 21 (4):
    357–368.
Coupland, N. and Nussbaum, J. (eds) (1993) *Discourse and Lifespan Identity*,
    London: Sage.
Eckert, P. (2004) 'Adolescent Language', in E. Finegan and J. Rickford (eds),
    Language in the USA: Themes for the Twenty-first Century, Cambridge:
    Cambridge University Press.
Gilleard, C. (2007) 'Old age in Ancient Greece: narratives of desire, narratives of
    disgust', *Journal of Aging Studies*, 21 (1): 81–92.
Gleason, J. (ed) (2008) *The Development of Language*, 7th edn, Boston: Allyn &
    Bacon.
Henneberg, S. (2010) 'Moms do badly, but grandmas do worse: The nexus of sexism
    and ageism in children's classics', *Journal of Aging Studies*, 24 (2): 125–134
Jolanki, O. (2009) 'Agency in talk about old age and health', *Journal of Aging Studies*,
    23 (4): 215–226.
Lee, M. M., Carpenter, B., Meyers, L. S. (2007) 'Representations of older adults in
    television advertisements', *Journal of Aging Studies*, 21 (1): 9–31.
Makoni, S. and Grainger, K. (2002) 'Comparative gerontolinguistics: characterizing
    discourses in caring institutions in South Africa and the United Kingdom',
    Journal of Social Issues, 58 (4): 805–824.
Maxim, J. and Bryan, K. (1994) *Language of the Elderly*, London: Whurr.
Schieffelin, B. and Ochs, E. (eds) (1987) *Language Socialization Across Cultures*,
    Cambridge: Cambridge University Press.
Williams, A., Ylänne, V. and Wadleigh, P. (2007) 'Selling the 'Elixir of Life': Images of
    the elderly in an Olivio advertising campaign', *Journal of Aging Studies*, 21 (1):
    1–21.

NOTE

1   Japanese has a very complex writing system. There are three types of script
     which are all used at the same time: kanji (Chinese characters for words of
     Chinese origin), hiragana (a rounded script based on syllables) and katana (a
     square-shaped script also based on syllables but used for words borrowed from
     languages other than Chinese).

CHAPTER 8

Language and social class

Eva Eppler

8.1 INTRODUCTION

> Class is a boring topic to write about. Big divides are not what people are interested in. But it's the most pressing concern – because other things spring out of it, like terrorism and instability.
>
> (Aravind Adiga, Man Booker Prize winner 2008,
> *The Guardian*, 14 October 2008)

Obviously neither Aravind Adiga nor I think that class is a boring topic to write about; otherwise we wouldn't be doing it! The recent downturn in the economy did make more people interested in social class again – partly because the recession was predicted to affect the middle class(es) most. In the end it has actually hit the working class(es) more. This already tells us something about why class matters.

In this chapter we will look at the relationship between socio-economic class and language, between social identity and status, and sociolinguistic variation. I don't think I need to make a special case for the fact that people talk differently, that there is linguistic variation. That should be clear by now. You also know that this variation is linked to different factors. It is linked to, for example, people's age (see Chapter 7), their ethnic background (see Chapter 6) and to where people come from in terms of geographical region (see section 8.3 and section 9.3). Linguistic variation is also linked to social class. Or, as

Penelope Eckert (1999: 3) puts it 'social groupings live very different lives, and as a result do very different things with language. It is no surprise then that this split frequently correlates with the use of sociolinguistic variables'.

This chapter begins by examining individuals' 'life chances' and the social hierarchies they create – that is, we begin with a definition of social class and the factors that contribute to determining social class. We then consider the relationship between regional and social variation and social position(ing) in the UK, the US and India, and how these relationships have changed in the twentieth and early twenty-first century, through **dialect levelling** and **standardisation**. I will then introduce you to some seminal studies from the late 1960s and early 1970s which systematically correlated linguistic variability with different social features.

During the 1980s, several researchers considerably re-thought aspects of social theories of variation. In the final section we will see that they came back with a changed view of the speaker, and consequently quite different types of studies of language and social variation. Rather than looking at the relationship between language and the large social groups individual speakers are members of, the more recent studies of social variation emphasise the role individuals play in positioning themselves in society. We will see that these more recent studies view linguistic variation as a social practice in which individuals actively construct their social identity (see section 9.6). Personally I think the truth lies somewhere between these two views. They are not mutually exclusive and several studies successfully combine them (eg Eckert 1999). At the end of the chapter you ought to be in a position to evaluate this shift and decide for yourself how much your linguistic behaviour is determined by your social background and/or how much you can create your own social identity through language use, clothing, gadgets and so on. But let's start by looking at what social class is.

8.2 WHAT IS SOCIAL CLASS?

Most of us have some kind of idea, intuitive or otherwise, about what social class is. When probed, we may start using words such as 'higher' or 'posh' and 'lower', and considering factors such as job, income, housing, family background. Language is an important factor in any discussion of social class, but it is one of many other indicators available. In this chapter, we will be looking at the detail of language in relation to class, but it is well to remember that other things help us attribute a class to people. We consider the clothing that people wear, perhaps including style and brands; we might also pay attention to the way people walk, stand and sit, or look at their 'manners'. All these features work together and we can usually make a judgement about people on this basis. (Whether we're right or not is another question altogether!) It's also worth remembering that what these features mean in terms of class will differ from place to place and time to time. Lastly, these features might not be consistent. Someone might be wearing 'posh' clothes and yet not talk in a 'posh' way.

Before we look at other people's definitions of social class, check your own intuitions by making a list of the major factors which you think combine to determine a person's social class. When you have a list, indicate the order of importance. How many factors did you come up with? Compare your list with a colleague's. Did you differ in terms of which factors you felt were the most important? Did one of you come up with anything that the other one didn't?

This activity may have shown that trying to define social class is not easy, and deciding exactly what criteria an assessment of someone's social class should involve isn't easy either. Fortunately, we do not have to reinvent the wheel and can take advantage of work in sociology in this area. This is also what many sociolinguistic researchers do who work on the relationship between language and social class.

Two components have been identified as fundamental in determining the life-chances of an individual or group: first, the objective, economic measures of property ownership and the power and control it gives to those who have it; second, the more subjective measures of prestige, reputation and status. The simplest kind of social stratification is based on occupational categories, with non-manual occupations being rated 'higher' than manual occupations. This method combines the two components just mentioned and demonstrates that factors other than income are important in the assessment of social status. A plumber might earn a great deal more than an accountant, but in many societies, the plumber would be considered to be of a lower social class.

American social anthropologists W. Lloyd Warner and colleagues (1960) included information on occupation, income, wealth, education, family and close friends, speech, manners and so on in their Index of Status Characteristics – the tools they developed for assessing social class among populations under investigation. Other less reliable classification schemes for social distribution define social class solely in terms of occupation (eg the National Opinion Research Council (NORC) in the US, the Standard Occupational Classification (SOC) the in the UK, and the Australian Standard Classification of Occupations (ASCO)). Most of these occupationally based social class schemes propose three ('upper', 'middle', 'lower'), or even five divisions:

1. Professional etc occupations.
2. Managerial and technical occupations.
3. Skilled occupations (non-manual/manual).
4. Partly skilled occupations.
5. Unskilled occupations.

While individual occupations have been reallocated to different classes, the overall shape of the structure has changed very little during the past sixty years. It is always advisable to adjust these indices and measures for local conditions when the system is used in other industrialised societies, but otherwise they offer a set of procedures that sociolinguists can rely on to place an individual speaker in the social hierarchy. To summarise our discussion of social class so far, traditionally, the term has been used to define and analyse identities and relations between groups located at different levels of the socio-economic hierarchy. We have seen that the notion of class links together and summarises many aspects of an individual's life: main source of income, educational and family background (which may influence cultural tastes and political associations), speech, manners and so on.

8.2.1 Thinking beyond occupation

A variation of the social class index is the linguistic market index (Sankoff and Laberge 1978, based on the notion of 'linguistic market' from Bourdieu and Boltanski 1975). It aims to examine the correspondence between an individual's socio-economic position and the extent to which her/his situation in life requires them to use the standard language. This model allows an understanding of the power that non-standard language use can have. Drawing on this work, Eckert writes:

> One will have little chance of succeeding in the diplomatic corps if one does not possess a range of knowledge that marks one as the 'right kind' of person: the right table manners, the right style of dress, the right ways of entertaining guests, the right language … this is equally true if one is to be accepted in a peasant village or in an urban ghetto (Woolard 1985) – what is 'right' depends on the market in which one is engaged.
>
> (1998: 67)

The **linguistic market** allows us to understand status in any context. If you want to be a successful lawyer, you may need the **symbolic capital** that matters in this linguistic market. Specifically, you'll probably need to be fluent in Standard English and in legal language. However, if you want status in a hip-hop community, you'll need to be proficient in the language genres that are prestigious in that environment (see section 9.6).

The social class stratification in the industrialised countries we have discussed so far is not universal. Although rapidly emerging as an industrialised country, traditional Indian society is stratified into different castes. Roughly speaking, castes are ranked, hereditary, closed social groups which, like social class, are often linked with occupation. Because caste membership is hereditary, castes tend to be more rigidly separated from each other than social classes are, and there is less possibility for movement from one caste to another, despite socio-economic advancement. Although this is a considerable simplification of the actual situation, there are 'big [social] divides' in Indian society. This is what Aravind Adiga, the Indian-born author who won the 2008 Booker Prize, is talking about in the opening quote to this chapter. And the big divides in Indian society are also reflected in language use. We will discuss this further in the next section on **regional and social variation**.

8.3 SOCIAL AND REGIONAL VARIATION

I would like to illustrate the relation between regional and social variation in India based on data from Kannada, a Dravidian language spoken in south India. The data in Table 8.1 are taken from Trudgill (1995: 24) and show a selection of linguistic forms used by Brahmins, the highest caste, and the corresponding forms or variants of the speech of the lower castes, in two towns which are about 250 miles apart – Bangalore and Dharwar.

Table 8.1 Brahmin and non-Brahmin linguistic forms in Bangalore and Dharwar

	Brahmin		Non-Brahmin	
	Dharwar	Bangalore	Dharwar	Bangalore
'it is'	ede	ide	ayti	ayti
'inside'	-olage	-alli	-aga	-aga
Infinitive affix	-likke	-ok	-ak	-ak
Participle affix	-o	-o	-a	-a
'sit'	kut-	kut-	kunt-	kunt-
reflexive	ko	ko	kont-	kont-

Activity 8.2

Compare the linguistic forms produced by members of the Brahmin and non-Brahmin castes in Dharwar and Bangalore and try to decide if social or regional differences in language are bigger.

The first three examples ('it is', 'inside' and the infinitive ending) show that the Bangalore and Dharwar forms are the same for the lower castes ('ayti', '-aga' and '-ak'). The Brahmin caste has forms which are not only different from the other castes, but also different from each other in the two towns. This means that the 'higher' caste forms are subject to more regional variation than the 'lower' caste form (we will compare this to the class varieties in England in a moment). The last three examples in Table 8.1 (the participle affix, 'sit' and the reflexive) show that there is more similarity within social groups than for geographical groups. This means that, overall, social differences in language use are greater than regional differences.

Let's compare the situation in India with that in England. This time I'm going to illustrate the relation between social and regional variation with two diagrams from Trudgill 1995: 20–30). Figure 8.1 represents social and regional variation in accents (pronunciation), while Figure 8.2 represents social and regional variation in dialects (grammar and lexis).

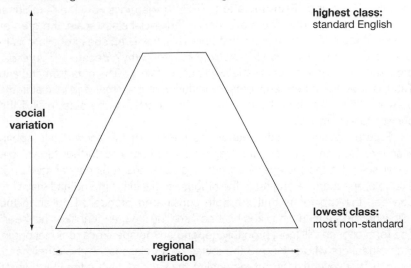

Figure 8.1 Social and regional variation in dialects

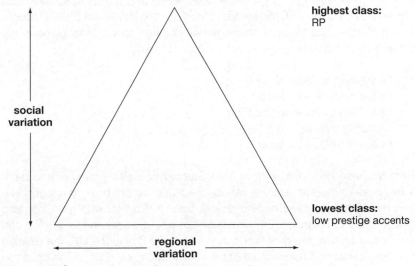

Figure 8.2 Social and regional variation in accents

Compare the relation between regional and social variation in the UK, as graphically represented in Figures 8.1 and 8.2, with the situation in India. Is it similar or different?

Activity 8.3

Figure 8.1 represents variation in pronunciation – that is, **accents**. It shows that speakers at the top of the social scale (ie at the top of the triangle) tend to pronounce the words they use with the same accent, roughly, **Received Pronunciation** (RP), regardless of their regional background. The further we move 'down' the social class scale, the greater spread of regional pronunciation we find. This, however, does not allow us to answer the questions posed in Activity 8.3 yet. Why? Because Figure 8.1 presents social and regional variation in accents only. The data from India in Table 8.1, on the other hand, present variation in grammar *and* lexical items (ie words). We therefore have to look at Figure 8.2 to be able to find the answer to Activity 8.3.

Figure 8.2 shows that speakers as the top of the social scale speak Standard English with very little regional variation. The further 'down' the social scale (ie the triangle) we go, the greater the regional variation. For example, speakers belonging to the highest social class in England may vary between the two forms that are both considered Standard English in the following, 'he's a man who likes his beer' and 'he's a man that likes his beer'. The form chosen will most probably depend on the speaker's regional origin. From speakers who belong to the lower social classes, on the other hand, we may hear several different regional forms such as 'I is' (in the Northwest), 'I are' (in the Midlands), 'I be' (in the Southwest) and the regional form that happens to coincide with the standard 'I am' (in the North and East) (Trudgill, 1995). Further examples of the regional variation found among the lower social groups from the same source are as follows:

> *he's a man at likes his beer*
> *he's a man as likes his beer*
> *he's a man what likes his beer*
> *he's a man he likes his beer*
> *he's a man likes his beer*

Each of these sentences differs from Standard English grammar and each belongs to a different regional variety. Because we are now comparing like with like – that is, grammar and lexical items in English with grammar and lexical items in Kannada, the Dravidian language of South India – we can now safely answer the question posed in Activity 8.3. In the UK, the relation between social and regional variation is exactly the reverse of the situation in India. In India we found social distance more differentiating than geographical distance. In England, on the other hand, regional variation is greater among the lower social classes.

Although we had to differentiate between Figures 8.1 and 8.2 to make a valid comparison with the Kannada data in Table 8.1, the two figures are quite similar in that they only differ at the 'top'. Figure 8.2 has a 'pointy' top because there is little regional variation in the RP accent, whereas there is a little bit of regional variation in the Standard English dialect. Generally, however, a **dialect** is often associated with a particular **accent**, so a speaker who uses a regional dialect will also be more likely to have the corresponding regional accent (this is why Figures 8.1 and 8.2 are so similar). It is also important to point out that these diagrams are representative of the situation in England only: in other countries, Germany and Poland for example, it is more likely that individuals who belong to the higher social classes will also speak with a regional accent. Even with reference to Britain, these two diagrams are generalised representations of regional social variation – of course it is possible for a member of the working class to speak Standard English and /or use RP. (This kind of linguistic **agency** is emphasised by the more recent sociolinguistics studies we will discuss towards the end of this chapter.) I included the two diagrams because they give a useful illustration of the traditional relationship between regional and social variation in Britain, and they allow us to make a comparison with the situation in India. This comparison also reveals one of the most fundamental truths about the relationship between language and society: the more **heterogeneous** or diverse a society is, the more heterogeneous or varied its language.

If this is the case, what are the effects of increasing mobility, urbanisation and globalisation on the relationship between regional and social dialects? Is language use becoming less varied as a consequence? For British English the answer seems to be 'yes'. David Brittain and Paul Kerswill, two British sociolinguistics, have confirmed what many people who travel in Britain have been observing since the beginning of the twentieth century: there are fewer differences between ways of speaking in some parts of the country today. This process has been called **levelling**: a **convergence** of accents and dialects towards each other, so that many differences between them disappear. One example of this process is the replacement of the two 'th' sounds by 'f' and 'v' so that 'thin' is the same as 'fin', and 'brother' rhymes with 'lover'. This is a characteristic London feature which has spread to the Southeast, Central and Northern England and the Lowlands of Scotland, but is only sporadically heard in Cardiff, Liverpool and Edinburgh (Kerswill 2001). Another interesting example of social class related accent levelling is the pronunciation of the vowel/**diphthong** in words such as 'bite' and 'bride' in Hull in northern England. In RP, the first vowel in both words is a diphthong (ai). In Hull, however, 'bride' is pronounced 'brahd' (not 'braide') among older working-class speakers. Working-class adolescents in Hull still observe this distinction, but middle-class adolescents use the more southern pronunciation in all contexts.

This example shows that dialect levelling is associated with socioeconomic changes in the twentieth century. It appears to have been caused by several interrelated factors: urbanisation due to the loss of rural employment, changes in people's networks (a loss of traditional networks and an expansion of the range of individual personal ties), and a change in social roles within the family (both men and women meet people from a wider range of geographical and social backgrounds). All these trends have led to widespread dialect contact (especially in the suburbs), dialect levelling and standardisation. We have already come across the term 'Standard English' as a class dialect. The term **standardisation** in this context therefore refers to the fact that, during the last century, many families have abandoned traditional rural dialects in favour of a type of English that is more like the urban speech of the local town or city. These new dialects are more like Standard English in grammar and vocabulary. As already indicated, the mechanism for standardisation lies in the kinds of **social networks** people have. People involved in socially varied networks will meet people with a higher status (most typically at work) and may accommodate their speech to them. This phenomenon is called upward convergence. But standardisation is far from a universal force (Kerswill 2001), as we all know, various aspects of regional speech are being preserved, despite dialect levelling.

One example that illustrates how modified regional dialects resist becoming completely standardised is Estuary English.[1] Until recently, Estuary English was no one's mother tongue, but people converged on it from two directions: from 'below' and from 'above'. The people who arrive at it from below have been upwardly converging their speech as they increase their social status. They, for example, eliminate grammatically non-standard features, such as double negatives and the word 'ain't' (see section 10.3), and they avoid the most stigmatised phonetic features – for example, the h-dropping that features prominently in the film *My Fair Lady*. People who arrive at Estuary English from above converge downward from Received Pronunciation (RP). This is why, according to the *Sunday Times*, Estuary English speakers cover the middle ground 'between Cockney and the Queen' (Rosewarne 1994). Cockney is the 'traditional' working-class dialect spoken in the East End of London.

Estuary English is much debated by linguists. It does, however, speak to arguments of homogenization and the idea that class is no longer relevant. It also exemplifies issues around language change.

> Estuary English is much debated by linguists. It does, however, speak to arguments of homogenization and the idea that class is no longer relevant. It also exemplifies issues around language change.
>
> (Kerswill 2001)

Some journalists have interpreted dialect levelling, standardisation and especially Estuary English as signs of a move towards a 'classless society'. I doubt this is the case, but we would need more research to establish this. As has been mentioned, the idea that *all* varieties are becoming the same is simply not true.[2] Rather, these linguistic phenomena do show us that that there is a consistent trend towards greater regional and social mobility and that there is a move away from the 'posh' accent (RP), at least among people who try to reach a wider audience and don't want to get ridiculed (see section 8.5).

8.4 VARIATIONIST SOCIOLINGUISTICS

The aim of variationist sociolinguistics is to correlate linguistic variation (the **dependent variable)** with **independent variables** such as social

categories, style or the linguistic environment. Dependent linguistic variables can be anything from slightly different pronunciations of certain sounds,
to constitutive word parts (**morphemes**), to words (**lexical items**), to
grammatical constructions. As this chapter focuses on social class, we'll
mainly be looking at which concrete quantifiable independent variables[3]
(that contribute to determining social class) correlate with which **dependent linguistic variables**[4] in the most seminal sociolinguistic studies of the
1960s. We will pay particular attention to the variety of treatments of social
class, how class correlates with linguistic variation, and how the findings
from these correlations have been interpreted. The classic studies of linguistic variation are all based on the traditional ways of defining social class we
examined in section 8.2.

8.4.1 Labov's department store study

In the early 1960s the American sociolinguist William Labov conducted a
survey of the relationship between social class and linguistic variation in
New York City (1966). In this famous 'department store' survey, Labov
defined social stratification by the prestige of the three department stores
he investigated: Saks, Macy's and Klein's. The relative prestige of the stores
was in turn established by a number of independent factors such as the
location of the store, the relative cost of goods in the three stores, and in
which newspapers they advertised. On these criteria, Saks was identified as
the most prestigious store, Macy's scored in the middle, and Klein's was
identified as the least prestigious one. Labov assumed that by selecting
stores from the top, the middle and the bottoms of the price scale, he could
expect first, that the customers would be socially stratified, and second, that
the sales people in each of the department stores would reflect this in their
speech styles. The second assumption is based on sociological research
which suggests that salespeople and cashiers tend to borrow prestige from
their customers, or at least make an effort in that direction. I have always felt
that this is a rather risky assumption, but as we'll see, it works.

Labov wanted to find out whether the presence or absence of a
pronounced 'r' in words such as 'car', 'fourth' and 'floor' was determined by
speakers' social class. In New York City, the prestige variety has **post-
vocalic 'r'** (ie, the /r/ sound is pronounced after vowels in this accent), and
lack of the feature is associated with less prestigious ways of speaking. If
you are English, it's important to note that this situation is the reverse of that
in the UK, where the prestige accent (RP) is 'r'-less (ie, 'car' is pronounced
/ka:/, and 'floor' is pronounce /flo:/, where the colon indicates a long vowel
sound). Labov believed that the more prestige speakers have or borrow
from their customers, the more instances of post-vocalic 'r' he would find in
their speech.

Labov's method of observation was to approach sales assistants in each
store and ask the location of particular sales item, to which he knew the
answer would be 'fourth floor' (in which, as the spelling indicates, there are

two places where it is possible to pronounce post-vocalic 'r', namely fourth floor). Labov also believed that speakers would tend to shift towards a very carefully articulated, more prestigious pronunciation of the word when paying more attention to their speech (see section 9.6). In order to test this, he pretended not to have heard the **informant**'s response, and asked them to repeat 'fourth floor'. In this way, Labov elicited a more 'careful' speech style, in addition to the 'casual' style of the first response. Figure 8.3 presents a simplified version of the results of Labov's department store investigation.

Figure 8.3 shows how often the two post vocalic 'r's in 'fourth floor' were pronounced in relation to the number of times it could have been pronounced. The first response and the repetition of 'fourth floor' are plotted on the horizontal axis. The vertical axis shows the actual pronunciation of post vocalic 'r' as a percentage of the number of times it could have been pronounced. The continuous line at the bottom of the graph shows that salespeople form Klein's pronounced the 'r' infrequently, with a small increase on each occasion they had the opportunity to repeat it (from slightly under, to slightly over 10 per cent of the time). Speakers from Saks and Macy's pronounced the 'r' in a similar pattern of frequency to each other, although informants from Saks pronounced the post-vocalic 'r's more often (as the interrupted lines show). Speakers in all three stores showed a tendency to increase the rate of 'r' pronunciation when they repeated 'fourth floor' – that is, when, according to Labov, they paid more attention to their speech. Labov's results show that the presence or absence of the prestigious post-vocalic 'r' is related to the prestige associated with the three department stores, and thus with social class. The pronunciation of 'r' in words such as 'car', 'fourth' and 'floor' was indeed more common for speakers wishing to project a higher social position. I expressed my scepticism about Labov's second assumption, that salespeople borrow prestige from their customers, or at least make an effort in that direction, but when Joy Fowler replicated Labov's study in 1986, she found almost exactly the same pattern of social stratification. Replication of results is as close as we can get to

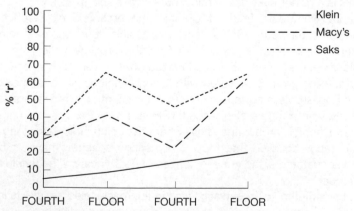

Figure 8.3 Simplified version of Labov's results (Source: Labov 1972a: 52)

'proof' that the phenomenon under investigation is real, and we can thus say that the presence of post-vocalic 'r' in the accents of New York City speakers is socially stratified.

In later studies, Labov relied more on concrete, quantifiable independent variables that contribute to determining a speaker's position in the social class hierarchy than in the department store study. In the Lower East Side study (1966), for example, he used a scale of socio-economic class based on the occupation, education and income of the informants; in his Philadelphia neighbourhood study, he constructed a socio-economic class index based on education, occupation and residence value to discover the social location of the innovators of linguistic change. In all these studies, Labov showed that there is a correlation between dependent linguistic variables and independent variables, such as social class and gender. With hindsight and knowledge of the research done on language and gender in the last fifty years (eg Pichler and Eppler 2009), I still find it fascinating that the first correlation between dependent linguistic variables and speakers' sex I am aware of in the literature takes up only five (out of 655) pages in Labov's (1966: 310–315) New York City's Lower East Side study.

8.4.2 Trudgill's Norwich study

The other large-scale sociolinguistic investigation into the relation between language use and social class we are going to look at in detail was conducted by the British sociolinguist Peter Trudgill in Norwich, England in the late 1960s and early 1970s. Trudgill set up a social class index based on occupation, income, education, locality and housing. To gather information on the sensitive issue of income, Trudgill showed informants a card with salary and wage ranges. He then asked his participants to pick the range which best described their occupational status. Thanks to this clever technique, nobody refused to give the requested information. In his research report, Trudgill observes that with five factors contributing to his social class index, it would be possible to examine each separately and determine which one, or which combination, provides the greatest explanatory power for the study of linguistic variation. Such a study would be really interesting, but to the best of my knowledge, it has never been done.

Trudgill's primary aim was to find out whether social factors play a part in the way the people of Norwich speak. He assumed that the higher a person's social class, the closer to the prestige variety (Standard British English with Received Pronunciation in this case) their speech would be. To test this hypothesis, Trudgill randomly selected sixty speakers from the electoral register from four separate areas of Norwich.

Like Labov, Trudgill assumed that speakers tend to shift towards the prestigious variety when paying more attention to their speech. Based on this assumption, Trudgill elaborated Labov's distinction between 'casual' and 'careful' style (implicit in Labov's first and repeated response) and created situations of varying degrees of formality or attention paid to speech: reading lists of individual words; reading a passage of text (containing words from the word list); interview style; and finally the least formal style produced when telling a funny story.

Trudgill examined several **linguistic variables** to explore the correlation between social class index and linguistic variation. One of them was a syntactic variable, the realisation of third person singular verb forms with no third person singular marker (eg 'he go' rather than 'he goes'). Another linguistic feature Trudgill was interested in was the way in which speakers pronounced '-ing' at the end of words such as 'writing', 'singing' and 'running'. He believed that the higher the social class of the speaker, the more likely they were to say, for example, 'singing' rather than 'singin'; by contrast, the further down the social scale the informant was placed according to the social class index, the greater the likelihood of them saying 'singin' rather than 'singing'.

Based on the percentage of non-standard forms ('-in') produced by the informants, Trudgill was able to persuasively divide them into five social groups: Middle Middle Class, Lower Middle Class, Upper Working, Middle Working and Lower Working Class (MMC, LMC, UWC, MWC and LWC respectively). The vertical axis of Figure 8.4 shows each social group's score for the dependent linguistic variable – that is, the number of times they used the non-standard '–in' as a percentage of the number of times they could have said '-ing'. A score of 0, for example, indicates exclusive use of '–ing' (as in the prestige variety), while a score of 100 signifies exclusive use of the non-standard form '–in'.

Activity 8.4

Compare the scores for the non-standard form '–in' in Figure 8.4. Speakers associated with which social class (on the basis of their linguistic production and the social class index) score highest in all styles? Speakers from which social class score lowest in the formal and casual styles? Why does Figure 8.4 not show a score for word lists and reading passages for Middle Class speakers?

Figure 8.4 shows that for the pronunciation of '–ing', the higher the social class of the speakers, the closer their speech is to the prestige variety – that is, the lower their score for the non-standard form '–in'. When reading word lists or passages of text, the Middle Middle Class speakers use no non-standard forms at all; this is why they score 0 for the two most formal styles in Figure 8.4 (WLS and RPS). Conversely, Figure 8.4 illustrates that Lower Working Class speakers score highest in all styles. This means that they use the highest number of non-standard forms in all 'styles' or situations of formality. When in their most casual speech style, the speakers associated with the lowest social position in fact only use '–in' (and thus score 100 per cent). The assumption that speech moves closer to the prestige variety in direct

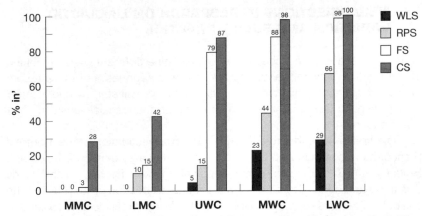

Figure 8.4 Results of Trudgill's sociolinguistic survey, Norwich (Source: Trudgill 1974: 92)

proportion to an increase in formality (and thus attention to speech) is also borne out by this study. Based on her own research conducted in the US, Eckert supports Trudgill's interpretation that the variable reduction of '–ing' reflects (and constructs) formality or informality. She concludes that 'the socioeconomic stratification of this variable ... may be more associated with class differences in formality and attitudes about formality' (Eckert 1999: 221).

Like Labov's research in the US, or Horvath's (1985) study of social class in Sydney, Australia, or Haeri's (1997) sociolinguistic investigation of Cairo's population in Egypt, Trudgill's (1974) Norwich study illustrates that the higher a person's position on the social scale, the closer their **linguistic variety** is to prestige norms. Another interesting point suggested by these classic studies is that, when speakers wish to, they can change the way they speak in accordance with the demands of the situation (see section 9.6.1). Trudgill's participants' speech, for example, moves closer to the **prestige variety** when the situation demands it. Labov's informants did exactly the same when repeating the words 'fourth floor'.

The idea that the way people speak is not completely determined by their social and regional background, ethnicity or gender has become very influential in recent sociolinguistics. Researchers today place more emphasis on speakers actively creating a social, regional, ethnic and gender identity for themselves by, for example, adopting linguistic forms or **styles** associated with speakers from various backgrounds. What is so important about these early studies, however, is that they have confirmed that language users rightly tend to associate particular linguistic forms with specific kinds of speakers or contexts of speaking. Without forming associations between linguistic variables and categories of speakers, the next step, naturalising and ideologising these sociolinguistic associations, would not be possible. This is the main focus of more recent research.

8.5 NEW DIRECTIONS IN RESEARCH ON LINGUISTIC VARIATION AND SOCIAL PRACTICE

In the last section of this chapter we will examine different ways of looking at the relation between language and social categories and more recent studies of social stratification in language use. We will start by briefly introducing two studies that use concepts other than social class in their investigations.

The first is Sankoff and Laberge's (1978) investigation of the Montreal Francophone community in Canada. In this study they employ Bordieu and Boltanski's (1975) concept of the linguistic market. The aim of this study was to measure the extent to which a speaker's situation in life requires the use of the standard language. Sankoff and Laberge first calculated a linguistic market index, constituted on the basis of judgements about each informant's economic context (based on occupation, job description, information about parents and or spouses). This information was provided by sociolinguists familiar with the Montreal Francophone community. They then examined the tendency to use the standard variant for a selection of relevant dependent linguistic variables. This study is innovative in that it uses individuals intimately familiar with the community under investigation to rank speakers according to their position in society. It also focuses more specifically on language use. Note, however, the factors that contribute to the linguistic market index are almost identical to the ones used to determine a speaker's social class in older studies.

The other study is Milroy's (1980) investigation of working-class networks in Northern Ireland. They also study speakers in an urban area, Belfast, but on a different scale from the survey-type studies (Labov's survey of New York City, and Trudgill's study of Norwich). They focus on the meaning and function that local everyday forms of speech have for small, close-knit, territorially based communities. Indirectly, this study thus also investigates why dialect levelling and standardisation do not eliminate linguistic variation (see section 8.2).

For studies trying to determine what can be learned about language from the differences in linguistic behaviour of people in different social positions, it is important that the determinants of social position have explanatory power for the use of language. In other words, it is crucial that the features of social class that are chosen are actually relevant to linguistic variation. It is equally important that the social groupings used in research are recognisable for the individuals involved; this is why later sociolinguistic research focuses on more local and self-defined groupings, such as social networks (Milroy 1980) and communities of practice (Wenger 1998).

Milroy (1980), for example, objects to class-based studies because, for her, large groupings derived from calculation of an index of some kind 'do not necessarily have any kind of ... reality' (1980: 14). Membership in a particular group that someone else has decided on does not necessarily form an important part of the speaker's own definition of his/her social identity. You might work as an accountant, but your social identity might be best captured by your semi-professional football career. Milroy's research therefore focuses on small, close-knit, local networks. The 'strength' of these networks depends on the degree to which the people who form them all know each other (**density**), and on the extent to which individuals are bound to one another by more than one relationship (**plexity**); for example, two people might be cousins and friends or friends and workmates.

The **communities of practice** model builds on the fundamental postulate of network analysis that individuals create personal communities that provide them with a meaningful framework for solving the problems of their day-to-day existence. Communities of practice are thus simultaneously defined by their membership and also by the common undertaking (and a shared repertoire of resources) that brings these people together. Communities of practice are groups of people that form to share what they know, to learn from one another regarding some aspects of their work, to contribute to a common purpose, and to provide a social context for that work. For many sociolinguists, network analysis and communities of practice help move away from what they see as a tendency to pigeon-hole speakers according to pre-determined categories and instead focus on self-defined social groups by recognising common practice in explaining linguistic behaviour.

Because of their different focus, studies that try to understand the particular local meanings speakers associate with linguistic varieties (and only optionally link them to more abstract large-scale notions, such as social class or gender), call for different methods, different types of data collection, and different types of analysis. For example, they tend to study groups of individuals who the investigators have some degree of familiarity with; they stress naturally occurring vernacular data (they do not include word lists or reading passages); and they tend to use **qualitative** (rather than **quantitative**) methodology.

8.5.1 Eckert's Belten High study

All these shifts are represented in the – by now classic – new generation study of linguistic variation and social practice by Penelope Eckert (1999). Eckert spent two years familiarising herself with the social landscape in several suburban Detroit high schools during which she collected natural speech data from various groups and individuals. In all the schools she observed, Eckert found a strong opposition between two social groups, referred to as 'jocks' and 'burnouts'. The jocks are school-oriented and embody middle-class culture; the burnouts are locally oriented and embody working-class culture. Eckert furthermore observed that the distinction between the 'jocks' and the 'burnouts' could realistically be judged to affect linguistic behaviour. She set out to demonstrate this.

The linguistic variables Eckert focuses on are predominantly vowels which are involved in language change in some parts of America (Northern Californian cities). This is important, because for change to happen, there has to be some pre-existing variability and heterogeneity. If this existing variation is noticed by speakers, as it was by the high school students Eckert studied, it lends itself to use by speakers for (social) differentiation and stratification. That is, the different forms can be used to signal affiliation to particular groups and identities (see Chapter 9). This is exactly what the adolescents investigated by Eckert do.

Eckert correlated the dependent linguistic variables she had chosen with the social categories she found in the schools. The mixed quantitative and qualitative analysis she carried out revealed that all the correlations she found relate the use of variables to social categories and to the practices and groups that constitute these categories. For example, Eckert found that the burnouts (and particularly the burnout girls) spearhead the use of a particular set of variables that lead to the above mentioned language change; and the jocks (and particularly the jock girls) lag in the change of this set of variants. Of all the variables covered by Eckert, the ones with the starkest social distribution are ones that are not undergoing change: double negatives and (ay) raising. Double negative may well be the most commonly stigmatised variable in the English language. Extreme raised (ay), on the other hand, occurs virtually exclusively in utterances that are directly related to key burnout cultural themes: alienation from school, restricted/classified substances, trouble, fights and disagreement. Eckert (1999: 219) concludes that 'the use of extreme raising is inseparable from the construction of burnout identity'.

Eckert's 'jock' and 'burnout' study is included in the sociolinguistic research reviewed in this chapter not only because it is famous, but also because it combines elements from variationist sociolinguistics (the correlation of phonological variables with social categories, for example, or the use of some quantitative/statistical analysis), with many of the new directions in research on linguistic variation and social practice. For example, Eckert carefully studied the environment under investigation (the high schools) for two years and fed this information into the analysis (also known as **ethnographic** research). She only used natural speech data and interpreted her data qualitatively (as well as quantitatively). She showed that variation carries predominantly local social meaning, but that it is systematically related to global patterns, such as the use of double negatives. Eckert views (linguistic) style and identity construction as creative rather than reactive processes (see section 9.6). Labov's informants, for example, were said to *react* to his request to repeat 'fourth floor' by moving their pronunciation towards the more prestigious variety. Eckert, on the other hand, shows how individual high school students *construct themselves* as 'jocks' or 'burnouts' in terms of their language, clothing, attitudes and behaviour. Most importantly, she shows how associations between a linguistic variable (eg double negatives) and a category of speakers (eg burnouts) renders that variable available for association with stereotypes associated with the category (eg being anti-school) and thus enables it to be consciously and rationally used to create intentional content or meaning (eg it can be used by new students to express anti-school sentiments).

The other reason why I chose Eckert's study is because the analysis is refined and the interpretations are careful. She, for example, clearly spells out why she emphasises creative **agency**, 'to counter the prevailing emphasis in the literature on norms and on the constraining effect of social groups' (2000: 215). She clearly states that – with the exception of heavily stigmatized linguistic features such double negatives – individual linguistic variables cannot take on interpretable social meaning unless they group with other features to form an identifiable style. A **style** therefore is a set of features, not just one thing all by itself (see section 6.5). Eckert clearly differentiates which linguistic features/variables are most easily controlled (eg lexical items, **discourse markers**, fixed expressions, intonational patterns) and which are not as easily adopted (eg phonological variables or vowel quality). And although she frequently looks at what individual speakers do, she stresses that the production of style and social meaning is a collaborative effort. This is the flip side of the coin: linguistic variables and linguistic styles become meaningless if others can't interpret them. For example, the identities and linguistic features of 'jock' and 'burnout' can't be said to be durable markers, if newcomers to one of the high schools Eckert studied cannot interpret what it means to be a 'jock' or a 'burnout' or identify who belongs to which group.

Most recent studies of social class combine several of the concepts we discussed in this chapter (factors contributing to social class, the notion of networks, linguistic markets, communities of practice), but almost exclusively work with linguistic elements that are a) easily identifiable, b) easy to adopt in at least a stereotypical fashion and c) therefore readily available for meaning negotiation.

8.6 SUMMARY

This chapter has focused on the relationship between language and social class, without losing sight of other principles of organisation that social class interacts with, such as ethnicity, gender and age. The link between linguistic variation and social class may be perceived (based on prevailing attitudes towards speech varieties), or it can be based on assessment of a speaker's social class calculated by a variety of means derived from sociological or ethnographic research. We saw that social variation is always linked to regional variation, but that this relationship can take different forms (for example in the UK and in India), and that it can change over time. Regional dialects can, for example, level out, or move towards the standard. We then looked at two classic variationist studies which suggest that the higher a person's social class (or at least the higher the social class they align themselves with), the closer their speech is to the standard variety used in formal situations. These studies take social categories as more or less given, and focus on individual speaker's use of variation as an indicator of their place in relation to them. We then observed how, for many sociolinguists, the counting, measuring and correlating of linguistic variables with different forms of social stratifications was too mechanistic and deterministic. They took new directions in research on linguistic variation and social practice by looking more locally, stressing the linguistic agency of speakers, and focusing on the social meaning of variation. Recent research is interested in how speakers actively use the associations between linguistic variables and categories of speakers to create their own social identity (eg as 'jocks' or 'burnouts'). Speakers are now seen as constructing, rather than representing broad social categories.

FURTHER READING

Ash, S. (2004) 'Social class', in J. K Chambers, P. Trudgill and Schilling-Estes, N. (eds), *The Handbook of Language Variation and Change,* London: Blackwell, 402–422.

Britain, D. (2005) 'The dying dialects of Britain?' in A. Bertacca, (ed), *Historical Linguistic Studies of Spoken English: papers read at the 11th Italian Conference on the History of the English Language, Pisa, 5–7 June 2003.* Online: http://homepages.tesco.net/~david.britain/13.pdf.

Gos, M. W. (1995) 'Overcoming social class markers: preparing working class students for college', *The Clearing House,* September 1995.

Kerswill, P. (2001) 'Mobility, meritocracy and dialect levelling: the fading (and phasing) out of Received Pronunciation', in P. Rajamäe and K. Vogelberg (eds), *British Studies in the New Millennium: The Challenge of the Grassroots,* Tartu: University of Tartu, 45–58. Online: www.teachit.co.uk/armoore/lang/dialect. PDF.

Labov, W. (1972c) 'Academic ignorance and black intelligence', *The Atlantic,* 72.06.

Rampton, B. et al (2008) 'Language, class and education', in S. May and N. H. Hornberger (eds), *Encyclopaedia of Language and Education,* 2nd edn, Volume 1: Language Policy and Political Issues in Education, Heidelberg: Springer, 1–11.

NOTES

1 See John Wells's website on this variety www.phon.ucl.ac.uk/home/estuary/home.htm.
  See also www.bbc.co.uk/routesofenglish/index.shtml (Kerswill 2001).

2 Nor is it true in the USA. See *The Linguistic Atlas of North America,* Labov, Ash and Boberg (2006). You can see a preview of this at www.mouton-online.com.

3 Independent variables range from social context to phonetic context, as the following makes clear

Social factors:	age, class, gender, ethnicity, friendships
Stylistic factors:	formal, informal
Linguistic factors:	preceding/following word, preceding/following sound

4 The following provides some examples of dependent linguistic variables

am I/be I/are I/bin I	**am/be/are/bin**	(British dialects)
he's cool/he cool	**be/Ø**	(US Black English Vernacular)
you was there/you were there	**was/were**	(British and US dialects)
he don't care/he doesn't care	**don't/doesn't**	(British and US dialects)

CHAPTER 9

Language and identity

Suzanne LaBelle

9.1 INTRODUCTION

Language is one of the ways in which we order the world around us. It is also central to how we create and reinforce our view of ourselves and others. This chapter looks at the ways in which identity is created and reflected through language use and how we can use language to highlight or downplay certain aspects of identity. We look at how setting and relationships can influence how we use language to show our identity. We then closely examine identity creation and reception, style and language variation. We also discuss to what extent individuals act as agents, or wilful actors in the world, in determining their personal and group representations.

9.2 WHAT IS IDENTITY?

All the topics we've looked at so far can be clearly considered to be part of identity. While these are quite specific categories (age, gender and so on), we find the same kinds of changes in thinking about identity as we found when trying to define these features. Identity is commonly thought of as one's conception of self in the world, something solid and relatively stable. Generally, we don't think about our identity as being something we need to think about or worry about, but something we might have acquired in the past and is somehow 'just there'. Looking at an individual's language use, however, reveals that we all have multiple identities. It might be useful to think of these identities in terms of the different relationships you have with people. In terms of language, our language use with our close friends and that with strangers differ in systematic and observable ways. We all behave differently in our various social roles; we have identities as friends, as the children of our parents, as colleagues with our workmates. Of course, language is only one of the things that changes.

The way people present themselves to the world, and the way in which they are perceived and evaluated by others are all relevant to the concept of identity. It's important to remember at the start that we have control over only some parts of our identity. The degree to which an individual can exercise **agency**, or control, in presenting him or herself to others in the world varies according to the society they live in, the way in which their language encodes social categories, and all of these may change over time. We can talk about this control over certain aspects of presentation of individual identity as **agentive** – that is, the parts of our identity we have control over can be said to be agentive. Different cultures allow individuals more or less leeway in determining their identity and having that self-determination accepted by others. For example, in the United States a person of mixed African and European heritage would be seen by the majority culture as 'African American'. There, the category of race is non-agentive for those of mixed backgrounds.

Social factors such as age, ethnicity, gender and social class, group membership or affiliation are more or less agentive depending on the **ideology**, or worldview, of the culture in which you live. For example, gender has traditionally been a non-agentive feature of identity for most cultures; you are expected to display a set of behaviours based on the rules that your culture had set out as appropriate for those with male and female bodies. However, in many cultures that is changing, due to individuals with internal gender identities which do not match their culturally expected external identities. In the UK for example, within the last decade, a person born into a female body but who identifies as male and then undergoes gender reassignment is able to change their birth certificate to match their reassigned gender. In claiming a public right to self-determination, to be who they feel they are on the inside, individuals create new ways of expressing these identities. Changes in agency for a social category such as gender are not easily accomplished. Because ideologies mean that some behaviours and identities are 'normal' and even 'natural', biologically determined or morally correct, resistance to change on the basis of 'nature' are frequently encountered by those looking to assert alternate identity.

Age in Western cultures is, in one sense, an unambiguously non-agentive factor of identity. One definition of age is absolute, determined by birth date and encoded in legal systems. Behaviours which are seen as acceptable for one age group, if practised by another are viewed as transgressive and sometimes, in the case of sexual activity or consumption of alcohol, illegal and punishable. Because the dominant ideology of a culture encodes only some behaviours as natural, and powerful, not all identities are created equal. However, there is some latitude in age identities, as it is possible to act 'younger' or 'older' in terms of language, dress and habits.

The social theorist Pierre Bourdieu (1984) sets out the concept of **symbolic capital**, or the prestige that individuals in a society gain based on the way they present themselves and through their relationships with others. Those who conform to what a given society thinks is the 'natural ideal' way of behaving have more power than those judged not to conform to the 'natural ideal'. So adopting practices that your society considers 'naturally good or prestigious' allows you to gain symbolic capital. The negative repercussions of displaying behaviours that are not valued by your culture is called **symbolic violence** by Bourdieu. This concept describes the actions taken to disenfranchise and disempower those who do not conform to their majority culture's ideologies. An example of this phenomenon is the success of more middle-class students in academic contexts in relation to those from poorer backgrounds. Bourdieu sees middle-class students as behaving, both physically and through their use of standard language, in a way that means their success is expected by teachers, who are also typically from the same class background. Examining how we use language with regard to large-scale social categories such as age, gender and class is just one way of approaching identity studies. By looking at what individuals do to create and reflect their identity through language we can see the concept of identity is multidimensional.

Identities are multifaceted, and may change over time. What is an important aspect of personal or group identity at one time and in one place is not necessarily the most important piece of identity at another. As a native of New England, I would identify with others from that region when interacting with other Americans – that is, for other Americans, my New England origins are meaningful and relevant. When interacting with people from outside of the US, I would claim a connection with other Americans from different regions – that is, when speaking to non-Americans, it will usually be my country of origin that is immediately relevant, rather than my more local identity. Likewise with language, within the US features of my language that mark me out as a New Englander, using 'wicked' as an adverb for example, are salient, though outside the US, this feature would be subsumed within other linguistic variables that mark my talk as American: the use of 'elevator' instead of 'lift' together with the pronunciation of 'r' after a vowel (**post-vocalic 'r'**). In this way, context can help determine which aspects of identity we choose to focus on.

9.3 REPRESENTING YOURSELF THROUGH LANGUAGE: DIALECT AND IDENTITY

Using certain pronunciations, terms or grammatical constructions can mark out individuals as being from a certain class (see Chapter 8), geographic area (see Chapter 8), ethnicity (see Chapter 6), gender (see Chapter 5) or age group (see Chapter 7). Additionally, looking at how geography and language interact helps to show how identity is related to language use. Some of these features are things we may not be aware of in our own speech; however, other people will hear them and may make assumptions about us and associate us with particular identities.

If we consider geography first, and look at how linguists map differences in language, we can see how linguistic identities begin to emerge. **Dialectologists** traditionally define geographic dialect boundaries by looking for bundles of **isoglosses**. An isogloss is an idealised geographic boundary between the use of one linguistic variable or feature and another.[1] You can think of isoglosses as like lines on a map which divide countries or other areas; they are often represented in exactly this way. However, isoglosses mark variation in speech rather than being territorial boundaries. For example, in Rhode Island in New England in the US, the word for a drinking fountain is a 'bubbla'. Speakers in the neighbouring dialect regions wouldn't use this term for a 'drinking fountain'. The transition area from 'bubbla' to 'drinking fountain' would form an isogloss. Boundaries such as this may be determined by pronunciation or grammatical differences as well, not just by vocabulary differences. As I acquired language in the area that many isoglosses can be shown to define as 'Rhode Island', part of my linguistic identity is 'Rhode Islander'. Those who hear me use 'bubbla' and who have the social and linguistic awareness to mark that term out as being limited to certain geographic areas can categorise me in this way.

Bundles of features work together to present your linguistic identity to the world. If we take the case of 'bubbla' we can make this very clear. Whilst an American from New England might recognise 'bubbla' as a Rhode Island expression, the term is also used in parts of New South Wales in Australia to mean 'drinking fountain'. Simply hearing someone use this term is not enough to know anything about where they come from; other information is required to know whether the speaker is from Australia or New England, features such as pronunciation and use of certain grammatical constructions. Finally, use of the term won't mean anything to the hearer if they don't know what a 'bubbla' is or where this term is used. Labelling individuals through their use of linguistic variables is part of a larger categorisation system that assigns individuals to groups.

9.3.1 Group labelling

The recognition of 'bubbla' as Rhode Island dialect brings up a very important issue in the relationship between language and identity. It is only through perception by others, in an oppositional relation, that group identities can be formed. Like language itself, identity needs an audience to make it meaningful. Claims to group membership will be assessed by those within and without the group and the authenticity of the claim to that membership will be a result of whether **in-group** or **out-group** members hold power (see section 6.6.1). For example, an issue in US Native American **identity politics** is whether 'blood' or 'culture' (Sturm 2002) holds more sway in claiming the label 'Native American'. For historical reasons in the US, some Native American communities integrated African American and White American individuals into their societies. This leaves individuals in these communities, who do not match up to some majority US culture ideas of what a Native American is meant to look like, open to the critique that their claim to that identity is not valid. At issue here is who has the right to determine an identity label (see Chapter 6). The people with power decide the legitimacy and authenticity of claims to group labels. The power to make these determinations is also a relative thing. While there may be legal definitions of what it means to be a member of group, these may be very different from the group's own definition. For example, the Mashantucket Pequot Native American community has an economically successful resort and casino in Connecticut in the US. Membership in this Native American community is restricted to descendants of those who officially affiliated themselves through birth records with the community before the resort was established in 1992. This means that there are those who may be the legal descendants of the Pequot nation according to the US government's administrative records who are nevertheless disqualified from claiming that identity due to policy within the Native American group.

Despite a general tendency to group individuals based on their language use into social categories, the language variety that each of us speaks is unique and subtly different to those from similar age, ethnic, geographic and class origins. This language of the individual is called an **ideolect**. Part of assessing the sociolinguistic world is how an individual measures the distance between their own ideolect and that of those they are interacting with.

This is most obviously true when an individual has more than one linguistic system at their disposal. Such a person would be able to **code-switch**, from one system to the other, depending on their desire to be part of or distance themselves from those around them (see section 6.8). For example, someone who speaks both Welsh and English may choose to use Welsh when monolingual English speakers are present. This would obviously exclude some people from the interaction and, as such, would be a way of distancing the English speakers. The creation of and perception of group and individual identity through language can be multilayered. **In-group** and **out-group** norms interact to establish categories and belonging.

Think about words that may make up your own ideolect, or ones which may be used only by your family or friend groups. For example in my family we would call the 'television remote control' a 'button pusher'. These may be words that other people use but with a different meaning. List as many words as you can think which have this small community of use. How did you come to use them? How would you feel if others started using these terms?

Activity 9.1

9.4 NAMING

The most obvious way in which we negotiate the world through language is by what we choose to call ourselves. In many cultures, names consist of a label to show who is closely related to an individual; a label that is unique to that individual, given by parents to children. Different cultures choose to show different relationships through their naming practices. In English-speaking countries, traditionally the father's family name gets passed on to the children as a surname, and women change their surname from their father's to their husband's if they marry. In many cultures special rituals are carried out to officially name children, welcoming them into that culture. This practice is frequently associated with a religious ritual. In Christian churches, a baptism asks parents and others, who receive a special relationship label 'godparent', to raise children in that faith, and announces the name of the child to others in that religious community. In the Catholic church, children must take a first or middle name in memory of a saint when baptised, and again when confirmed as adults in the church. Jewish naming ceremonies can involve ritualised circumcision for male children and the bestowing of a Hebrew name on both male and female children.

Icelandic names reflect the gender of the individual in both fore and surnames as well as paternal ancestry. So Anna Jónsdottir would be the child of Jón Einarsson and the sister of Gunnar Jónsson, as 'dottir' is Icelandic for 'daughter' and 'son' for 'son'. Greek names reflect gender in fore and surnames. Children receive their father's surname, and special endings are added to the child's surname if the child is a girl. So Eleni Yannatou would have a brother Yannis Yannatos. Russian names include a name derived from the father's name as a middle name, meaning 'son of' plus their father's first name for males, and 'daughter of' for females. Names in Arabic-speaking countries show a similar phenomenon, but for parents, where 'father of' may be appended to a man's name if he becomes a father.

9.4.1 Access to naming

Who uses a name, and how they choose to style it is determined by social distance, the formality of the language use situation, and the desire of speaker to show solidarity with or separateness from, respect or disdain, for the addressee. Typically this means that the closer you are socially to your **interlocutor** the more likely they will be to use a less formal version of your name. So, your sister might call you by a nickname, but you would not expect to hear your doctor's receptionist do so. Parents ordinarily use their child's first name or a term of endearment when addressing their offspring, but may use their full name in anger if a child has done something wrong and are to be punished. The parent uses the full name in such cases as a way to indicate social distance to the child, in opposition to what is usually a close relationship.

Name use may be **asymmetrical** when those involved want to make power relationships obvious. Those with less power will use titles, and politeness markers when addressing those who they perceive to have more power. If you were to meet the Queen of England you would address her as 'Ma'am' or 'your Majesty' to show respect for her status. In many English-speaking communities children may use 'aunt' or 'uncle' plus a first name to address adult friends of their parents, as a way to show both closeness, and respect. 'Aunt Mary' is more familiar than 'Mrs Smith' and yet more respect-ful than 'Mary'.

Because naming is connected to relationships, speakers may attempt to manipulate social distance through terms of address. When a beggar styles a request for money as 'Spare any change, mate?' they are looking to reduce the **social distance** between themselves and their addressees by choosing a term of address, 'mate', which would put them in the same social group as their addressee. The hope is this will create feelings of solidarity in their addressee and encourage giving.

Physical context and heightened emotional state can override social distance norms around use of terms of address. Emergency situations will allow politeness and deferential language norms to be ignored. So you could address the Queen without her title, yelling 'Hurry, move, move now!' if you could see she was in imminent danger. Situational formality can also influ-ence naming practices. For example, when I was an undergraduate, two of my sociolinguistics lecturers were married to each other. In class, they expected us to call them by their first names. However, if they were lecturing separately and referring to the work of their husband or wife, they would use their spouse's full name. The formality of academic context overrode their usual naming styles.

Names frequently become associated with certain social categories; for example, in English-speaking cultures there are relatively few names which can be used for both males and females, such as Alex or Sam. Gender is usually a social category made overt in naming practices. Think about which other social categories are made obvious through naming. Make a list of first names of younger and older people you know. Do any patterns emerge? What about social class, or ethnic origin? Are there repercussions when names do not match up to obvious or expected social categories? Why might that be the case?

Activity 9.2

What might be some reasons individuals or organisations choose to change their name? Many times performers take on 'stage names': why would an artist such as singer Lady Gaga prefer that name to Stefani, the one her parents chose for her? It isn't just performers who change their names: journalist Kate Hilpern in the *Daily Mail* (19 September 2009) discussed her name change, both first and surname, which she took up upon turning 18, and how her father reacted negatively, saying 'I was unprepared for my dad's devastation'. Why might this journalist's father have felt 'devastation' at his daughter's name change?

Activity 9.3

9.5 SOCIAL RELATIONS AND GRAMMATICAL FORM

Each language and culture chooses to encode certain social relationships grammatically, either through **morphology** or special vocabulary. These might take the shape of a codified system of address or calling, or the marking out of a pronoun for formal or informal use.

In some languages the act of trying to get someone's attention from afar involves use of a special case, a type of form change to show that the noun is functioning in this specific way. The special form used in the 'calling' context is known as the **vocative**. The vocative case is a grammaticalisation of socially directed speech. It is a special marker that tells the named person they are being searched for or spoken to. For example, in Polish, nouns in the feminine gender are **suffixed** with either '-o', '-u' or '-i' when calling. Traditionally in Welsh, for the vocative, the initial sounds of certain nouns are changed. Welsh for 'god', 'duw' [dyu], would be pronounced with an initial voiced 'th' [ð] sound rather than an initial 'd' [d] when praying, for example. In Arabic the particle ﺎﻳ 'ya' [ja] is added before a noun to indicate calling. In English we do not have a special form change for names when calling, but we do have a special particle, 'O', as in 'O John, where are you?' or classically 'O Romeo Romeo, wherefore art thou Romeo?' (meaning, 'O Romeo, Romeo, why are you [called] Romeo' (*Romeo And Juliet* 2 ii: 33)). We also use a rising and falling intonation, lengthening the stressed syllable when we call to someone or something from afar. This intonation pattern is unique to that linguistic environment and helps listeners and others recognise who is being addressed (even if you're just calling for your cat).

9.5.1 Pronouns, politeness and power

Relationships can also be encoded through use of special pronouns. Some languages allow for a polite/informal distinction amongst second person pronouns, 'you' in standard English. French has 'tu' [ty] as informal and 'vous' [vu] as formal, Welsh 'ti' [ti] as informal, 'chi' [xi] as formal, German 'du' [du] as informal and 'Sie' [zi], in Finnish 'sinä' [sinæ] is informal, and 'te' [te] formal. Deciding whether to use formal or informal pronouns can be quite a complicated social procedure, which involves weighing up how well you know an individual, how formal the environment is, and whether you want to show solidarity with or distance from your addressee. It may be thought of as similar to the decision to use someone's full name and title or just first name or nickname in English. Use of the inappropriate pronoun can lead to your addressee feeling you are trying to be too familiar, or thinking you are unfriendly, depending on the context.

Pronouns can also be a way of creating and reinforcing group identities and displaying power. For example, a doctor may call on the power of their profession when giving a diagnosis, through use of the plural pronoun 'we': 'We feel you should follow this treatment option'. Or a teacher may say 'We think it is best for you to retake this class' when it is likely in fact to be the opinion of just one individual. Use of 'we' here allows the speaker to metaphorically take more authority, to show their interlocutor they should be obeyed. Additionally, as discussed in Chapters 3 and 4, classifying individuals as like 'us' and like 'them' allows the speaker to focus in on similarities or differences between themselves, their listeners and others in the world. These uses for pronouns help to create boundaries around behaviour, they act as markers to help us manage and coordinate complex social relationships. If you recognise your culture has an 'us' and 'them' divide and see yourself as fitting into one of these groups, such as 'criminal' and 'law-abider', that may influence your behaviour. You may do things to live up to or down to your label; this is arguably a type of linguistic determinism. Pronouns serve as a shorthand for these divisions.

9.6 LANGUAGE VARIATION: STYLE

As you become used to your own society's language norms, you become aware that certain types of talk are prestigious in certain social contexts. For example, when you go to a job interview you would use more formal language than you would when talking with friends. You change the way you talk to conform to the language norms of the context you find yourself in. Adopting the style, or shifting your talk towards a style which has prestige within a certain domain of use, can be a way of attempting to gain power in that domain.

In the mid 1990s, a Canadian rapper called Snow had an international hit with the song 'Informer'. Snow was a white reggae artist from Toronto in Canada but adopted a Caribbean English pronunciation when he rapped and sang, and included Jamaican Creole vocabulary such as 'irie' [airi], to mean 'good', in his songs. Snow chose not to use his native Canadian English for singing. Caribbean English has prestige in the domain of reggae music, as it is the code through which the genre originated. Knowing that and borrowing that form, Snow was trying to make his audience think of his music as more like that of previously successful reggae artists. Caribbean English was used in an attempt to reference success and power in that domain.

Linguists have looked at exactly this issue, though in a different time and place. Peter Trudgill (1983a) looked at the Americanisation of accent for British performers during the 1960s and 1970s. He found that at the start of their careers, groups such as the Rolling Stones and the Beatles, used dialect features such as **post vocalic 'r'**, making their language more like American English than British. He noted that American English had prestige in the domain of rock and roll and adopting features of American English may have been a way to reference legitimacy and success in that domain. Trudgill (1983a) also noted that as these performers' careers developed, they began using their native dialect features with greater frequency. As their power in the domain of rock and roll increased, there was less of a need to modify their linguistic forms.

9.6.1 Theories of style shifting

As the discipline of sociolinguistics has developed, different ideas about how perception and production of style functions have held sway. Labov (1972a) explained 'style' in relation to the attention paid to speech by the speaker. The less attention paid, the more informal the situation – that is, the more unguarded the speech, the closer to the **vernacular** the speech was said to be. For example, we tend to pay much less attention to our speech among friends and much more if we were reading written text aloud. Labov's department store study (1966) (see section 8.4.1) measured style in this way, by asking sales clerks to repeat their response to his queries to measure the socially variable pronunciation of 'r' after a vowel in New York City. This repetition meant that Labov was able to gather two styles of speech and compare pronunciations between the first casual response, and the second more careful response. By looking at any differences between the two, he could say something about which forms were prestigious or powerful in more formal contexts.

There are other things that alter the kind of language we use with others. Alan Bell (1984) showed that attention paid to speech was not enough to explain style shifting, and developed a theory of **audience design**. His study of the language used by DJs working in a New Zealand radio station showed that the same individual, when broadcasting to a local audience, was more likely to use different pronunciations of 't' than when they were broadcasting to a national audience. The expectation the DJs had for what their audience were used to hearing in a local or national context was enough to change the pronunciations those DJs used. Bell argued that the DJs associated certain pronunciations with certain types of audiences. Sounding 't' as a voiced stop, so that 'writer' would sound like 'rider', was more common in the broadcasts for the local radio station. Using this pronunciation was associated with non-standard speakers locally. Thus, in less formal broadcast contexts, such as a local show, where DJs wanted to show solidarity with local vernacular speakers, they would use the linguistic form they associated with that group. When broadcasting on the national radio station, however, this pronunciation was used much less. The DJs were designing their speech towards their perceived expectations of their audience, a type of **accommodation**. Giles and Powesland (1975) write that accommodation:

> can be regarded as an attempt on the part of the speaker to modify or disguise his persona in order to make it more acceptable to the person addressed ... One effect of the convergence of speech patterns is that it allows the sender to be perceived as more similar to the receiver than would have been the case had he not accommodated his style of speaking in this manner. But in addition, speech accommodation may be a device by the speaker to make himself better understood.
>
> (1975: 159)

There are limitations to the audience design theory of style shifting however. Schilling-Estes (2007) notes that speakers will sometimes change their talk in a way that doesn't directly relate to the needs of their audience, neither promoting solidarity through accommodation nor promoting social distance through non-accommodation. A speaker may change their style to show affinity with a group which is not present even in the imagined audience for their talk. A speaker may use features associated with a group because of their own relation to the group. For example, if a police officer witnessed an extraordinary event such as a UFO flying overhead, he may use occupation-related register when describing it to a journalist, in the following way: 'I was *proceeding* towards the vehicle when I saw it', rather than 'I was *walking* towards the car when I saw it'. His choice of words would be related to identity as a police officer rather than attention paid to speech or design for the journalist, his audience.[2] A 'speaker design' theory allow us to explore further factors that influence the way people talk.

Schilling-Estes (2007: 389) states that when style in language is understood in terms of speaker design, then it becomes clear that identity is not fixed, but something that can be reshaped and constructed, as language varies according to context and also changes according to how the speaker wants to be perceived. A speaker may adopt the style of a group they wish to be seen as a member of, regardless of the effect this may have on their interlocutor. They may also attempt to create and reinforce new local

---

Read the following extract from the Police Service in Northern Ireland, written in Ulster Scots, a language of Northern Ireland closely related to English. Read the extract aloud, and then attempt to translate it into English with the help of the brief glossary beneath the text. Ulster Scots has faced difficulties in gaining acceptance as a written language as some think features of the language are simply informal or local variants of English. As an English speaker, are there features in the text you wouldn't associate with an official or formal register? What are they? How does the way you think about identity and language influence your perception of Ulster Scots?

Wittins anent the Polis Service in Norlin Airlan in the Ulster Scots

The Polis Service o Norlin Airlan is aa sat for makkan Norlin Airlan saufer, wi progressive, professional polisin. We ar ettlet at makkan our services apen tae the haill commontie. We hae sat contact wittins and heid screeds furth ablo. Gin ye be needin onie farder wittins in yer ain leid, obleeged gif ye wad get ahauld o us.

(www.psni.police.uk/ulster_scots.pdf)

Glossary

wittins	information
anent	about
ablo	below
leid	language
ettlet at	trying to

Activity 9.4

sociolinguistic norms. It is important to consider the multifaceted and moveable nature of the production of linguistic identity. Identity is a changing and evolving concept, rather than a static one, where even long-standing social categories may be considered more or less important by an individual in different contexts over the course of their lifetime.

Beliefs around how language and social structure interact can allow individuals to adopt a particular stance towards language use. Once group language use associations are fixed, individuals may make short-term use of features associated with these groups in order to reference association with that group, or to demonstrate their familiarity with that group. Rampton (1995), discussing Creole use by non-Black children in London for talk domains of 'toughness' or 'coolness', calls this phenomenon **crossing** (see section 6.8).

Activity 9.5

Think about the motivation for the 'ummmmm' in the following sentence:

'I, ummmmm, don't like them.'

How could this filler could be caused by audience design? What else could it be caused by?

Activity 9.6

Read the following sentences. Note down which ones might be used by a native speaker of English. Answers are found at the end of the chapter. What in your own experience tells you whether a linguistic form 'counts' as signalling native speaker identity?

1. We hate going there anymore.
2. You might could get one.
3. A: I like cake
   B: So don't I, I like cake too.
4. I'll be there just now, I'll try to get there after I finish all this work.
5. These clothes need cleaned.
6. I'm stuffed, I'm after eating lunch!

9.7 PRODUCTION OF GROUP IDENTITIES

Language can be the means of classifying individuals into groups, and a means by which we express our group identity. One way of looking at group expression through language is the way even groups of people with nothing much in common in terms of age, ethnicity and so on, may develop their own ways of speaking with each other. **Quantitative** sociolinguists find that around the world, language variation can be associated with identity features.

A nice example of how language can be used to delineate group identity comes from sign language practices in Northern Ireland. Historical religious disputes in the region means that Catholic and Protestant communities today interact separately in many contexts. Woll and Sutton Spence (2007) recount how British Sign Language is used by the Protestant deaf community in Northern Ireland, and Irish Sign language by the Catholic deaf community. They state that the two languages are not related to each other, nor are they related to English. Use of one or the other sign languages correlates here with religious affiliation.

A similar, though less extreme example, exists for Northern Irish English. McCafferty found that for the production of the diphthong [iə], identity as Protestant or Catholic influenced pronunciation (McCafferty 1999). This is found in words such as 'face'. Penelope Gardner-Chloros (1997) found that in the French bilingual city of Strasbourg, choosing to use Alsatian German or French in department stores transactions depended upon how social class and age interacted. In her study of a suburban Detroit high school in the US, Penelope Eckert (1989) found that high school students created local social and groupings 'jocks' and 'burn-outs' unrelated to the class or group affiliation of their parents (see section 8.5.1). Membership in these local groups is linked to use of urban Detroit language variables. Finally, Mees and Collins (1999) found that gender and social class influenced use of glottal stop in place of 't' in Cardiff English. Identity and language use form a complex web in the creation and display of social categories. In order to show your group affiliation through language, first you need to be aware of what certain linguistic forms may indicate. This might not be straightforward. Eckert points out that the same feature can have various meanings that depend on the speaker and the context. Looking at marked pronunciation of /t/ at the end of words, she notes that it can be used by Americans to reference British English, by 'nerd' girls to identify as intelligent, and by Orthodox Jewish children to demonstrate qualities of masculine intelligence (2003: 50).

Social theorists also consider the way that production of new identities can be handled. For example Hebdige (1979) discusses the concept of **'bricolage'**, or the use of cultural symbols with an agreed meaning in a new way to produce a new identity. For his analysis of punk rock style, a symbol such as a Mohawk haircut is an example of bricolage. The haircut was originally associated with a group of Native Americans, but was then appropriated by punk rockers, allowing them to create a new identity with the existing symbol. Another linguistic example would be the use of 'he' by lesbians or 'she' by gay men to refer to a fellow gay person. Here the symbol is the pronoun, and its appropriation helps to create a common identity, not one where gender identity is in question, but where non-majority culture sexuality is recognised.

Individuals who come together to perform some behaviour or engage in a common activity form a **community of practice**, where, whilst engaging in that activity, they create and reinforce their social identity (Holmes and Meyerhoff, 1999; see also section 8.5). Part of this activity and identity is related to language use. Labov's (1972b) early work on the language of gang members inspired this conception of linguistic identity. He found there was a positive correlation between embracing group values, being part of the social core of a group, and the frequency of use of linguistic variables associated with that group. He found that for gang members in New York City, those on the periphery of the gang used fewer linguistic features associated with gang culture than those in core social positions.

9.7.1 Perception and linguistic identities

Theorising about the perception of linguistic variation begins with Labov's (1964) ideas about how important linguistic difference is to speakers. Labov divides linguistic variables into **indicators** and **markers**, depending on whether speakers who use these forms **style shift** when using them. An indicator describes variation which is obvious to those who are external to a social group as marking out that group. Indicators are not socially evaluated by members within that group. These forms do not show style shifting – that is, they don't change, regardless of whether the context is casual or formal. This contrasts with a marker, which is language variation subject to style shifting because it is evaluated socially by the in-group. An example of a marker would be the use of glottal stop and 't' in many varieties of British English. Speakers are aware that in more formal contexts use of 't' is preferred to glottal stop. It is evaluated as showing greater power, and so speakers may modify their speech accordingly.

Finally, a **stereotype**, according to Labov, is when the association with a variable becomes so well known and has attracted such negative or archaic associations that the form is actively avoided by in-group speakers. Labov cites the traditional 'oi' pronunciation of 'ir' in New York City English as an example; 'thoidy-toid street' for 'thirty-third street'. For those outside New York City, this is a shorthand way of referencing a New York accent, though not in fact much used by New York speakers anymore. Another stereotype would be the use of the term 'bobby' for police officer in British English. The term is rarely if ever used by British speakers but is still used as a shorthand by outsiders, non-British English speakers, to reference this community's dialect. Its popularity as a stereotype dates from a time when the term was current in British English and became widely known to all English speakers.

Out-group awareness very much determines the status of a form as indicator, marker or stereotype. Johnstone (2009) notes that it is only when in-group members notice that their community's variety is different from outsiders' talk that a new way of referencing local identity through language becomes available to those speakers. Johnstone notes how this heightened awareness of the difference between in-group and out-group talk took hold for her Pittsburgh Pennsylvania **informants** from the 1960s onwards:

> Pittsburghers could then begin to vary the usage of regional forms in their own speech, depending on what they need to accomplish, or were

heard as accomplishing in interaction: whether they were trying to sound more local or supra-local, more careful or more relaxed, more working class or less so.

(2009: 12)

It is only through perception of groups' linguistic difference that **styles** can emerge. If people don't notice the difference, it can't be used to demonstrate identity. Sometimes noticing difference works against social cohesion. Jack K. Chambers (2002) discusses a phenomenon where social group affiliation seems to inhibit any perception of linguistic difference. Chambers notes the seemingly widely experienced, though little-noted phenomenon of cases where difference exists but it is not noticed at all. He illustrates this with the case of 'Ethan', a native speaker of English in Toronto Canada, who was not able to hear the non-native variety that his parents spoke.

Ethan was well into his school years before he was consciously aware that his parents' English was foreign-accented. This, too, is typical of children raised in households where the parents are fluent ESL [English as a Second Language] speakers. The innate [accent] filter works so efficaciously as to inure the developing native speakers to sounds and forms that would be false steps in the acquisition process as the children go about acquiring the indigenous accent of their peers. Accordingly, instead of learning to ignore the foreign-accent features in their parents' speech, a presumably tedious process, children simply fail to hear them. Consequently, they fail to recognize their parents' speech as different from their own.

(Chambers 2002: 117)

Chambers's account, 'The Ethan Experience', highlights the importance of social cohesion between parent and child, as well as noting that this can override the perception of linguistic differences between the parents' talk and the child's talk. Perception of difference seems to be governed by social distance.

9.8 SUMMARY

In this chapter we looked at how naming practices, pronoun use, dialect and style contribute to the creation of linguistic identities. We also examined how identity is a complex construction of agentive group membership and reaction to classification by others and how linguists attempt to study the ways in which we categorise the world through identity labelling. Identity encompasses these and other issues discussed in chapters on gender, age ethnicity and social class and language standardisation.

ANSWERS TO ACTIVITY 9.5

All the examples are native speaker constructions.

1. This is used by speakers in Ohio/Pennsylvania in the US; 'anymore' means 'nowadays'.
2. This is used by Southern speakers, especially in North/South Carolina in the US. The use of two modals is a way of mitigating modality even more than the use of one would do.
3. Used in Southeastern New England in the US; 'so don't I' means the same as 'so do I'.
4. This is from South African English; 'just' means an indeterminate time in the future.
5. This is found in various local dialects including parts of Scotland and Pittsburgh in the US.
6. This is found in Irish English, where 'after' means 'just finished'.

FURTHER READING

Beal, J. (2009) '"You're not from New York City, you're from Rotherham": dialect and identity in British indie music', *Journal of English Linguistics*, 37 (3): 223–240.
Bucholtz, M. (1998) 'Geek the girl: language, femininity, and female nerds', in N. Warner et al (eds), *Gender and Belief Systems: Proceedings of the Fourth Berkeley Women and Language Conference*, Berkeley: Berkeley Women and Language Group, 119–31.
Bucholtz, M. and Hall, K. (2004) 'Language and identity', in A. Duranti (ed), *A Companion to Linguistic Anthropology* Malden, MA: Blackwell, 369–394.
Bucholtz, M., Liang, A. C. and Sutton, L. A. (eds) (1999) *Reinventing Identities: The Gendered Self in Discourse,* Oxford: Oxford University Press.
Eckert, P. (2003) 'The meaning of style', *Texas Linguistic Forum,* 47: 41–53.
Gesser, A. (2007) 'Learning about hearing people in the land of the deaf: an ethnographic account', *Sign Language Studies,* 7 (3): 269–283.
Olsson, John (2009) 'The man with the baseball bat', in *Word Crime: Solving Crime Through Forensic Linguistics*, London: Continuum, 41–45.
Ramsdell, L. (2004) 'Language and identity politics: the linguistic autobiographies of Latinos in the United States', *Journal of Modern Literature*, 28 (1): 166–176.
Schilling-Estes, N. (2007) 'Investigating stylistic variation', in J. K. Chambers, P. Trudgill and N. Schilling-Estes (eds) *The Handbook of Language Variation and Change*, Oxford: Blackwell.

NOTES

1. You can see some maps in Labov's 'The Organization of Dialect Diversity in North America' at www.ling.upenn.edu/phono_atlas/ICSLP4.html.
2. See Fox, G. (1993) 'A comparison of "policespeak" and "normalspeak" a preliminary study', J. M. Sinclair, M. Hoey, and G. Fox (eds), *Techniques of Description: A Festschrift for Malcolm Coulthard*, Routledge: London, 183–195.

CHAPTER 10

Language standardi[s/z]ation

Suzanne LaBelle

10.1 INTRODUCTION

Which spelling of the second word in this chapter title is correct? 'standardisation' or 'standardization'? Do you think one form is 'better' than the other? Would it depend upon who was using the word? Your intuitions on which form is correct/better depend upon attitudes to Standard English, where you acquired English, and perhaps where you now live. Growing up in the US, I would have said the 'z' spelling, but after a decade in the UK, I would use 's'. The switch was determined by the domain for my language use. It first happened for me when writing for work, as the expectation of the UK audience was to use 's', and eventually this work use spread to all my writing.

All written forms of language are in some way a representation of their spoken equivalents, but this is not always straightforward. Different varieties of English have standardised spelling in different ways. In fact, not every language in the world has a fixed written form: some languages have no writing systems at all; others have not agreed upon one written form, and leave choices up to individual users. However, once the speakers of a language agree a fixed written variety, that variety comes to be viewed as the standard by which other varieties are judged.

Think again about which form you think is 'correct' for 'standardisation'. What it would mean if someone used the [s/z] form you were not expecting? Would it make you question their identity or their education? Would it depend upon your social experience, whether you knew or agreed there was more than one standard? In this chapter we will look at how English developed its standard forms, and think about what social consequences there may be for users of non-standard varieties. We will look at techniques linguists use to get at attitudes about language, and work through some examples relating beliefs about non-standard language to beliefs about speakers of those varieties.

10.2 LANGUAGE PLANNING

So how do we obtain agreed-upon standard forms? Standardisation can take place for both written and spoken language and is supported through their use in powerful cultural institutions. Received Pronunciation (RP) used to be widely recognised as the pronunciation or accent of a spoken prestige variety in British English. However, as Tench remarks, 'The word *received* has largely lost its meaning of "generally accepted" and is now no longer applicable in modern (British) society as other "educated" standard accents of a regional variety are increasingly favoured' (2003: 427). It was used by upper-class speakers, and for broadcasting on state sponsored media, the BBC. This has changed somewhat in recent years and one can hear national accents, Welsh, Scottish and Northern Irish amongst newsreaders, and regional accents in continuity announcements or as voiceovers for non-news or local programmes.

But how do we get individual language users to agree on common forms? When a culture goes about standardising a language, according to Haugen (1966), first a language variety is selected, which means that spellings and/or pronunciations and grammatical constructions are fixed or codified. Those doing the selecting and **codification** form a type of cultural elite – those with 'expert' status with regard to language. Selection and codification of a written language variety involves 'corpus planning' – that is, agreeing on which alphabet and spelling systems to use to encode a chosen variety, picking one form over another where variation exists. Language professionals, educators, editors, linguists and others are involved in corpus planning.

Once forms are selected and codified by this expert elite – perhaps formalised by a 'language governing body', the domain of use for those forms is expanded. So, if the spoken form of one community is chosen as the new national written standard, other communities within the nation will first need to accept the new forms, and then begin using them in new contexts. Haugen calls this 'elaboration of function'. Elaboration of function might mean developing a literary canon in the newly standardised variety, or using it in educational or scientific contexts, or for legal and governmental purposes. The domains of use that encode power are typically those which the new standard is meant to be used for. Its use then becomes a way of signalling that you have had access to powerful cultural institutions.

Table 10.1 Standardising language (Haugen 1966)

	Form	Function
Society	Selection	Acceptance
Language	Codification	Elaboration

Haugen's chart (Table 10.1) shows what a society does both culturally and linguistically when it standardises a language. Those with power in a given culture first select a form, which must eventually be generally accepted. They then codify that form, deciding on one variant as correct. For example, when a word enters the officially sanctioned lexicon, the dictionary, it may have had many forms circulating in the culture, but its inclusion usually coincides with a fixing of one form. The etymology of the spice 'coriander', for example, had variants 'coriandre' and 'coliander', 'corriandir' noted in the Oxford English Dictionary, before the present spelling was agreed. After codification, a society will expand the domains where that variant is expected to be used: an elaboration of its function. For example, for communities where creoles are used by the majority of the population in spoken language, there are creole activists looking for this to happen for the traditionally unwritten creoles; this is happening for creoles used throughout the Caribbean. Spelling forms need to be agreed (selection and codification) and then the domain of use expanded. This would involve using creoles for official purposes in government and education where they now frequently co-exist with a dominant and standardised European language.

'Status planning' involves the marketing of the newly agreed upon standard, working out how forms will be disseminated to users within the speech community. Practicalities during this process involve deciding who will have access to the standard, what teacher training will need to be undertaken, what official translations will need to be completed, how the new forms will become part of everyday life and what the cost of producing materials in a new written variety will be.

The consequence of selection of variety and codification of form is that positive associations are made with the variety selected; the appropriateness of that variety for use in high culture contexts comes to be seen as natural. Arguments are created to support the pure logic and beauty of the variety. This can be understood as a strategy of **prescriptivism**. As works of literature, philosophy, science and religion are conceived and disseminated through that variety, the code becomes inexorably intertwined with content. A further consequence of selecting a variety and elevating it to the position of standard is that users of other varieties become disenfranchised. Their forms are no longer just different, but different and not appropriate for use in powerful cultural institutions. Those varieties not selected acquire negative associations, of illogicality, ugliness, of a having a 'jarring' and uneducated nature. These attitudes may then be transferred to speakers of the non-standard varieties (see section 6.3.2). Use of a non-standard variety can become a marker for membership in a culturally powerless group.

10.3 ENGLISH AND STANDARDISATION

As we have seen, at issue in language standardisation is agreeing upon a written form, alphabet and spelling system. Ideally, a spelling system closely matches the pronunciation of a language, so that once the sounds of a language are encoded into symbols there is a one to one, sound-symbol correspondence. This makes learning to read a straightforward activity. Languages such as Italian where there is a close one sound to one symbol correspondence have fewer incidences of surface dyslexia, or the inability to pronounce unfamiliar new words than users of a language such as English does (Patterson et al 1985). English's spelling system is notoriously difficult for children and second language learners to acquire because many words' spellings are not obvious from their pronunciations. Take a word such as 'knife'. The 'k' and the 'e' are not pronounced, and the 'i', represents two vowel sounds together, a **diphthong**, [Λ] plus [I]. This mismatch between spelling and pronunciation in English was not always so dramatic. The spelling of 'knife' dates from a time when both the 'k' and the 'e' were pronounced, and the 'i' vowel was sounded as one, rather than two sounds. What happened? The pronunciation of English moved on, but the spelling system did not. Spellings change much more slowly than spoken forms do, because as a culture we invest in learning traditional written forms and police their use. Once a spelling is enshrined as standard, changing it to bring it closer to pronunciation, no matter how sensible that may be from a learner's perspective, will cause consternation from those who have already gone to the trouble to acquire the traditional form. The standard spelling becomes a thing of value in itself, quite apart from its relationship to the spoken language. There have been some attempts at change and reform in English spelling, but these have not been met with much success.

In the early twentieth century, the playwright George Bernard Shaw left assets in his will to conduct research into the English spelling system. The will set out a number of specific research questions including establishing:

> how much time could be saved per individual scribe by the substitution for the said [normal] alphabet of an alphabet containing at least 40 letters (hereinafter called the Proposed British alphabet) enabling the said language to be written without indicating single sounds by groups of letters or by diacritical marks, instead of by one symbol for each sound.
>
> (Re Shaw, Public Trustee *v.* Day [1957], 1 All ER 745, [1957] 1 WLR 729)

The courts held that this could not be allowed as the body Shaw wanted to create did not meet the legal requirements necessary. In short, they did not see a benefit resulting from the research and alphabet Shaw proposed. Justice Harman described other parts of the proposed programme as 'propaganda' and decided that Shaw's proposal was analogous to one for a political party. One might argue that the court's rejection of Shaw's proposal was a way of protecting the value of their own language variety and the investment they had made in it. Certainly the decision appears to conform with the law of the day, but some have suggested that the courts may rule differently on such matters now. Here we see the power of the court effectively overruling other forms of power. The court of public opinion, however, has an ongoing fascination for the 'rules' of Standard English (see Truss 2003; see section 1.2.1). Some of these rules have a curious history and are a result of practical convenience and the preferences of those in power.

English began the process of standardisation in earnest after William Caxton brought the printing press to England in 1476. Previously, documents written in English varied in their grammar and spelling conventions, depending on the geographic origins of the writer.[1] As books were copied longhand, and as such were highly prized, copying involved much work by specially trained scribes. However, the development of the printing press allowed for easier copying and allowed the publishing industry to establish itself. The technological advancement of the printing press came together with the philosophical movement of the Renaissance in Europe, the development of humanist values, which saw a broadening of access to education and literacy. English publishers now had a means and a market for their new industry. What they needed was a standardised form for their craft, so those setting the presses would be able to quickly reproduce texts that buyers would easily understand. Publishers chose the variety of English spoken in the south-east of England as the basis for their new standardised English. This variety was chosen as the market for books was largely composed of the upper and developing middle classes around London. This makes clear that corpus planning is sometimes done as part of a decision making in a commercial or pragmatic setting.

Later, this standard variety became sanctioned by the King and God, through its use in the King James Bible and as the language of empire as the English crown established colonies and expanded its territories. During the Enlightenment attempts were made to improve the English spelling system and also to establish guidelines for 'correct' usage of grammar variables. The prohibition on **multiple negation** – that is, having both 'doesn't' and 'no' in the sentence 'He doesn't have no money' – dates from this time. The argument goes that in mathematics two negatives make a positive, so why should the principle apply differently to language, if we want the best, most logical forms? So whilst native speakers of English understand 'He doesn't have no money' to be an emphatic form of the statement 'He doesn't have money', the standard tells us the sense of this sentence *should* be 'He does have money', using the two negatives equal a positive argument. The ideology of the standard as correct and other varieties as wanting is reinforced by views that its forms were more worthy because of their purity and logic.

There is nothing logical, or more pure about this version that became the written standard. For example, other languages such as French get along just fine using multiple negation; indeed, multiple negation can be found in Chaucer. We say no to multiple negation in Standard English because of the power that language experts exerted upon the language. To give you some further evidence that logic cannot be appealed to in explaining differences between the standard and non-standard forms, consider the case of 'ain't'. In English 'ain't' is a non-prestige variant; compare 'I ain't going' to 'I'm not going'. 'Ain't', however, fills a lexical gap that is otherwise left empty in English. Look at the conjugations in Table 10.2.

Table 10.2 'To be' in the negative

	Singular	Plural	Singular	Plural	Singular	Plural
1st	I am not	We are	I'm not	We're not	I _____	We aren't
2nd	You are not	You are not	You're not	You're not	You aren't	You aren't
3rd	She/He is not	They are not	She/he's not	They're not	She/he isn't	They aren't

'Ain't' fills in for the missing form 'amn't', and is used with other persons and numbers as well, giving a very regular logical paradigm, as shown in Table 10.3 (see Broadbent 2009).

Table 10.3 Ain't

	Singular	Plural
1st	I ain't	We ain't
2nd	You ain't	You ain't
3rd	He ain't	They ain't

However, because 'ain't' is associated with non-prestige speech and writing, the logic here is overlooked!

A further example of how non-standard English can express useful distinctions which the standard lacks relates to the singular and plural forms of 'you'. English used to have separate forms: 'thou' for singular and informal, and 'you' for plural and formal. Many other languages of the world you may be familiar with have these distinctions. Standard English has lost this, so we use 'you' in all cases. Non-standard Englishes have preserved these distinctions. So for some Lancashire and Yorkshire speakers in northern England the 'thou/you' distinction remains, and in the southern States in the US 'you' has become the singular and 'y'all' (from 'you all') the plural. Some southern US speakers go further, with 'you' deleted completely from the paradigm and 'y'all' taking on the singular meaning, and 'all y'all' used for the plural. In many parts of the English-speaking world – Liverpool in the UK, throughout the Republic of Ireland and the mid-Atlantic states in the US – 'you' is the singular and 'yous/youse' is the plural.

Just as the printing press had an influence on the standardisation of English, new technologies also have effects. We saw in Chapter 4 the way in which the possibilities provided by text messaging allow individuals to be creative with language in new ways. Arguments have also been made about other technologies driving change in what is considered 'standard'.

Can you think of any other examples where non-standard English constructions, either in grammar or vocabulary, present a more logical or regular pattern than the standard? Make a list of non-standard forms you know and think about the logic behind them. Why do you think these forms are not more widely embraced or haven't taken on a more prestigious place in English?

British PM Gordon Brown was forced to make a public and personal apology to the mother of a slain British soldier after the handwritten letter of condolence he sent was found to have twenty errors. *The London Evening Standard* reported the mother, Mrs Janes, as saying that the letter was disrespectful: 'When ... the letter is littered with 20 mistakes, they offer no comfort. It was an insult to Jamie and all the good men and women who have died.'[2] Brown misspelt 'condolencs', and 'colleagus' amongst other errors. If Mrs Janes could understand what Gordon Brown meant, why was she insulted by his spelling? Why did Brown feel the need to apologise? Why would this exchange be news?

Apostrophes, for example, are a subject of much discussion in terms of their correct use in, for example, place names. The Australian Committee for Geographical Names, in its *Guidelines for the Consistent Use of Place Names,* 'explains that leaving [apostrophes] out "facilitates the consistent matching and retrieval of place names in database systems such as those used by the emergency services"'.[3] Meanwhile, in the UK, some local authorities have banned the use of apostrophes in public signage, while the Apostrophe Protection Society works to protect this punctuation mark.[4] While these are small organisations, with a limited sphere of influence, there are bodies that take responsibility for standard language in a more official and far-reaching way.

Some language cultures establish institutions whose sole function is the adjudication of whether certain forms are acceptable as standards in that language. For example, in France the Academie Française officiates in this capacity. Norway has the Norwegian Language Council, and Mandarin Chinese has the National Languages Committee. At issue for linguists and educators is what exactly defines Standard English? Is it a set of spelling conventions, a set of pronunciations, grammatical forms, or a certain register or style? English has no institution charged with creating or delineating the standard, so certainty about whether one form or another is 'correct' is frequently down to listing what has been proscribed, or not allowed (Trudgill 1999 in Jenkins 2003). We have writing style guides that suggest we should not end sentences with prepositions such as 'up' or 'on', and that we should not split infinitives, such as 'to go', by inserting an **adverb** between as in 'to boldly go'. The latter 'rule' is based on the eighteenth-century idea that English should be more like the prestige language Latin. In Latin it would not be possible to create either construction because of the **morphology** of the language; in Latin, the infinitive is one word. But the lack of a clear authority and the vagueness as to what counts and does not count as part of the Standard means that creating a cohesive set of forms that are definitively 'in' is illusive, at least without such an official body.

10.4   GLOBAL STANDARDS/GLOBAL ENGLISH(ES)

Further complicating matters is the position that English finds itself in today as a language of global communication. In the aftermath of European colonialism, languages such as English began to be spoken by groups with increasingly loose cultural ties to Europe. The reason that standardisation/standardization variants came about is linked to American nation building and the power of speakers to determine local language norms. Once the United States established itself as politically free from the UK, there was social space available for creating new language standards. America did not need to look to England for its government and in a similar way was free to develop **language norm**s, spelling conventions of its own. 'Z' spellings in suffixes such as '-ize' date from the 1820s when the first US dictionaries of English were developed. Noah Webster in developing the first US dictionaries argued that the 'z' spelling more accurately reflected the Greek etymology of the suffix, and that it should be preferred to the 'French' −ise variant (Hargraves 2003).

The myth of genetic transmission means that for English in colonial contexts, a select group of nations outside of Britain are allowed to innovate, to claim some form of ownership over their local variety internationally. These nations are the first wave of British colonialism where English settlers supplanted local populations in large enough numbers to create a kind of English culture outside of England. The unstated assumption, until evidence to the contrary is provided, is that white speakers received their English in a parent−child relationship that dates back to English settlement. This idea of the way language is handed down is the myth of genetic transmission.

The nations of Ireland, Canada, the United States, Australia, and New Zealand are classed by Kachru (1992) as inner circle nations. Kachru notes these nations can develop norms of English, acquire the language natively, and claim ownership rights over the language. Outer circle nations, in Kachru's design, are those which are norm developing, where English is acquired as a native language but in competition with local languages which have official status and are used by the population regularly. Nations where English is used as a lingua franca, but do not have official status are deemed expanding circle nations. A **lingua franca** is a language that is not native to either speaker or listener but is used for communication where learning one or the other native languages is not practical.

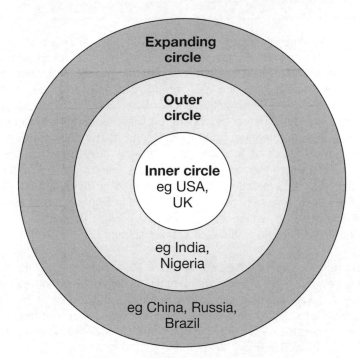

Figure 10.1 Kachru's concentric circles

Expanding circle nations depend upon inner circle nations for language norms and traditionally may not claim ownership over the language (see Figure 10.1). The question of ownership is central to the evolution of English as a global language. At issue for language planners of a language such as English, which has become a tool of international trade and commerce, are the rights that non-native users of the language have to modify and change the language. What right of ownership do you have to a language where you are not a native speaker, but where your use of that language may not ever entail an encounter with a native speaker? Linguists such as Jennifer Jenkins suggest that in English as a Lingua Franca (ELF) contexts, not all inner circle variety norms and standards should be enforced. Jenkins suggests, for example, that an EU English might not include phonologically marked sounds such as 'th' both [θ] and [ð], instead replacing them with [s] and [z] or [f] and [v], or [t] and [d] (Jenkins 1998). There is widespread recognition of other standards by speakers of inner circle English. Indeed, speakers from outer circle areas may well be native English speakers. The ranking suggested by the circles above still exerts strong power. Jenkins asks why speakers who are not using English with native speakers strive only for native speaker norms? The perceived value of inner circle varieties seems to be a contributory factor.

Read the following selection from the novel *Ella Minnow Pea*, a story of a fictional post-colonial English-speaking island nation Nollop, whose most famous inhabitant coined the sentence 'The quick brown fox jumped over the lazy dog' and was immortalised with a plaque of the sentence in the capital's main square. Over time, letters from the plaque fall off the sign, and the governors interpret this as divine intervention and ban the use of the letters that have fallen off. The book charts the new written standards as they develop. After you have read the selection, try to rewrite the passage using standard spellings. Can you understand the original? Which letters are missing? What does this tell you about the relationship between certain sounds in English? What about the flexibility of the writing system we use? What do users of the language do to innovate within a prescribed standard?

I regret to tell yew most greephos news: Mannheim is mort. I no that yew new him, were phrents with him. That yew ant he ant his assistant Tom were worging still on the Enterprise 32 shallenge. How it happen is not easy to tell: he yoose an illegal letter in interphew aphter poleese see him ant Tom going threw wintow into yew-niphersity hall-trespassing.

(Dunn 2001: 165)

10.5   PIDGIN AND CREOLES AND STANDARDISATION

Not all cases of global English fit nicely into the concentric circles paradigm. Pidgin and creole languages are special types of language varieties. A pidgin is an emergency communication language, a highly variable simplified variety, with no native speakers, used when one group encounters another but social prohibitions prevent normal second language acquisition taking place. Linguists see **creoles** as the blossoming of a **pidgin** into a fully developed language once they acquire native speakers in a second generation. Standardising pidgin and creole languages is an especially contentious issue as most have little history of writing, and exist in a complex relationship with their **lexifier** (the language which gives most of the vocabulary to the pidgin or creole) or with another official standard language. Romaine (1997 [1990]) discusses problems that arise in attempting to use written forms of Tok Pisin, an English lexified expanded pidgin used in Papua New Guinea. Puns in English such as 'eggcellent' to sell a brand of eggs, would be difficult for a Tok Pisin reader, because though many words in Tok Pisin derive from English, the word for 'egg', 'kiau', is taken from the local Papua New Guinean language, Tolai. Cultural and linguistic mismatches between written Standard English and local Tok Pisin forms mean that advertising strategies such as these, which play on phonological similarities, can be inappropriate for the Tok Pisin audience.

Language planners in creole contexts need to be aware of the issues which may arise in trying to allow, what the poet Kamau Brathwaite called, the development of 'nation language' or local linguistic standards. There may be positive attitudes towards the historical Standard, the lexifier, as in Jamaica where English and Jamaican Creole are used, or in island nations such as Aruba, where Dutch is the official language, but a Spanish lexifier Creole Papiamentu is used by the majority of the population in everyday circumstances. These positive attitudes are entrenched in the educational and legal systems. Moving towards a new standard would mean changing these positive attitudes. In these cases, standardising spoken creoles, creating written forms, causes clashes between speakers who have already invested in Standard English/Dutch as the language of officialdom and high culture.

10.6 LANGUAGE ATTITUDES

As we have seen, a consequence of language standardisation is the develop- ment of certain attitudes towards users of more or less powerful language varieties. Attitudes about a language variety are not just derived from its similarity to the standard but also come about through codified indexical relationships between linguistic form and groups in the world. There are several ways to investigate language attitudes. One is to simply ask people what they think about certain codes. However, people may be reluctant to express negative attitudes when directly questioned for fear of causing offence. **Matched guised** testing was developed to determine a group's language attitudes without direct questioning. In this methodology, a bilingual or bidialectal speaker records a monologue in each of their language varieties. Each variety is played to an audience, and that audience is asked to make judgements about the speaker, ranking them for friendliness, intelligence, trustworthiness and the like. As all factors about the speaker are the same for both recordings, save the code in which the monologue is delivered, linguists suggest that any disparity between the rankings will be down to attitudes the audience has about the language variety. These tests help reveal embedded prejudices about and preferences for language varieties.

10.6.1 Attitudes and education

In the United States, a widely used non-standard variety of English, African American Vernacular English (AAVE), is popularly used and a prestige variety in R&B, hip-hop and rap. However, it has met with serious reactions to its use in the most innocuous of official educational contexts. A controversy about teaching Standard English emerged in the mid-1990s in California in the USA, when the Oakland California school board, in response to many African American children falling behind their white counterparts in reading, devel- oped a program for recognition of AAVE. They suggested a teacher training program be implemented, whereby AAVE features would be explained to teachers to enable them to better meet the needs of their AAVE-speaking students when teaching them to read English. An example of how children who use this dialect would be helped by special training can be seen when we look closely at a feature of the dialect. Third person singular 's', as in 'he walks' is optionally absent from AAVE, so for a listening comprehension exercise where children hear a story and are tested on their understanding of what happened, dialect-based misunderstanding might arise. In a sentence such as 'The cats sleep' children who use the non-standard variant would not have enough information to know the number of cats doing the sleeping, as the two clues which tell the number of cats would be obscure; specifically, the plural 's' on the noun will be hidden by its position next to the 's' at the start of 'sleep'. In speech, these would be indistinguishable. The final 's' on the verb in the singular is optionally absent in this dialect. The student, when asked how many cats there were, would be guessing. A wrong guess would not be assessed as a dialect problem, but as a comprehension one. Assessing dialect differences such as this as comprehension errors could put AAVE-speaking children at a disadvantage scholastically. The school board's resolution led to much discord in the non-AAVE community. The media spun the story to suggest that teachers would be using AAVE in the classroom in place of English, and the outcry this engendered ultimately led to the board dropping their teacher education provisions. The issue has not gone away. As Baugh comments, 'Although considerable time has elapsed since Oakland educators passed their controversial Ebonics resolution, many of the linguistic and educational problems they articulated have yet to be resolved' (2000: 3) (see section 6.3.2).

Debates about education are common in language standardisation (and prescription) discussions and can come from various points of view. While the Oakland case can be read as an attempt at inclusion, a recent policy shift in Arizona is rather different. The Huffington Post, a website in the United States, reported in April 2010 on a controversial law passed by the Arizona state legislature in relation to immigration. The new law allows police to stop and search anyone it suspects of being an illegal immigrant. However, changes to educational policy have also been made.

> [T]he Arizona Department of Education has told schools that teachers with 'heavy' or 'ungrammatical' accents are no longer allowed to teach English classes.
>
> (2010)[5]

Exactly what this means is far from clear. Indeed, it is difficult to see how an accent can be 'ungrammatical'. What it means for a teacher who is considered not to speak 'proper' English is, on the contrary, very clear:

> Teachers who don't meet the new fluency standards have the option of taking classes to improve their English ... but if they fail to reach the state's targets would be fired or reassigned.

Language attitudes are often reported in a way that suggests they are harmless and amusing. We are told which are attractive and which are not. However, when such attitudes are used to exclude speakers from education, it becomes clear how important it is to understand where these ideas come from so that they can be appropriately challenged.

Activity 10.4

The following is an exchange between two characters in the popular cartoon *South Park*, the African American student 'Token' and the young white and racist 'Cartman'. The boys are trying to come up with ways for their school television news program to win in the ratings against a rival student who is televising videos of puppies. Cartman suggests that Token's language might be the thing keeping the boys from winning the ratings war.

> CARTMAN: Ah, Token, can I have a quick word with you? Look, Token, I, I know the guys are having trouble bringing this up with you, but uh ... Well the thing is, Token, we ... we really need to revamp your whole TV persona.
>
> TOKEN: Huh?
>
> CARTMAN: You see Token, people really enjoy seeing African-Americans on the news ... Seeing African-Americans on the news, not hearing them. That's why all African-Americans newspeople learn to talk more ... wha, how should I say ... white. Token, all the great African-American newspeople have learned to hide their ebonic tribespeak with a more pure Caucasian dialect. There's no shame in it, and I think it'll really help our ratings.
>
> (Trey Parker 2004, *South Park* episode 'Quest for Ratings')

What conclusions can you come to about ebonics/African American Vernacular English based on Cartman's characterisation? According to Cartman, what domain is appropriate for its use? What is the consequence of not using Standard English in his eyes? How have attitudes about language become conflated with attitudes about groups in this example?

10.7   LINGUISTIC IMPERIALISM AND DIGLOSSIA

We have looked at the issues that arise within one language culture when different varieties of a language are evaluated as having more or less social value by speakers. It is also important to examine what the consequences are for languages when social evaluation of language varieties lead to the abandonment of one variety in favour of another.

Linguistic imperialism is the imposition of one culture's language upon another culture. This frequently coincides with increased social power for the linguistically dominant group. The right to use the language system of one's choosing in public and official capacities is closely associated with the continuation of group identity. In the aftermath of European colonialism, many of the world's languages are under threat. The spread of major languages of international business and commerce, such as English, mean speakers shift away from less powerful languages. When a language dies, a particular view on interpreting the world, what is worthy of being encoded in grammar, as well as original canons of literature and folklore, are lost. This philosophical and literary loss frequently also coincides with the loss of status for speakers of a minority language. When a nation is under the yoke of linguistic imperialism, access to education, legal and governmental services, and other formal institutions of state may be unavailable to minority speakers, and this can lead to disenfranchisement and civil unrest.

Sometimes when a language ceases to be the means of everyday communication, it comes to be preserved for ritual purposes, acting as a means to promote group identity. For example, up until the 1960s Latin was used in Catholic church services, despite it not being the language of church-goers anywhere. In northern Chile, the Atacama people have Cunza, a local language no longer spoken in everyday life in the region, but used for ritual purposes (Rodriguez 1991). Other groups seek recognition of their language and identity outside such restricted spheres.

When a marginalised linguistic group, such as French Creole speakers in Haiti, invest in their identity as users of a minority language, opposition movements can arise to try to gain power for these speakers. In Haiti, since the 1960s, the Creole has been an official language of Haiti, though agreeing on written forms for this traditionally spoken language has proved problematic, with a high incidence of variation amongst taught varieties. Schieffelin and Doucet note, 'As of 1980 eleven proposed spelling systems could be identified' (1992: 431) for Haitian Creole. Standardisation of linguistic form is more difficult for a variety that has historically been power-less, and without fixed spellings. Schiffman (1996) discusses how the language policy in India evolved after it gained independence from Britain. The newly formed government attempted to promote regional Indian languages alongside Hindi and English. This 'three language formula' was a compromise (Schiffman 1996), recognising how powerful the Hindi identity had become in the nationalist movement as well as recognising English's historical place as a language of colonialism, and allowing regional languages some official status locally.

It is important to look closely at national language policy and planning to tease apart who is driving linguistic change and for what reason. As Chew argues in relation to Singapore, using English may be a pragmatic and finan-cial decision, rather than the realignment of culture and identity: 'language is seen not so much as an emblem of culture and nationhood but as an impor-tant economic resource' (2007: 74). While it is tempting to blame English as a language for the death of less powerful languages, this may be too simple and may result in missing real causes of inequality. The English language does not have power of itself, it is invested with it by people with particular interests. Tollefson and Tsui write: 'A key finding … is that language policies are always linked with broader social, economic, and political agendas that usually have priority over pedagogical and educational concerns' (2007: 262). We see this even in contexts where English is the norm.

Betsy Evans (2010) examines the ideologies and values surrounding language in her paper which describes the defeat of an English only bill in Ohio. While the legislation was proposed because of values of unity and national identity, she argues that it may have been defeated on more immediate financial grounds – that is, the state wanting to encourage overseas investment. Language values are not always straightforward as they interact with other cultural values. For example, the desire to promote English as the official language in some parts of the US may come into conflict with the importance of individuals' autonomy and 'the right to speak whatever language they want' (2010: 169). Thus, 'English-only legislation is underpinned by a cultural consensus about national identity that can be challenged by its own complexity. Therefore, such legislation is subject to being overruled by more salient transitory practical issues such as the local economy' (2010: 169).

Conforming to the official or dominant language appears to be under-stood as a requirement of good citizenship in other countries. In 2007, the British prime minister was reported as believing 'immigrants had a "duty to integrate"' which 'included learning English language'. This duty has also been formalised, though not with legislation about language as such: 'Ministers have also opted to make anybody who wants to stay here perma-nently to sit a citizenship test written in English' (Slack 2007). This appears to be a common view as 'A Mori poll for the Commission found that 60 per cent of people surveyed agreed that the biggest barrier to "being English" was not speaking the language' (Waugh 2007: 7). Still, as Evans points out, in the US at least, holding such a view does not necessarily rule out support for multilingualism.

Whatever the particular configuration of values, there are always some ideologies at work. These manifest in relation to position and power, as social prestige and access to language do interact in multilingual and

A magazine advertisement for designer lamps 'I guzzini' in English language international lifestyle magazine *Wallpaper* (September 2008) featured a photo of a lamp and a one sentence description in Italian. At the bottom of the advert was written in English 'If you don't speak the language of the country where great design was born please look up pizzakroba at iguzzini.com'. What is the purpose of advertising in Italian without an English translation in an English-language publication? Who does it privilege? Why might that be more than worth the cost of using a language most readers will not understand?

Activity 10.5

perhaps especially in post-colonial societies, privileging some and disempowering others. Prestige and language variety interact internationally as well in different domains. Look at the following activity to explore how prestige operates for Italian and English in the domain of design.

In many cultures, and where there has been a history of linguistic imperialism, access to standard varieties is policed. This can lead to the phenomenon of **diglossia**, where the language used by the majority is not the language used for official purposes. The label diglossia was first used by Ferguson (1959) in relation to the language situation in Arabic-speaking nations. He noted that local varieties of Arabic were very different from the classical Arabic used for religious and educational purposes. Ferguson gives us a method for classifying the domains of use that each language in a diglossic society fulfils for its speakers. (H) varieties fulfil high prestige, official roles, and (L) varieties fulfil low prestige or everyday functions. Though classical Arabic and local varieties are related genetically – that is to say, one form evolved out of the other at some time in the past – this is not a prerequisite for diglossia. Fishman (1967) labels this non-related language variety situation as 'extended diglossia'. The Aruban Creole case, where Dutch exists as the official or (H) language and Papiamentu, the Spanish Creole is the (L) language, is one such example. English culture was in a diglossic situation after the Norman invasion of 1066. The (H) language after the invasion was Norman French, the (L) was Middle English. Norman French terms for cooked meat, such as 'mutton' for 'sheep' and 'pork' for 'pig' date from this time, when English speakers would be preparing food for French nobility. Today, increasingly in many cultures, English is the (H) language supplanting local varieties. The usefulness of English in a global market is undeniable, but rethinking the ways in which it might co-exist with local languages may lead to a more equitable power sharing, and enfranchisement through bilingualism.

10.8 SUMMARY

Language varieties differ not just in their forms but also in the way they are used by speakers to gain access to and protect their status. If a culture chooses to promote one variety of speech or writing as a standard for high culture purposes, then that can have both positive and negative implications for language users, as associations of strength, logic, beauty and correctness become inextricably linked to the standard form. Deviations from the standard come to be viewed as holding opposing values. Linguists work to tease out the stereotypes which link speakers and varieties. Education about non-standard dialects can lead to enfranchisement for users of these varieties. English's journey with standardisation is an ongoing one, as it becomes a language of global communication, and the idea of who 'owns' English becomes revised. Reflecting upon why standards look the way they do can help to break down imposed social barriers based on access to prestige varieties and judgements about language use.

FURTHER READING

Evans, B. (2010) 'English as official state language in Ohio: market forces trump ideology', in H. Kelly-Holmes and G. Mautner (eds), *Language and the Market*, London: Palgrave.

Graddol, D. (2006) *English Next*, British Council.

Jenkins, J. (1998) 'Which pronunciation norms and models for English as an International Language?' *English Language Teaching Journal*, 52 (2): 119–126.

Jenkins, J. (2009) 'English as a lingua franca: interpretations and attitudes', *World Englishes*, 28 (2): 200–207.

Kachru, B. (2000) 'Asia's Englishes and World Englishes', *English Today*, 61: 18–22.

McArthur, T. (2001) 'World English and World Englishes: trends, tensions, varieties, and standards', *Language Teaching*, 34 (1): 1–20.

Milroy, J. and Milroy, L. (1999) *Authority in Language: Investigating Standard English*, London: Routledge.

Trudgill, P. (1999) 'Standard English what it isn't', in T. Bex and R. Watts (eds), *Standard English: the Widening Debate*, London: Routledge.

NOTES

1   This allows for the localisation of such manuscripts. That is, linguists can examine the spelling variations and then be reasonably certain about where the text was transcribed. See the Middle English Grammar Project (MEG) http://uis.cp-prod.uis.no/research/culture/the_middle_english_grammar_project/project_summary/.

2   9 November 2009, www.thisislondon.co.uk/standard/article-23766369-browns-spelling-mistake-shows-no-respect-says-grieving-mother.do.

3   www.worldwidewords.org/articles/apostrophe.htm.

4   www.apostrophe.org.uk/.

5   www.huffingtonpost.cois allows the localm/2010/04/30/arizona-ethnic-studies-cl_n_558731.html.

CHAPTER 11

Projects

11.1 INTRODUCTION

In this chapter, we provide some ideas about projects you could do to explore the topics introduced in this book. The best way to find out about what language is and what it means is to go and see how the language around you is being used. In the chapters so far, you have read about some of the research that sociolinguists do. The important point to remember is that every language community, every text, every utterance can tell us something new. The way that you use language, the way that communication occurs with your friends or in your family is all valuable sociolinguistic data. But as you may have realised already, a lot of this data passes us by. We're so accustomed to using language to do things that we don't normally pay much attention to how we do this. We seem to know instinctively what works and what is appropriate, but think about how difficult it would be to explain these rules to someone new to the language situations that you know.

The projects will give you some idea of what sociolinguists do when they conduct research. It should give you an understanding of the kind of work involved, how long particular kinds of investigations take and what kinds of questions we can ask. Most importantly, we hope that in doing some of these projects (or designing your own) you'll realise that the language that you use is just as interesting, and complex, and worthy of consideration, as the examples that have been given throughout the text.

Some of these projects are based on particular topics that have been covered. However, more often than not, it will be helpful to consider topics and approaches from a variety of perspectives rather than just those suggested by a particular chapter in the book. For example, the close analysis that can be done through transitivity analysis is useful in all kinds of contexts. Likewise, recording and transcribing conversation is an excellent way to examine the tiny details that we're not generally aware of when participating in, or even listening to, conversations.

There are some skills that are useful to have, and some issues to bear in mind when you're conducting research. We deal with that first. There are a lot of useful guides for different kinds of data collection and analysis and we list them in the further reading.

11.2   DATA COLLECTION

11.2.1 What are data?

This is a question that is often asked. Pretty much anything can be data. What your data are will influence what you can do with them and what kinds of things you can say about them. Sociolinguists work with spoken and written data. Obviously, written data can be easier to work with as you don't need to transcribe it. You shouldn't look for data, written or otherwise, in the library. You need to go out into the world. You might be interested in the way a particular group uses language; in the past, the easiest way to get data such as this was to find magazines or other popular publications aimed at or written by this group. Now, the internet provides endless data!

Spoken data are also out in the world. What you're looking for is what people actually do; not what they think they should be doing. So while looking at data from the radio or television can tell you about how people use language in these contexts, it can't really tell us how people use language otherwise. The best way of obtaining spoken data is to record the people you know. While there are ethical issues involved (see BAAL guidelines), if you ask permission to record your family or friends at some time over the coming week, and they consent, chances are they will have forgotten about what you plan to do. In this way, you get spontaneous, natural conversation. These are the kind of data that were used in Chapters 5 and 8. Sociolinguists like to use these kind of data because it reveals how people really talk.

If people are conscious of the fact that they are being recorded, they're more likely to 'perform'. The problem, of course, is that usually the researcher (you) has to be present, or wants to be present, when the recording is taking place. The problem raised by the presence of the researcher and the desire to get natural speech is usually spoken about in terms of the 'observer's paradox'. The paradox is that you want to observe, to be present, but exactly this presence may change the way in which people speak. There are a number of methods of getting around the paradox. Asking informants whether you can record them some time in the future is a possible solution. Jennifer Coates asked her male informants to record themselves (2002).

William Labov argues that asking for a story about an emotional event will also reduce the amount of attention people give to their speech performance. One of his methods was to ask informants about a time their life was in danger; the so-called 'danger of death' narratives.

There might not be a good way, or even any way, of overcoming this problem. It is something you need to consider when you're analysing your data, especially in terms of what you can claim about their 'natural' way of speaking. Is there, for example, any evidence that the speakers are or are not aware of being recorded? Do they constantly refer to the fact of being recorded? One former student (now an academic) provided excellent proof when arguing her informants had forgotten they were being recorded (a couple had volunteered to record themselves each evening). In the data being analysed, one partner wanted to move their interaction to a more intimate level!

It's impossible to be inside someone's head and know for certain whether they are aware of being observed. This doesn't mean that you can't trust your data. It just means you have to think carefully about *what* you can trust the data to tell you.

11.2.2 Transcribing

Once you have your recorded data, you need to transcribe it. Transcription is a time-consuming process. It's important to have as much detail as possible if you're going to be able to say something about the way people are interacting. So while you might normally delete all the 'uhms' and 'ahs' and self-corrections, when you're transcribing data, you need to keep all of that in. It can take a few times of listening to figure out what people are saying, so you need to be patient and listen to your data more than once. It also helps if you record your data in a place and with a recorder that will give you a good sound quality. While conversations in a nightclub may be very interesting to analyse, they will be very difficult to transcribe. Choose somewhere where there isn't a great deal of background noise, and start with conversations that don't have too many people (three or four is more than enough). You can see the transcription conventions that have been used in this book below. You'll also notice that in multi-party conversations, it's useful to use a stave when you transcribe (see examples 10–13 in Chapter 5). This gives a very clear visual indication of who is speaking when. As we've also noticed during this book, pauses, overlaps and interruptions can be very important (see section 5.6.2).

11.2.3 What to do next?

Once you have your data, you need to analyse it. It helps to keep a clean copy and you should always make a backup of recorded data immediately. Analysing data takes time. You need to spend time looking at it and thinking about it. It helps to have more than one copy of written data so you can look for different things. If the written data are electronic, it can help to rearrange the parts. This allows you to compare small chunks (for example) side by side and also allows you to see patterns. Everyone has their own methods for working with data and these projects should help you research and develop your own methods by trying out different ones to see what works for you.

When I'm looking at data, I have two general starting places. The first involves looking at your data to see if anything 'jumps out at you'. Note it down then try to figure out why you noticed it. Is it something very unusual (for the speaker or the situation)? Is it something you don't understand? Is it something that appears in more than one place in the text or the conversation? If you notice something like this, you have a 'lead'. Keep asking yourself questions about it; if it recurs, is it always from the same speaker? How do other speakers react? What comes next?

The second starting place is useful when nothing 'jumps out at you'. Look at the kinds of variation we find in language. If we consider transitivity analysis, for example, we can look at whether active or passive verbs are used. Go through your data systematically and chart the usage (different coloured highlighters can be useful for this). Is there a pattern? What might the pattern mean? What pronouns are used? What verb **tenses**? This way of working is always productive. It may seem to be mechanical, but paying attention to one feature at a time is an excellent way of focusing your analytical mind. Remember, there is always a pattern. Language is a system and it follows rules. With patience, and attention to detail, you can discover and describe these rules. Further, when you're working with data, it will usually be impossible to say *everything* about it. If you're going to say anything meaningful about what the patterns are, you have to focus on a small number of features. If you've spent enough time with your data, the analysis will always provide more than you can write up in a paper of reasonable length.

11.2.4 Questions to ask

In the following, we will suggest features that you might look for and questions that you might ask of your data. But it's important to remember that there is a connection between the data you have and the questions you can ask of the data. This will seem obvious, but it is easy to get carried away when you get enthusiastic about a topic and forget that the data may have nothing to do with the topic you have suddenly become intrigued by. If you have conversational data from men in their twenties, you obviously won't be able to say anything about how women behave in conversations, or about how older or younger men might behave. Crucially, though, you also won't be able to say anything about what these same men might do in the presence of different people (women, older men, and so on). Every data set has specific limitations. This isn't a bad thing. It allows you to focus on a small area and pay it proper attention. The goal of this kind of research is not to come to conclusions about the whole of the human race. You just need to be able to say something about how these people use language in this situation. Because of this, choose your data set carefully. For example, if you want to explore the way people of your own age text each other, you shouldn't include in your data texts from your parents or from advertisers.

11.3　PROJECTS

Project 1: mini dictionary

Language changes all the time. While **lexicographers** constantly update dictionaries, the process is slow. In any case, some words or expressions don't stay around for very long. Over the course of at least a week, keep a notebook with you and write down all the words and expressions you suspect you wouldn't find in a dictionary. It may be the case that the word is common, but the particular meaning is not. When you have a list, think about what they mean (their definition) and how they can be used. Your task is to compile a mini-dictionary of novel linguistic terms in your speech community. You might need to sit down with friends and test their intuitions about how terms can be used. If it's an adjective, can it be used only about people or also about things? If it's a verb, what kind of subject can it take? Does it need an object? Find at least six words and write as full an entry as you can. Look it up in a good dictionary (such as a full version of the Oxford English Dictionary). Does it appear there? Does it have the same meaning?

　　Example: in British English, 'bang' can be used in specific collocations as an intensifier; for example, 'bang on time', meaning exactly on time or 'bang up to date', meaning completely up to date. When I learnt this term I used it as intensifier in all kinds of situations. To express the shaggy nature of my toothbrush, I said 'bang old toothbrush'. A competent member of the speech community told me that this was not allowed.' 'Bang' can only be used as an intensifier in a very limited set of circumstances.

Project 2: political speech

In this project, the task is to examine a political speech in detail. Choose a recent speech by a politician from your country or area. Then choose another, either from the same politician to a different kind of audience or on a different topic, or from a different politician; but choose a speech that is similar in some way to the first. For national politicians, you can often find transcripts of speeches on the government website. Don't rely on this, but you can use it as a starting point to save some transcription time. You'll need a speech that has an audio version too. Transcribe it, including pauses, stress on particular words, hesitations and mistakes. You might also find it useful to make a note of speed if this varies throughout the speech. It's a good idea to transcribe any laughter or applause from the audience too.

Look at each speech individually. What is the goal of the speech? Is it intended to inform or persuade? Is it an emotional or a rational speech? How is the argument constructed? You will need to provide evidence from the specific linguistic choices made to justify what you say about the speech. For example, if you think that it is an emotive speech, you will probably look for particular word choices (recall the paradigmatic axis). What register is used? Is it formal or informal? There are any number of tools and concepts you can use for this task. It's a good idea to look at Chapters 2, 3 and 4 for an idea of what might be appropriate. Compare the similarities and differences between the two speeches. What might this allow you to say about these particular political speeches and how they use language?

Project 3: your own many voices

This is in some ways a difficult project and you might like to team up with a colleague and exchange data. The task is to see how your own use of language changes in different situations. Over the course of a week, record yourself in different situations. You won't want to analyse all the data, but you should have a good selection. Recording much more than you need means that you can discard the parts where you're aware of the recording and thus work only with natural, spontaneous data. You will probably have conversations with friends, conversations with family, talk in a work context, talk in a service encounter. It's fine to record telephone conversations for this.

Choose a small amount from each of the different contexts, about a minute, and transcribe them. Are there any differences in the way you talk? Do you address people differently? Do you use different words? Do you speak in a more standard way in some contexts? Thinking about the different kinds of variables examined in this book (age, gender, ethnicity and so on), which are relevant in the way your language changes? Remember, that while your age will stay the same, the people you talk to will vary. The same is true of the other variables.

Project 4: conversational politics

Record a conversation that involves a group of people. You might choose your family or a group of friends. The task is to see whether some participants have more power than others in the conversation. Is there someone who interrupts more than other people? Who asks questions? Who chooses topics of conversations? Whose contributions are responded to or laughed at? There is always a dynamic in conversations that, to a greater or lesser extent, all participants contribute to. Note that sometimes the most powerful participant in a conversation is a child or baby (or even the television). Try looking at Ochs and Taylor (1992) to see how they analysed conversations.

Project 5: playing with register

Find a comedy programme, a short sketch or scene will do. There is a wealth of such data on the internet. The task is to examine it using Fairclough's analytical tools of voice, style, mode and activity type (see section 4.3.2). Do these tools help explain why the scene is humorous?

Project 6: representation of women/men

This project looks at the representation of women or men and involves written data. Choose a topic to limit your data and allow for comparison of data. For example, you might want to look at news stories where a woman/ man is involved, how a female/male politician or celebrity is written about, or how health and fashion features aimed at women/men are constructed. You can collect data from newspapers, magazines, television, radio and/or the internet. What words are used to address and describe women/men? What adjectives are used? What values and ideologies underlie the representations you are working with? Remember, that just because you expect something to be in your data, it doesn't mean that it isn't significant. It's important to defamiliarise the data you look at. In short, what would a being from another world conclude about these creatures called 'women' from looking at your data?

Project 7: titles around the world

The titles *Miss* and *Mrs* are historical reminders of a time when women were regarded as the responsibility, or indeed the property, of their fathers and husbands. While women's political and economic rights have changed considerably in many countries, the English language still allows us to mark the marital status of women in ways that do not exist for men. Is women's marital status marked in other languages? If so, how? You'll need to spend time with translation dictionaries to gather this data. How can people avoid title and surname conventions when they get married? Investigate the use of titles and surnames in same-sex civil partnerships, which are frequently referred to as 'marriages'. You might need to look at announcements in newspapers or coverage of celebrity same-sex partners to gather the data here. How might these partnerships eventually affect the language system?

Project 8: identity forms

These days, when you apply for a job or a course of study, you are usually required to fill in a form about your ethnicity, age, nationality and disability status. Collect as many of these as you can – a local careers office or job centre would be a good place to find these. What categories are included?

Are all the forms the same? Are there gaps? From the categories and the labels and language used, is it possible to tell what is considered 'normal' or unmarked? Is there any significance to this?

Project 9: friendly talk

The following extract captures the talk between Ardiana, Hennah, Rahima, Varda and Dilshana – five 15-year-old Bangladeshi girls from London, UK (Pichler 2009). Overall these girls align themselves with a modified version of a discourse of arranged marriage – that is, they very much accept that their families will play a role in finding their future spouse. However, the girls object to certain forms of arranged marriage, in particular to being married to boys from Bangladesh. In addition, as with all groups, there is always a certain amount of negotiation of different positions and discourses that takes place before a consensus can be found. In the following example, analyse both the conversational style (see section 5.6; see also Pichler and Eppler 2009) and the different types of discourses in the following extract of talk and consider if and how they inform the girls' construction of (gender) identities within their friendship group. Then, get some friends to talk about what they think about marriage, whether arranged or not. Record and transcribe some of the conversation. Analyse it in the same way as you analyse the extract following. Are the discourses the same? Are they realised differently?

(1)
Ardiana   EXCUSE ME I LOVE MY BOYFRIEND here right I don't wanna

(2)
Ardiana   get married to somebody else I don't /**know**
Hennah   (-)   [(inn]it) (.)
Rahima   (-) innit ma[n]
Varda   (-) {- - - laughs - - -}

(3)
Ardiana   [but then
Hennah   {amused}he may be gorgeous but then again he mig[ht have a

(4)
Ardiana   again (a] ha-)
Hennah   (a)   ]   personality like a (.) **ape** or **some**thing=

(5)
Ardiana   =YEAH:: [that's] true (.)
Dilshana   [yeah]   (.) yeah when they come to England

(6)
Ardiana   they just wanna get
Hennah   [(they just]xxx-)
Dilshana   yeah they just lea[ve you man]

(7)
Ardiana   married to girls from London [because like they are Londoni]
Varda   [yeah because of the passport]

(8)
Ardiana   (.) **yeah** [they are from London they are British] they are British
Varda   (.)   [they want their passport inn]it
Dilshana   (ah [::) *{agreeing}*

(9)
Ardiana   and they wanna come to this country as well
Varda   (-) *{swallows}* they
               want

(11)
?Varda   the passports (the British) passport

Project 10: little bits of data

Michael Hoey identified a particular kind of text, the discourse colony: 'a colony is a discourse whose component parts do not derive their meaning from the sequence in which they are placed' (Hoey 1986: 4). Thus, personal ads in a magazine or newspaper constitute a discourse colony. Entries in a phone book also constitute a colony, though these will have a particular alphabetic sequence. Because the colonies have small component chunks, they make excellent data for analysis. First, identify the discourse colony you want to examine (personal advertisements, job advertisements, etc). Then, decide what variable you're interested in. For example, you might to compare job advertisements from the public and private sector. Alternatively, you might want to compare the same kind of colony from different publications, perhaps comparing letters to the editor from magazines read by women to those in magazines read by men. Try to keep everything the same except for this one variable. You'll need to analyse the texts closely, paying attention to their syntax, lexical choices and structure. What do you find, and why do you think the texts are structured in the way they are?

Project 11: children's television

At certain times of the day, usually morning and afternoon, television channels broadcast programmes for children. These are often cartoons or other series, joined together with sections in which hosts of the programme conduct competitions, interview celebrities and so on. Focusing on the hosted sections, transcribe parts which are addressed directly to the audience (the camera/children). Is there anything distinctive about the way the audience is addressed? Is a specific vocabulary or tone used? Does language speed up or slow down? Are there any features of Child Directed Language? Compare this with any conversation with adult guests.

Project 12: data in plain sight

Sometimes the most interesting data to analyse is that which you probably never considered worthy of examination. In 2009, Veronika Koller examined the Christmas catalogue of a major British retailer, Boots the chemist (2009). She examined the difference in written text between sections aimed at men and those aimed at women. Her results demonstrate a clear gendering of products and audience. The travel industry is full of companies which target particular consumers. Some companies organise fun exciting holidays for young adults, others design holidays they think will appeal to older people. Gather data from two or three companies with a special customer in mind. You may be able to do this by looking on the internet, but paper brochures from a travel agent are also available. Look at the language used to describe the holidays and to address the reader. Pay attention to the other representational choices that are made. What kinds of colours are used in the material? What do the photographs show? Working with such data lends itself to quantitative research. Choose about six very specific features and conduct quantitative and qualitative analysis on them. You might find van Leeuwen (2004) useful to look at.

Project 13: email and texting

You have data in your own life. Many people now have mobile phones and use them to text (SMS). Save all your incoming and outgoing texts for a period of time. How long this should be depends on how active you and your friends are in terms of texting. How does text language differ from other kinds of written language? Are there differences in syntax, spelling and lexical choices? Are other symbols used? Finally, do text conversations share any features with face-to-face conversations? You can think about this by writing out an exchange of text messages as though it were a face-to-face conversation (using transcription conventions). Does this look like a 'real' conversation?

You might like to add a second component to this project. Once you have analysed your data and thought about why the use of language may be the same or different, interview some of your texters. You could ask them why they text (instead of phoning). Do they use language differently when texting? Have they noticed texting conventions? Has their language use in other areas changed because of texting? You might like to take notes when interviewing, but it's also very helpful to record the interview. You may not need to transcribe all of it, but transcribing some of the interview conversation with texters will give you very useful comparative material for deciding whether 'real' conversations and text conversations are similar or different.

Project 14: spam – good for something

Spam is the junk mail of the virtual world. But it is useful for something. Blommaert and Omoniyi (2006) argue that spam can tell us important things about globalisation. Gather some spam from your email account (make sure it's not something dangerous for your computer or so offensive you don't want to spend time with it). Try to gather a few examples of the same kind of text, and choose examples with more written language than pictures. Through detailed analysis of the language, try to identify features that could signal its identity as spam. What kind of features these will be will depend on the kind of text you're looking at (and how good the spammers are). You might find it helps to gather some examples of real texts of the same kind. You may not in fact find any distinctive features!

Project 15: blogs and vlogs

Blogs are a reasonably recent genre. Brown (2008) argues that they are sites of linguistic innovation. Lin and Tong (2009) suggest that particular identities are constructed and displayed in blogs. Choose some blog data. You might like to choose comparable material (about the same subject) from different bloggers, or you might like to follow an individual blogger over time (there are usually archives on their sites). If you'd like some transcription practice, you could choose to use vlog (video blogging) looking at social networking or YouTube sites. Genres have particular styles – because the blog/vlog is recent, there is no single profile of the genre yet. Look at the structure of the texts as well as whether they do anything new with lexemes or syntax. Are these features linked to the purpose of the blog? Do they succeed in portraying a particular identity? Are some forms of blogs more successful than others? To answer this last question, you'll have to think about what blogs are for. Look at a wide variety and see if there is a common generic purpose.

Project 16: language and the law

Forensic linguistics is a branch of linguistics that looks at language in a legal context. The law is all about language and about force. It's very often about the force of language. Many scholars have worked on the significance of public signs, their legal significance and their linguistic force. Signs that detail legal rules are everywhere, from parking signs to conditions of entry for shopping centres. Collect as many examples as you can. What you will find depends on your local area, though parking lots are excellent places, as the contractual terms are often detailed near the entry for the car park. Look at the kinds of syntactic choices that are made. Pay attention to modals and pronouns. What kinds of transitivity choices are made? Are the notices clear? Would you say they constitute information, requests or warnings? Base your argument on the features you've examined.

Project 17: what's in a name?

Patrick May, in *The Seattle Times*, wrote about a change observed in the naming of internet company names (2010).

> Born of too much brainstorming or not enough sleep, the names come flying out of nowhere — Crocodoc, Yext, Nowmov.
> They turn nouns into adverbs (Answerly) or aspire to become brand-new verbs in true 'I-just-googled-her' fashion.
> And in the process, they drop vowels like a clumsy waiter (Flickr), spell perfectly good words backward (Xobni) and insert punctuation points where they have no business being (Center'd).

Find names of new companies, you'll need at least twenty (though the more the better), from any area and see what kinds of linguistic creativity is used in coming up with new company names. Finding the data may not be easy and will be time consuming but you can do it online. You might like to use the handy tool, Web Corp: webascorpus (www.webcorp.org.uk/). If you search for 'internet start up company' you should retrieve names of companies. You might also try searching in online newspaper corpora.

Project 18: your own

Usually the most fascinating project you do will be the one you come up with yourself. Some of the ideas above have come from students that I've taught and who have asked to work on something specific. You might start with something you're passionate about, or by wanting to explore something you've noticed. Make sure you keep the project doable, and don't get too sidetracked by issues that you can't investigate. Find a feature of language (one may well be enough) that you can focus on. It's good to have a focus. Right at the start think it all through; talk it over with a colleague. You can anticipate most of the problems if you think carefully about all the steps you need to take to get from data to final discussion. Looking at what linguists work on can also give you ideas.

11.4 EXAMPLES OF RESEARCH

There is a great deal of research happening all the time in the field of socio-linguistics. You might like to look at some of the research being published in specialist journals. Your place of study may have access to these, but there are often some articles and issues that are free to look at. Even looking at the abstracts will give you a good idea of the kind of work that researchers are doing.

> *Communication and Medicine*
> *Critical Discourse Studies*
> *Discourse and Society*
> *International Journal of Speech Language and the Law*
> *Journal of Language and Politics*
> *Journal of Sociolinguistics*
> *Language in Society*
> *Language Variation and Change*
> *Text & Talk*

It is becoming more usual for large research projects to have websites that detail the work they're doing. You might be interested in the following.

> LWP – Language in the Workplace www.victoria.ac.nz/lals/lwp/research/index.aspx
>> This research looks at language in the workplace from a number of different perspectives.
>
> Buckeye Natural Speech Corpus http://buckeyecorpus.osu.edu/
>> A collection of data from Columbus, Ohio, USA. Here you can see the material researchers have gathered and the publications coming from this work.

For a whole list of links to ongoing research projects, which gets updated: http://linguistlist.org/sp/Projects.html.

11.5 RESOURCES

There are a great many resources available online which may be useful for your own research or project work. Some of them have been mentioned already.

> *Ethics* – BAAL (British Association of Applied Linguistics)
>> Recommendations on Good Practice: Student Project Version www.baal.org.uk/about_goodpractice_stud.pdf (accessed 25 January 2010).

Blogging Linguist – Language log http://languagelog.ldc.upenn.edu/
nll/
This is a blog which a number of linguists contribute to. It is and
interesting and often amusing insight into the concerns of linguists,
especially in relation to language in the real world.

Computers and Language – Sociolinguistics and Computer Mediated
Conversation: http://sociocmc.blogspot.com/.

Dialects

■ American Dialect Society – www.americandialect.org/.
■ BBC – Voices – www.bbc.co.uk/voices/. Hear samples of different
   accents and dialects.
■ International Dialects of English Archive – http://web.ku.edu/idea/.
   While this is a resource for actors, the international perspective is very
   useful.
■ Language Varieties – www.une.edu.au/langnet/. A site from Australia
   with language varieties you might not find elsewhere
■ Languages in Ireland Website – www.uni-due.de/IERC/. A great deal
   of information including an aural map.
■ 'Sounds Familiar? Accents and Dialects of the UK' – www.bl.uk/
   learning/langlit/sounds/index.html.Multimedia. Pages at the British
   Library.
■ The Speech Accent Archive – http://accent.gmu.edu/. English accents
   from around the world.

Dictionaries

■ Links to a variety of different dictionaries – http://linguistlist.org/sp/
   Dict.html.
■ Some online resources of different varieties of English:
   ■ www.singlishdictionary.com/
   ■ Dictionary of American Regional English – http://dare.wisc.edu/
   ■ Macquarie Dictionary of (Australian) English –www.macquariedic-
      tionary.com.au.

Law and Language – Forensic Linguistics Institute
http://www.thetext.co.uk/index.htm
A site with texts that you can analyse and information about what
forensic linguists do.

Lists of and for linguists – Linguistlist.org
This website has a number of different areas which you may find useful,
from dictionaries to information about current research projects.

11.6 TRANSCRIPTION KEY

(With thanks to Pia Pichler)

{laughter}	non-verbal information
xxxxxx {laughing}	paralinguistic information qualifying underlined utterance
[.....]	beginning/end of simultaneous speech
(xxxxxxxx)	inaudible material
(......)	doubt about accuracy of transcription
((.....))	transcriber's comments or descriptions
'......'	speaker quotes/uses words of others
CAPITALS	increased volume
%......%	decreased volume
bold print	speaker emphasis
>...<	faster speed of utterance deliver
/	rising intonation
yeah:::::	lengthened sound
-	incomplete word or utterance
~	speaker intentionally leaves utterance incomplete
=	latching on (no gap between speakers' utterances)
(.)	micropause
(-)	pause shorter than one second
(1); (2)	timed pauses (longer than one second)
.hhh; hhh	in-breath; out-breath
Bengali	translation of Bengali *utterance* into English

FURTHER READING

Cameron, D. (2001) *Working with Spoken Discourse*, London: Routledge.

Carter, R., Goddard, A., Reah, D., Sanger, K. and Swift, N. (2007) *Working with Texts: A Core Introduction to Language Analysis*, Adrian Beard (ed), London: Routledge.

Cukor-Avila, P. (2000) 'Revisiting the Observer's Paradox', *American Speech*, 75 (3): 253–254.

Hillier, H. (2004) *Analysing Real Texts: Research Studies in Modern English Language*, Basingstoke: Palgrave.

van Leeuwen, T. (2004) *Introducing Social Semiotics*, London: Routledge.

Wray, A., Trott, K. and Bloomer, A. (1998) *Projects in Linguistics: A Practical Guide to Researching Language*, London: Arnold.

NOTE

1   Thanks to Isobel Scott-John for her expertise and patience in inducting me into the British speech community.

Glossary

AAVE   African American Vernacular English.

accent   features of speakers' pronunciation that can signal their regional or social background.

accommodation   adjusting the way one speaks to be more like a real or imagined interlocutor.

active and **passive**   are terms which refer to the voice of the verb. In the active voice the sentence has a structure where the 'doer' (agent) of the action is in the subject position and the 'done-to' (affected) is in the object position. This contrasts with the passive where the 'done-to' is in subject position and the agent becomes optional. *Active*: 'Tom hit Bob'; *Passive*: 'Bob was hit by Tom' or 'Bob was hit'.

activity type   closely related to genre and used to analyse speech situations; one of Fairclough's four categories used in the analysis of genre. However, Stephen Levinson (1979) uses the term to refer to events that can be defined by their goals and the constraints on the kinds of contributions that can be made (whether verbal or non-verbal).

address forms   expressions used to refer to a person when you are talking to them directly. Address forms can vary according to the context of use and the relationship between the speaker and hearer. Variation can involve the use of 'titles' such as *Ms, Dr* or *Reverend*; whether or not a person is called by their first name; and in some languages, the form of the second person pronoun as in the *tu/vous* distinction in French. (See also **honorific**.)

adjective   a class of words which is generally used to describe or modify a noun. The adjectives in the following examples are in small capitals: 'The LUCKY cat ran away.' 'The PERSIAN cat ate my trout.' 'That cat is BIG.'

adverb   a class of words that is generally used to describe or modify a verb, but can also modify other parts of speech which are not nouns. They signify when, where, how, or to what extent happened. The adverbs in the following examples are in small capitals: 'The girl QUICKLY solved the problem.' 'The dog wagged its tail FURIOUSLY.' 'He came to class LATE because he was tired.'

agency/agentive   agency is having control of something – that is, being in the position of agent (in terms of transitivity analysis). See also **active**.

Amerindian   a general name for the languages spoken by the native peoples of North and South America.

arbitrariness of the sign   de Saussure argued that there was no inherent connection between combinations of sounds or letters and the concepts which they refer to. The fact that different languages label concepts differently; for example, French speakers using *arbre* for what the English speakers call *tree*, supports this.

asymmetry/asymmetrical see **symmetry**.

audience design   the notion that speakers will take into account whom they are addressing and alter their speech style accordingly.

auxiliary verb   see **modal auxiliary verb**.

back channel support   the feedback that listeners give to speakers, by verbal expressions such as *mmm, uhuh, yeah*, and by nodding, frowning or other facial and body gestures. See also **minimal responses**.

BBC   the British Broadcasting Corporation (BBC) is the oldest and most prominent television and radio broadcasting company in the UK, with several national television and radio channels. Supported by public funds, it has a reputation for good quality programming which reflects established norms and values.

bilingual   strictly, having two (bi-) languages, but also used for someone who speaks more than one language.

bricolage   from the French meaning, roughly, 'tinkering' but more like 'DIY'. It refers to the way signs and symbols can be used to create new meanings, but placing them in novel contexts or combinations.

citizen journalism   a kind of user-generated content, where local people provide material for broadcast or publication in news outlets.

code-switching   the change from one language to another, often in the same piece of talk.

code   a term sometimes used instead of 'language' or 'dialect' to refer to a linguistic system of communication. There are also non-linguistic communication codes such as dress codes or gesture codes.

codification   a process where scholars analyse and record the vocabulary and grammatical patterns of a language. For English, much of this codification took place in the eighteenth century. The vocabulary and grammatical patterns that were written down in dictionaries and grammar books then became 'rules'.

collocation   refers to the co-occurrence of words. Some words are in frequent collocation such as *happy* and *event* as in 'happy event'. Collocation can also affect the meaning of a word in a particular context. For example *white* in collocation with *wine* denotes a different colour from *white* in collocation with *snow*.

communicative competence   in contrast to **competence** and **performance**, communicative competence is what a speaker needs to do to construct appropriate utterances in a speech community.

communities of practice   a group of people who come together for a common aim or activity. Communities of practice often develop their own ways of using language. The model is influenced by a move in sociolinguistics to look locally at language use, as opposed to large-scale variationist investigations.

competence and performance   competence is opposed to performance, in a distinction made by Chomsky. Competence refers to the grammar, or the rules of the language which need to be followed for grammaticality. Performance is what people actually do in their speech. See also **communicative competence**.

compound   a term used to describe a noun created by combining two other nouns. The meaning of the compound derives only partly from the meaning of the words that make it up. For example, a *blackberry* is a dark purple rather than a black berry.

conative   one of Jakobson's six functions of language which draws attention to the addressee-oriented nature of language.

connotation   the personal associations conjured up by a word, although they are not strictly part of its definition. For example, a *spinster* is an adult female human who has never been married, but for many people this word also carries connotations of 'old', 'unattractive' and 'not sexually active'.

consonant   a speech sound made by partially or completely obstructing the airflow from the lungs. The italic letters in the following examples represent some of the consonant sounds in English: '*s*a*t*', '*believe*', '*man*'.

convergence   a process in which speakers change their speech to make it more similar to that of their hearer, or to that of other people in their social group. When applied to the convergence of whole dialects or accents it is also termed **levelling**.

covert prestige covert means 'hidden' or 'non-obvious'. Sometimes speakers use a seemingly less prestigious or non-standard language variety to identify with a group that uses that variety. Thus, the language variety of that group can have a covert prestige.

creole see **pidgin**.

crossing a process in which speakers of one group occasionally use the speech patterns of another group as a means of identifying with some aspect of that group (see also **covert prestige**). It is similar to **code-switching**, in that a change from one language to another is made; however, the second language is not 'owned' by the speaker in the sense that they may be seen as an illegitimate user of the variety.

cultural capital see **symbolic capital**.

defease the term used when an implicature is denied. Thus while 'It's cold in here' is conventionally heard as a request to close a window or turn up the heat, this implicature can be defeased by saying, 'It's cold in here but don't close the window.'

denotation the literal meaning of something, as opposed to **connotation**.

density see **social networks**.

dependent and independent variable when looking at sociolinguistic data, you will have a dependent and an independent variable. The independent variable is a factor which can be established independent of language variation, but is something you suspect will correlate with the variation. The specific language feature you examine is the dependent variable. Class, age, gender and ethnicity are very often used as independent variables in sociolinguistics. The dependent variable can be any feature of language (phonetic, syntactic, lexical). Consider the independent variable of class. In Trudgill's Norwich study, the dependent variable '-ing/-in' at the ends of words such as 'running' correlated with class: the 'lower' the class, the higher the presence of the '-in' variant. Independent variables can include such things as social factors (age, class, gender, ethnicity), stylistic factors (whether context is formal or informal), and linguistic factors (what words or sounds are in close proximity). An example of a dependent variable can be seen in relation to geographic location in the UK. The variants one finds for first conjugation of the verb 'to be' include I am/I be/I are/I bin, depending on where the speaker is from.

diachronic as distinct from synchronic; diachronic means looking at a situation as it changes over time.

dialect a variety of a language that can signal the speaker's regional or social background. Unlike accents which differ only in pronunciation, dialects differ in their grammatical structure – *Do you have ...?* (US) versus *Have you got ...?* (UK) – and in their vocabulary: *sidewalk* (US) versus *pavement* (UK).

dialect levelling a convergence of accents and dialects toward each other within a geographic region.

dialectologists those who study and document dialects.

difference theorists in respect of language and gender, those who argue that women's and men's languages are different though equal.

diglossia when there are two varieties of a language, the H (High) variety and the (L) low variety, used in the same speech community. They are used for separate, non-overlapping functions. The H variety is formally learnt and not used for everyday interaction. Sometimes the term diglossia is extended to describe the situation where two completely different languages are used in the same community, where one functions as the H variety and one as the L variety.

diphthong two vowel sounds connected such that it seems to be a single sound.

discourse used in linguistics with a range of meanings. It can refer to any piece of connected language which contains more than one sentence. It is also sometimes used to refer specifically to conversations. In sociology, it can be used to refer to the way belief systems and values are talked about, as in 'the discourse of capitalism'. The prevailing way that a culture talks about or **represents** something is called the **dominant discourse** – that is, the '**common-sense**' or 'normal' representation.

discourse marker   a word with a function more than a meaning, which is to structure speech. 'So', 'well', 'now', 'really' are all examples of discourse markers. They do have a function in displaying affect and also in structuring arguments.

divergence   a process in which speakers choose to move away from the **linguistic norms** of their hearer or social group. This can involve using a style or **language variety** not normally used by the group or even speaking an entirely different language.

dyseuphemism   see **euphemism**.

epistemic modal forms   see **modal auxiliary verb**.

Estuary English   the label for a dialect in the south-east of England, found roughly around the Thames river estuary.

ethnographic   a research methodology which seeks to describe a particular society or event through such methods as participant observation and interviews, usually over a long period of time.

euphemism   the use of an inoffensive or more 'pleasant' term as a substitute for one which might be unpleasant or taboo. For example, *passed away* is a euphemism for *died*. Euphemism can also be used to promote a more positive image; for example, *air support* for *bombing* or *preowned* for *second-hand*. Dyseuphemism is the opposite – that is, the use of a more offensive or less pleasant term.

field   see **register**.

first person pronoun   see **pronoun**.

foreground   to draw attention to something; this is a visual metaphor – that is, something that is put in the foreground is made more prominent. This can also be done linguistically, through the use of marked terms, stress in speech or other modes of emphasis.

generic   generally, an expression which is used to refer to a class of things. For example, a distinction is drawn between the generic use of *man* in *Man has walked the earth for millions of years* where this term refers to humans in general and *I now pronounce you man and wife* where this term refers only to male humans.

genre   a 'kind' or 'type'. As used in discourse analysis it can refer, for example, to writing genres such as thrillers, scientific writing or recipes. It can also refer to other media genres such as talk show, documentary and soap opera.

glottal stop   a **consonant** made by a tight closure of the vocal chords followed by an audible release of air. It can be heard in several British accents where this consonant replaces the /t/ in a word such as *butter* pronounced *buh-uh*. The phonetic symbol for a glottal stop is /ʔ/.

grammatical gender   some languages attribute masculine, feminine (and sometimes neuter) genders to their nouns, as in French *la gare* (the station – feminine), and *le soleil* (the sun – masculine). This type of gendering is called grammatical for two reasons. First, the gender differentiation often has no correlation with 'natural' gender (there is nothing inherently masculine or feminine about a railway station or the sun), and therefore exists only in the language's grammatical system. Second, in languages which made use of such gender differentiation, there is typically grammatical agreement between the noun and its modifiers. Thus, if a noun is masculine, any determiners or adjectives that modify it must also be masculine, as in *le train brun* (the brown train). The same applies to the noun when it is feminine (as in *la table brune* – the brown table) or neuter.

hedges   linguistic devices such as *sort of* and *I think* which 'dilute' an assertion. Compare *he's dishonest* and *he's sort of dishonest; she lost it* and *I think she lost it.*

hegemonic (adj)/hegemony (n)   the common meaning of the concept originates in the work of Antonio Gramsci. While initially it was related to dominance and leadership in economic matters and means of production, it was later extended to include all forms of dominance and leadership, especially in relation to dominant (or hegemonic) ideologies (Gramsci 2000).

heterogeneity   difference, as opposed to homogeneity (uniformity).

homophone   see **lexical item**.

honorific   in general, refers to the use of language to express respect or politeness. More specifically it can refer to certain **address forms** which express respect such as *Sir/Madam, Your Highness, Reverend* and the 'formal' version of *you* in languages which make that distinction.

identity politics   coming together for social or political action or purpose on the basis of a common identity, whether constructed or not. Ethnicity and gender are common bases for such action.

idiolect   the language of an individual.

ideology   a set or pattern of beliefs.

imperative   in grammatical terms, a verb form, which is both a command and the simplest verb form in English. 'Come!' or 'Speak!' are both imperative forms.

implicature   a meaning which can be extracted but is implicit rather than explicit. For example, *a dog is for life, not just for Christmas* implies that some people regard dogs as a short-term rather than a long-term responsibility.

independent variable   see **dependent** and **independent variable**.

indicator   one of Labov's three kinds of linguistic variables. An indicator describes variation which is obvious to those who are external to a social group as marking out that group. Indicators are not socially evaluated by members within that group. These forms do not show style shifting – that is, they don't change regardless of whether the context is casual or formal. This contrasts with **marker** and **stereotype**.

informant   someone who acts as source of linguistic data or information.

in-group   a social group to which the speaker belongs. The **out-group** comprises people who do not belong to that group. For example, gang members may use certain expressions with each other that mark them as members of a particular gang or in-group. At the same time, the use of these expressions can differentiate them from members of other gangs, the out-groups in that situation.

interlocutor   another way of describing an addressee.

interpellation   from the work of Althusser, to describe the way people are addressed and positioned by ideologies.

interruption   variously defined as simultaneous speech and an utterance that stops the interrupted person speaking.

intertextuality   generally used to refer to the referencing of or allusion to one text by another. This may be done by obvious quotation, parody or borrowing any textual feature.

isogloss   an isogloss is an idealised geographic boundary between the use of one linguistic variable or feature and another.

jargon   a rather negative term for language used by a group that is difficult or impossible for those outside the group to understand. It is often associated with a specific profession.

L1 and L2   Language 1 and Language 2 – that is, a person's first language and their second language.

language norm   see **linguistic norm**.

langue   de Saussure's term for the perfect knowledge of a language that he believed we all have in our heads, in contrast to what he thought of as the corrupt versions of language we actually produce, which he called **parole**.

levelling   see **convergence**.

lexical item   term used by linguists for one of the senses of 'word'. This term is useful because while *loves* and *loved* are two different words in terms of their form, they still represent the same lexical item, the verb *to love*. Notice that we can also have two words with the same phonological form but which represent two different lexical items. An example is: *bark₁* as in 'the bark of a dog' and *bark₂* as in 'the bark of a tree'. Words like *bark₁* and *bark₂* are said to be **homophones**.

lexicographer   a maker of dictionaries – that is, someone who documents the changing meaning of works in a language.

lexifier   the language which gives most of the vocabulary to a pidgin or creole.

lexis   vocabulary.

lingua franca   a language that is not native to either speaker or listener but is used for communication where learning one or the other native languages is not practical.

linguistic determinism/relativism   also known as the Sapir–Whorf hypothesis, this is the idea that language influences thought. The strong version, linguistic determinism, holds that we cannot think outside the terms of our language. The weaker, and more credible form, holds that we tend to think in the terms of our language system.

linguistic imperialism   is the imposition of one culture's language upon another culture.

linguistic market   a way of understanding the **social/cultural capital** that speakers of particular varieties have. The linguistic market can be understood as the attitudes speakers have to varieties, what can be accomplished with them and thus which forms it is valuable to acquire.

linguistic norm   generally, a norm refers to 'standard practice'. **Speech communities** can differ with respect to the linguistic norms being followed. These norms can involve grammar (eg whether or not *I don't know nothing* is acceptable); pronunciation (eg whether or not *pie* is pronounced as 'pah'); vocabulary (eg whether the pedestrian walkway is called the *sidewalk* or the *pavement*); and the appropriate social use of language (eg whether or not you should address your parents as *Sir* and *Ma'am*).

linguistic variable   a linguistic item (phoneme, morpheme, lexeme, syntactic feature), which has identifiable variants the presence of which is variable.

linguistic variation   term referring to the many ways that language systems can change or vary with respect to their grammar, pronunciation and vocabulary. Language systems change over time. They also change or vary according to the geographical or social identity of their users and according to the situations in which they are used. See also **linguistic variety**.

linguistic variety   term with several meanings, but generally referring to an identifiable language system which is used in particular geographic or social situations and has its own linguistic norms. For example, the variety of English spoken in Birmingham, Alabama, will differ from that spoken in Birmingham, England. Within a geographic region there may also be varieties based on social class or occupation. Similarly, the variety of English used in casual conversations will differ from that used in academic writing.

marked   generally speaking, 'marked' means noticeably unusual. More specifically, marked terms refer to anything which deviates from the norm and this deviation is signalled by additional information. **Unmarked** linguistic forms are neutral in so far as they **represent** the 'norm', and carry no additional information. For example, the unmarked form *nurse* is often assumed to refer to a woman. To refer to a nurse who is a man, the additional term *male* is often added: *male nurse* (the marked form). The notion of markedness has also been applied to pairs of opposites such as *tall* and *short*, where *tall* is considered to be the unmarked term. We can see this in certain constructions where the use of the unmarked term seems more 'natural'. Compare: *How tall are you?* to *How short are you?* and *She's five feet tall* to *She's five feet short.*

marker   one of Labov's three kinds of linguistic variables. A marker is language variation which is subject to style shifting because it is evaluated socially in-group (unlike an indicator).

matched guise experiment   method of investigating people's attitudes to different languages. It involves **informants** listening to several recordings of the same 'script' spoken by the same speaker (or by other speakers matched for voice quality) but using a different language for each recording. The informants are then asked to judge each speaker's personal characteristics based on what they hear. Matched guise experiments can also be adjusted to elicit people's attitudes to different voice qualities, **accents** or **dialects**.

metalingual   literally, above the linguistic, thus, language used to talk about language. This comes from the model proposed by Jackobsen.

metaphor/metaphorical   figurative expression where a word or phrase from one area of meaning (semantic field) is used to refer to something from a different semantic field. Metaphorical expressions transfer some features from the first semantic field to the second. For example, *Her uncle is a snake* transfers features associated with snakes such as stealth, danger, evil, to a person. Rather than asserting that her uncle actually is a snake, it implies that he is like a snake in some respects. This contrasts with **simile**, where the comparison is made explicit rather than implied: *Her uncle is* LIKE *a snake.*

minimal responses   in conversations, the contributions that speakers make to show that they agree or that they are listening; for example, 'mm hm', 'yeah' and so on. See also **back channel support**.

mitigation   making an utterance less forceful, usually with epistemic modals, such as 'may', 'might' or with verb forms that indicate a lack of complete certainty, such as 'I think' (as opposed to 'I know').

modal auxiliary verb   the modal auxiliary verbs of English are *will, shall, would, should, can, could, must, may, might.* Modal auxiliaries have several meaning functions. One important meaning function is epistemic. That is, speakers use modals to express their attitude towards the 'certainty' of what they are saying. Note the meaning difference between *That is a bird* and *That could be a bird.*

modalities   different modes of communication, including speech, writing, and other visual modes. Most often this is used in the context of multi-modality, where more than one modality is used in a single communicative event.

mode   see **register**.

morphology   the study of the smallest meaningful part of language, the morpheme. Morphemes can be 'bound' or 'free'. Bound morphemes cannot stand by themselves, while free can. In 'smallest', 'small' is a free morpheme and '-est' is a bound morpheme.

multimodal   referring to communicative contexts which use more than one channel – that is, more than just speech or writing. The internet is multimodal as it facilitates written, spoken and visual modes of interaction.

multiple negation   see **negation**.

negation   sentences can be negated in English by using *not*: *I knew* versus *I did not (didn't) know.* They can also be negated by the use of other negative words such as *nothing, never, nowhere: I knew nothing.* The grammar of standard American and British English does not allow a sentence such as *I didn't know nothing* because it contains *multiple negation*, the use of *not* plus the negative word *nothing.* However, the grammatical rules of other **dialects** of English, as well as other languages such as Italian and Spanish, require the use of multiple negation.

Newspeak   term coined by George Orwell in his novel *Nineteen Eighty-Four*, where it referred to a special vocabulary invented by a totalitarian regime to manipulate people's thinking. This term has now passed into common usage to mean, loosely, new words or uses of words, but more specifically new words or uses of words in political jargon or propaganda.

nominalisation   grammatical process of forming a **noun** from another word class; for example, *organisation* is nominalisation of the **verb** *organise, happiness* is a nominalisation of the **adjective** *happy*.

norm   see **linguistic norm**.

noun   class of words which, generally speaking, name people or things, but more importantly share certain grammatical characteristics. For example, in English nouns (in small capitals) can be preceded by *the: the* MUSIC. They can be marked for plural: CAT/CATS. They can be modified by **adjectives**: *the big* BRIDGE.

noun phrase   a phrase with a **noun** or **pronoun** as its 'head'. A noun phrase can consist of a single noun or pronoun or a noun which has been premodified and/ or post-modified by other words or phrases. The following are examples of noun phrases (the 'head' is in small capitals): FIDO, HE, *the* DOG, *my big* DOG, *that expensive* DOG *from the pet shop.*

number   a grammatical category marking contrasts between the number of entities being referred to. English makes a number distinction between **singular** (one) and **plural** (more than one) as in: singular *cat* and plural *cats*, singular *I* and plural *we*. Number can also be marked on **verbs** as in singular *I am* and plural *We are*.

orthography   the writing system of a language and how words are spelled. For example, in English orthography both *so* and *sew* have different spellings even though they sound the same when spoken.

out-group   see **in-group**.

overlap   sometimes classified as a kind of interruption. An overlap is a brief instance of simultaneous talk which does not result in a speaker stopping what they were saying; it is distinct from **interruption**.

overt prestige   a type of prestige attached to forms of language use that are publicly acknowledged as 'correct' and as bestowing high social status on their users. See also **covert prestige**.

paradigmatic   as opposed to syntagmatic. The paradigmatic axis of language describes the way words are chosen from among all possible choices and, as a consequence, can be said to be meaningful. For example, to call a woman a 'girl' rather than a 'lady' depicts her as young. This is part of the structuralist view of language.

parallelism   when there is the same or similar syntactic structure in two or more parts of a text. This similarity asks the reader to understand the two parts in relation to each other. This is a stylistic choice common in persuasive speech.

parole   de Saussure's term for the language we actually produce, which may not match the system of **langue** in our brains because, de Saussure believed, of errors we make in the actual production of speech.

passive   see **active**.

pejoration   to acquire negative connotations or even denotations over time. Semantic perjoration is particularly common for words associated with women.

performance   see **competence**.

phatic   one of Jakobson's six functions of language. Phatic talk is often described as 'small talk' as its primary function is to build or sustain social relationships rather than, for example, to convey information.

phoneme   the smallest significant sound unit in a language. For example *bat, sat,* and *pat* are different words in English because they differ in their first sound unit. The sounds /b/, /s/ and /p/ are three of the phonemes of English. English has approximately forty-four phonemes, although this number varies slightly between accents.

phonetics/phonetic   the study of speech sounds, especially how they are made by speakers and perceived by hearers. Analysing the phonetics and phonology of a language generally involves looking at speakers' pronunciations.

phonology/phonological   the study of the sound systems of languages. It looks at what sounds are significant for a language (its **phonemes**) and the permissible ways that sounds can be combined in words. For example, the phonology of English would permit a word such as *tump* but not *mptu*. Analysing the **phonetics** and phonology of a language generally involves looking at speakers' pronunciations.

pidgin   simplified form of language (in terms of both vocabulary and grammar) which arises when speakers of different languages need a common means of communication, usually for trading purposes. Pidgins are not fully fledged languages and have no native speakers. A *creole*, while it may have developed from a pidgin, is a fully fledged language with native speakers. In its most 'standard' or **prestige variety**, a creole will closely resemble one of the original languages from which it came.

plexity   see **social networks**.

plural   see **pronoun** and **number**.

possessive   words or phrases indicating possession. In English this is indicated either by '*s* as in *Jane's book* or by possessive determiners such as *my/our/your/his/her/their book*.

post-vocalic 'r'   post-vocalic means 'after a **vowel**'. A speaker whose accent does not have post-vocalic 'r' will pronounce the 'r' only when it occurs before a vowel, as in *arise, trap* or *rip*. However, speakers whose accents contain a post-vocalic 'r' will pronounce the 'r' also in words where it occurs after a vowel at the end of a word, as in *floor*, and in words where it occurs after a vowel and before another consonant, as in *smart*.

prescription/prescriptivists   the view, and those who maintain that there are rules for 'correct' language use and that language users should abide by them.

prestige variety   when used with respect to language, it refers to a variety which society associates with education and high social status.

presupposition   a background assumption embedded within a sentence or phrase. The assumption is taken for granted to be true regardless of whether the whole sentence is true. For example *We will introduce a fairer funding formula* presupposes that the current funding formula is not fair.

pronoun   a class of words which can replace a **noun** or **noun phrase** in a sentence. This is an example from the English pronoun system:

first person	I/me	we/us
second person	you	you
third person	he/him, she/her, it	they/them

qualitative research   the collection and interpretation of textual (spoken/written) material for analysis and interpretation.

quantitative research   research that is designed to collect and interpret numerical data.

question tags   see **tag questions**.

received pronunciation or **RP** – the **accent** which is generally used by newsreaders on national television in the UK. Sometimes called a 'BBC accent' or an 'educated British accent'. An RP accent is not marked for a particular region of Britain, but is marked for relatively 'high' social class. It is thought that only about 3 per cent of the British population normally use RP.

referential   one of Jakobson's six functions of language. The referential function of language is what we might normally think of as information, or the denotative function of language, but also includes the ideas, objects and conventions which speakers share knowledge of.

register   the way that language can systematically vary according to the situation in which it is used. Different registers can be characterised by their sentence structure, pronunciation and vocabulary. Three factors that determine variation in register have been proposed: *field*, which refers to the subject matter of the discourse; *tenor*, which refers to the role being played by the speaker and the resulting level of formality in the situation; and *mode*, which usually refers to the medium of communication, such as speech or writing.

regional and social variation   see **linguistic variety**.

represent/representation   as used in discourse analysis, it is basically how the speaker chooses to refer to something or someone. For example, the same act could be represented as *terminating a pregnancy* or *killing an unborn baby* depending on the worldview of the speaker. Similarly, the same person could be represented as either a *terrorist* or a *freedom fighter*. See also **euphemism**.

rhetoric/rhetorical   the use of language to persuade or convince the hearer.

RP   see **Received Pronunciation**.

second person pronoun   see **pronoun**.

semantic derogation   a process in which a word can take on a second meaning and/or **connotations** which are negative or demeaning. Examples in English are the words *mistress, madam* and *spinster*. Compare these to their masculine counterparts *master, sir, bachelor*.

sign   the **arbitrary** combination of concept and label which exists in the minds of members of a **speech community**. De Saussure called the 'concept' half of the sign the **signified**, while he referred to the 'label' half as the **signifier**.

signified   see **sign**.

signifier   see **sign**.

simile   expression in which something is figuratively compared to something else. Unlike a metaphor, where the comparison is implied, the comparison in a simile is made explicit by the use of expressions such as *as, as if, like*. For example: *You're as red as a beet. He's working as if there's no tomorrow. She's like a tiger defending her young*.

singular   see **pronoun** and **number**.

social distance   a term used to describe the relationship between people in terms of a hierarchy of some kind. What influences social distance may include age, class and the like. It helps us understand why, for example, speakers may choose to use a formal mode of address rather than an informal one.

social network   a way of describing the way people are connected to each other in a community. Social networks can be closed (where everyone knows each other) or open. Closed networks are said to be dense. Networks can also be uniplex or multiplex depending on whether individuals have more than one relationship with each other. For example, if A is only a work associate of B their relationship is uniplex. If they are also related, or spend time together socially, they will be connected in more than one way and thus their relationship can be said to be multiplex.

speech community   a human group, defined either geographically or socially, whose members share a common **language variety** and set of **linguistic norms**.

speech event   a specific unit or exchange of speech which has a well-defined structure; for example, a greeting or a sermon.

standardisation   in relation to language codification, the regularisation of some aspect; for example, spelling or pronunciation. This standard is often based on written norms and may be decided by an institutional body. The term may also describe the process of dialects moving closer to a standard variety, a variety that is frequently based on written norms.

stereotype   one of Labov's three kinds of linguistic variables. A variable is a stereotype when the association of a group with a variable is so well known and has attracted such negative or archaic associations that the form is actively avoided by in-group speakers.

stratified/stratification   division into layers, where a layer can be 'above' or 'below' another layer. In terms of social stratification, people in any one layer share certain social characteristics and are 'equals' but differ from and are not 'equal' to people in other layers. One example of social stratification by class is: upper, middle and lower or 'working' class.

structuralism   the idea that the system of signs is structured, and that the meaning of signs depends on their position relative to other signs.

style   distinctive linguistic choices that are made; for example, the choice of words or a register. Style is also one of the categories used to analyse **genre**. **Style** is now also used to discuss the way people modify their language to effect a particular identity.

style-shifting   people do not always talk in the same way. They can shift their speech styles and this can involve using different words, pronunciations or even grammatical forms. Notice the style differences between: *singin'* and *singing*; *verdant* and *green*; *So I says …* and *So I said …* See also **audience design** and **register**.

suffix   a bound morpheme that attaches to the end of a word.

symbolic capital   from the work of Bourdieu, symbolic (or cultural) capital refers to assets that individuals accumulate based on their presentation, speech, relationships, education and so on. Like real capital (money), symbolic capital can be used to procure things.

symbolic violence   the way in which what society positively values results in the exclusion of those who do not align with these values.

symmetry   as used in linguistics, an equal balance between expressions; *asymmetry* is an imbalance between expressions. For example, Standard English shows symmetry between the **first person** singular and plural **pronouns** – *I/me* versus *we/us* (two forms for each). However, it shows asymmetry between the first and **second person** pronouns. There are four forms for the first person pronouns: *I/me* and *we/us* but only one form for the second person pronouns: *you*. Asymmetry can be seen also in some **address forms**: only *Mr* for men but *Mrs, Miss* and *Ms* for women. Symmetry and asymmetry can also refer to the distribution of speakers' rights to talk in given situations. In a trial, speakers' rights are asymmetrical. Lawyers have more rights to ask questions than the witnesses.

synchronic   as opposed to diachronic; looking at something at a particular point in time.

syntactic/syntax   grammatical rules which determine how words can be combined into phrases and sentences. For example, the syntactic rules of English permit the phrase *the nice book* but not **book the nice* and the sentences *Jane is happy* and *Is Jane happy?* but not **Is happy Jane?*

syntagmatic   as opposed to **paradigmatic.** The syntagmatic axis of language describes the way in which words are ordered in relation to each other, from left to right.

tag questions   a way of turning a declarative into a question by the addition at the end, 'it's good, *isn't it*'?, 'you are going, *aren't you*?'

tenor   see **register**.

tense   way in which grammatical information about time can be marked on verbs. In English there are two tenses – present: *I leave* and past: *I left*. Future time is not expressed by tense marking but by other constructions such as *I will leave* or *I am going to leave*.

thesaurus   a book of words arranged by meaning categories.

third person pronoun   see **pronoun**.

topical ambiguity   situation where the hearer needs to know the topic of the discussion in order to interpret a word correctly. For example, *a hit* means one thing in the context of talking about pop songs, another when talking about baseball, and yet another when talking about the internet.

transitive/intransitive   kind of verb used in a clause. A transitive verb requires a direct object in order to make sense, whereas an intransitive verb does not. For example, in *Lucy loves Fred*, 'Fred' is the direct object of the verb 'love'. 'Love' is a transitive verb and would be incomplete without its direct object, as you can see from *Lucy loves …* On the other hand, in *Fred snores*, 'snores' is an intransitive verb; there is no direct object and the verb is complete on its own. Not to be confused with **transitivity (model)**.

transitivity (model)   model used in the analysis of utterances, to show how the speaker's experience is encoded. In the model, utterances potentially comprise three components. (1) *Process*, which is typically expressed by a verb. (2) *Participants* in the process. The participant who is the 'doer' of the process represented by the verb is known as the *actor*. The *goal* is the entity or person affected by the process. (3) *Circumstances* associated with the process. In utterances such as *she cried* <u>loudly</u> or *he jumped* <u>from the cliff</u>, the underlined components provide extra information about the process, and can be omitted.

turn/turn taking   a turn is a contribution to a conversation; turn taking describes the way these conversational contributions are ordered – that is, who is allowed to speak and when.

unmarked   see **marked**.

user-generated content   material contributed by audience and viewers to media outlets.

variation   can be related to social variables or to other linguistic variables. See **linguistic variation**.

variationist   a branch of sociolingusitics which examines the way in which language differs among various populations according to, for example, geography, class, age and the like. Some argue that only variationist sociolinguistics is properly sociolingusitics.

verb   grammatical class of words, which commonly refer to 'acting' or 'doing', although many verbs such as *to seem* or *to know* do not quite fit into this meaning category. More importantly, verbs take characteristic forms or endings such as those marking tense and voice, and they perform a specific function in a sentence. The verbs in the following sentences are in small capitals: *She WAS elected president. I AM WALKING quickly. He LAUGHED a lot. They might WANT some. I HAVE SEEN her. Bob SEEMS nice. SIT there.* See also **modal auxiliary verb**.

vernacular   this word comes from the Latin meaning 'of the home'. It refers to the indigenous language or dialect of a speech community; for example, the 'vernacular of Liverpool' (UK), or 'Black English vernacular' (US). It is often used in contrast to the standard or prestige variety of a language.

vocative   the vocative case is a grammaticalisation of socially directed speech. It is a special marker that tells the named person they are being searched for or spoken to.

voice   see **active**.

voiced/voiceless   distinction used to classify **consonants**. Voiced consonants are produced with vocal cords vibrating as in the first consonants of *bat, din, zap*. Voiceless consonants are produced without vocal cord vibration as in the first consonants of *pat, tin, sat*.

vowel   speech sound made with no obstruction to the air flow from the lungs. The bold letters in the following examples represent some of the vowel sounds in English: *s**a**t, t**o**p, h**ea**lth, si**ll**y*.

References

ABC News (2009) 'Cutting Calories in Lunch Lady Land'. First broadcast on 20 October 2009. Online: http://abcnews.go.com/video/playerIndex?id=8875625 (accessed 9 May 2010).

Agha, A. (2004) 'Registers of Language', in Alessandro Duranti (ed), *A Companion to Linguistic Anthropology*, London: Blackwell, 23–45

American Dialect Society www.americandialect.org/index.php/amerdial/categories/C178.

American Psychological Association (2010) *The English-Only Movement Myths, Reality, and Implications for Psychology*. Online: www.apa.org/pi/oema/resources/english-only.aspx (accessed 10 May 2010).

Ash, S. (2004) 'Social class', in J. K. Chambers, P. Trudgill and N. Schilling-Estes (eds.), *The Handbook of Language Variation and Change*, London: Blackwell, 402–422.

Atkinson, K. and Coupland, N. (1988) 'Accommodation as ideology', *Language and Communication*, 8: 821–8.

Bauer, L. and Trudgill, P. (eds) (1998) *Language Myths*, Harmondsworth: Penguin.

Baugh, J. (2000) *Beyond Ebonics: Linguistic Pride and Racial Prejudice*, Oxford: Blackwell.

Baxter, J. (2008) 'Is it all tough talking at the top? A post-structuralist analysis of the construction of gendered speaker identities of British Business leaders within interview narratives', *Language and Gender*, 2 (2): 197–222.

Becker, J. (1988) 'The success of parents', indirect techniques for teaching their preschoolers pragmatic skills', *First Language*, 8: 173–182.

Bell, A. (1984) 'Language style as audience design', *Language in Society*, 13 (2): 145–204.

Bell, A. (1998) 'The discourse structure of news stories', in A. Bell and P. Garrett (eds), *Approaches to Media Discourse*, Oxford: Blackwell, 64–104.

Berlin, B. and Kay, P (1969) *Basic Color Terms*, Berkeley and Los Angeles: University of California Press.

Blastand, M. (2010) 'Migration v ageing population – a tricky trade-off', *BBC News Magazine*, 19 November 2009. Online: http://news.bbc.co.uk/1/hi/magazine/8368230.stm (accessed 15 April 2010).

Blommaert, J. and Omoniyi, T. (2006) 'Email fraud: language, technology and the indexicals of globalization', *Social Semiotics*, 16 (4): 573–605.

Boletta, W. L. (1992) 'Prescriptivism, politics, and lexicography: a reply to Jane Barnes Mack', *ILT NEWS*, 92 (October): 103–111.

Boroditsky, L. (2001) 'Does language shape thought?: Mandarin and English speakers' conceptions of time', *Cognitive Psychology*, 43: 1–22.

Bourdieu, P. (1984) *Social Critique of the Judgement of Taste*, London: Routledge.

Bourdieu, P. (1991) *Language and Symbolic Power*, Cambridge: Polity Press.

Bourdieu, P. and Boltanski, L. (1975) 'Le fétichisme de la langue', *Actes de la recherché en sciences sociales*, 2: 95–107.

Boussofara-Omar, N. (2006) 'Learning the "linguistic habitus", of a politician: a presidential authoritative voice in the making', *Journal of Language and Politics,* 5 (3): 325–8.

Broadbent, J. (2009) 'The *amn't gap: the view from West Yorkshire', *Journal of Linguistics,* 45: 251–284.

Brown, D. W. (2008) 'Paris Hilton, Brenda Frazier, blogs, and the proliferation of celebu-', *American Speech,* 83 (3): 312–325.

Bucholtz, M. and Hall, K. (2004) 'Theorizing identity in language and sexuality research', *Language in Society,* 33 (4): 501–547.

Butler, J. (1990) *Gender Trouble: Gender Trouble: Feminism and the Subversion of Identity,* London: Routledge.

Butler, R. N. (1969) 'Age-ism: another form of bigotry', *The Gerontologist,* 9: 243–246.

Calasanti, T. and King, N. (2007) '"Beware of the estrogen assault": ideals of old manhood in anti-aging advertisements', *Journal of Aging Studies,* 21 (4): 357–368.

Cameron, D. (1995) *Verbal Hygiene,* London: Routledge.

Cameron, D. (1997) 'Performing gender identity: Young men's talk and the construction of heterosexual masculinity', in S. Johnson and U. Meinhof (eds), *Language and Masculinity,* Oxford: Blackwell. Also in Coates, J. and Pichler, P. (eds) (2011) *Language and Gender: A Reader,* 2nd edn, Oxford: Blackwell.

Cameron, D. (ed) (1998) *The Feminist Critique of Language,* 2nd edn, London: Routledge.

Cameron, D. (2001) *Working with Spoken Discourse,* London: Sage.

Cameron, D. (2003) 'Gender and language ideologies', in J. Holmes and M. Meyerhoff (eds), *The Handbook of Language and Gender,* Oxford: Blackwell, 447–467. Also in J. Coates and P. Pichler, (eds) (2011) *Language and Gender: A Reader,* 2nd edn, Oxford: Blackwell.

Cameron, D. (2005) 'Relativity and its discontents: language, gender, and pragmatics', *Intercultural Pragmatics,* 2–3: 321–334.

Cameron, D. (2007) *The Myth of Mars and Venus,* Oxford: Oxford University Press.

Cameron, D. and Kulick, D. (2003) *Language and Sexuality,* Cambridge: Cambridge University Press.

Cameron, D. and Kulick, D. (2006) *The Language and Sexuality Reader,* London: Routledge.

Carter, R., Goddard, A., Reah, D., Sanger, K. and Swift, N. (2007) *Working with Texts: A Core Introduction to Language Analysis,* A. Beard (ed), London: Routledge.

Casagrande, J. (1948) 'Comanche Baby Language', reprinted in Hymes, D. (ed) (1964) *Language in Culture and Society,* New York: Harper & Row.

Chambers, J. K. (2002) 'Dynamics of dialect convergence', in L. Milroy (ed), *Investigating Change and Variation through Dialect Contact,* special issue of *Sociolinguistics* 6: 117–130.

Chambers, J. K. and Trudgill, P. (1980) *Modern Dialectology,* Cambridge: Cambridge University Press.

Chew, P. G. (2007) 'Remaking Singapore: language, culture and identity in a globalized world', in A. B. M. Tsui, and J. W. Tollefson (eds), *Language Policy, Culture, and Identity in Asian Contexts,* Mahwah, NJ: Lawrence Erlbaum, 73–93.

Chittenden, M. (2010) 'Martin Amis calls for euthanasia booths on street corners', *The Sunday Times,* 24 January. Online: www.timesonline.co.uk/tol/life_and_style/health/article6999873.ece (accessed 15 April 2010).

Clancy, P. (1986) 'The acquisition of communicative style in Japanese', in B. Schieffelin and E. Ochs (eds), *Language Socialization Across Cultures,* Cambridge: Cambridge University Press.

Coates, J. (1996) *Women Talk. Conversation between Women Friends.* Oxford: Blackwell.

Coates, J. (1998) *Language and Gender: A Reader.* Oxford: Blackwell.

Coates, J. (2002) *Men Talk. Stories in the Making of Masculinities*, Oxford: Blackwell.

Coates, J. (2004) *Women, Men and Language*, 3rd edn, London: Longman.

Coates, J. and Pichler, P. (eds) (2011) *Language and Gender: A Reader*, 2nd edn, Oxford: Blackwell.

Coupland, N. and Nussbaum, J. (eds) (1993) *Discourse and Lifespan Identity*, London: Sage.

Coupland, N., Coupland, J. and Giles, H. (eds) (1991) *Language, Society, and the Elderly: Discourse, Identity, and Ageing*, Oxford: Blackwell.

Coupland, J., Nussbaum, J. and Coupland, N. (1991) 'The reproduction of aging and agism in intergenerational talk', in N. Coupland, H. Giles and J. Wiemann (eds), *Miscommunication and Problematic Talk*, London: Sage.

Coupland, N., Bishop, H., Evans, B. and Garrett, P. (2006) 'Imagining Wales and the Welsh language: ethnolinguistic subjectivities and demographic flow', *Journal of Language and Social Psychology*, 25 (4): 351–376.

Cromer, R. (1991) *Language and Thought in Normal and Handicapped Children*, Oxford: Blackwell.

Cruikshank, M. (2003) *Learning to be Old: Gender, Culture, and Aging*, Lanham, MD: Rowman & Littlefield.

Crystal, D. (2005) *How Language Works: How Babies Babble, Words Change Meaning and Languages Live or Die*, Harmondsworth: Penguin.

Crystal, D. (2007a) *The Fight for English: How Language Pundits Ate, Shot, and Left*, Oxford: Oxford University Press.

Crystal, D. (2007b) *Words, Words, Words*, Oxford: Oxford University Press.

Crystal, D. (2008) *Txting: the Gr8 Db8*. Oxford: Oxford University Press.

Cukor-Avila, P. (2000) 'Revisiting the observer's paradox', *American Speech*, 75 (3): 253–254.

Daily Telegraph (2009) 'Britain's top 50 most eligible bachelors', 14 June. Online: www.telegraph.co.uk/news/newstopics/celebritynews/5531303/Britains-top-50-most-eligible-bachelors.html (accessed 6 May 2010).

Dave, L. (2009) 'The rise of Iran's citizen journalists', *BBC News online* 30 July. Online: http://news.bbc.co.uk/1/hi/technology/8176957.stm (accessed 3 May 2010).

DeFrancisco, V. L. (1991) 'The sounds of silence: how men silence women in marital relations', *Discourse and Society*, 2 (4): 413–424. Also in J. Coates, and P. Pichler (eds) (2011) *Language and Gender: A Reader*, 2nd edn, Oxford: Blackwell.

de Saussure, F. (1966) *Course in General Linguistics*, C. Bally and A. Sechehaye (eds) with A. Reidlinger, and W. Baskin (trans), London: McGraw Hill.

van Dijk, T. A (1998) 'Opinions and ideologies in the press', in A. Bell, and P. Garrett (eds), *Approaches to Media Discourse*, Oxford: Blackwell.

van Dijk, T (1999) 'Discourse and the denial of racism', in A. Jaworski and N. Coupland (eds), *The Discourse Reader*, London: Routledge, 541–558.

van Dijk, T (2004) 'Racist discourse', in E. Cashmere (ed), *Routledge Encyclopaedia of Race and Ethnic Studies*, London: Routledge, 351–355.

Dixon, R. M. W. (2002) *Australian Languages: Their Nature and Development*, Cambridge: Cambridge University Press.

Dunn, M. (2001) *Ella Minnow Pea*, London: Metheun Publishing.

Dymond, J. (2010) 'As Europe's power grows, we need to cling to our separate languages', *The Guardian*, 25 April: 38. Online: www.guardian.co.uk/comment-isfree/2010/apr/25/europe-languages-jonny-dymond (accessed 2 May 2010).

Eades, D. (1996) 'Legal recognition in cultural differences in communication: the case of Robyn Kina', *Language & Communication*, 16 (3): 215–227.

Eades, D. (2000) 'I don't think it's an answer to the question: silencing Aboriginal witnesses in court', *Language in Society*, 29: 161–195.

Eades, D. (2003) 'The politics of misunderstanding in the legal system', in J. House, G. Kasper, and S. Ross (eds), *Misunderstanding in Social Life: Discourse Approaches to Problematic Talk*, Longman: London, 199–226.

Eakins, B. W. and Eakins, R. G. (1979) 'Verbal turn-taking in faculty dialogue', in B. L. Dubois and I. Crouch (eds), *The Sociology of the Languages of American Women*, San Antonio, TX: Trinity University, 53–62.

Eckert, P. (1989) 'The whole woman: sex and gender differences in variation', *Language Variation and Change*, 1 (1): 245–267.

Eckert, P. (1998) 'Gender and sociolinguistic variation', in J. Coates (ed), *Language and Gender: A Reader*, Oxford: Blackwell. Also in J. Coates, and P. Pichler (eds), (2011) *Language and Gender: A Reader*, 2nd edn, Oxford: Blackwell.

Eckert, P. (2000) *Linguistic Variation as Social Practice*, Malden, MA: Blackwell.

Eckert, P. (2003) 'The meaning of style', *Texas Linguistic Forum*, 47: 41–53.

Eckert, P. (2004) 'Adolescent language', in E. Finegan and J. Rickford (eds), *Language in the USA: Themes for the Twenty-first Century*, Cambridge: Cambridge University Press, 361–374.

Eckert, P. and McConnell-Ginet, S. (1992) 'Think practically and look locally: language and gender as community-based practice', *Annual Review of Anthropology*, 21: 461–490.

Eckert, P. and McConnell-Ginet, S. (1995) 'Constructing meaning, constructing selves: snapshots of language, gender and class from Belten High', in K. Hall and M. Bucholtz (eds), *Gender Articulated. Language and the Socially Constructed Self*, London: Routledge, 468–508. Also in J. Coates, and P. Pichler (eds) (2011) *Language and Gender: A Reader*, 2nd edn, Oxford: Blackwell.

Eckert, P. and McConnell-Ginet, S. (2003) *Language and Gender*, Cambridge: Cambridge University Press.

Edelsky, C. (1993) 'Who's got the floor?', in D. Tannen (ed), *Gender and Conversational Interaction*, New Yord: Oxford University Press, 189–224.

Eder, D. (1993) '"Go get ya a french!": romantic and sexual teasing among adolescent girls', in D. Tannen (ed), *Gender and Conversational Interaction*, Oxford: Oxford University Press, 17–31.

Edwards, J. (1994) *Multilingualism*, London: Penguin Books.

Eisikovits, E. (1989) 'Girl-talk/boy-talk: sex differences in adolescent speech', in P. Collins and D. Blair (eds), *Australian English: The Language of a New Society*, St Lucia, Qld: University of Queensland Press, 35–54. Also in J. Coates, and P. Pichler (eds), (2011) *Language and Gender: A Reader*, 2nd edn, Oxford: Blackwell.

Ervin-Tripp, S. (1979) 'Children's verbal turntaking', in E. Ochs and B. Schieffelin (eds), *Developmental Pragmatics*, New York: Academic Press.

Evans, B. (2010) 'English as official state language in Ohio: market forces trump ideology', in H. Kelly-Holmes and G. Mautner (eds), *Language and the Market*, London: Palgrave, 161–70.

Fairclough, N. (1992) *Discourse and Social Change*, Cambridge: Polity Press.

Fairclough, N. (1995a) *Critical Discourse Analysis: The Critical Study of Language*, London: Longman.

Fairclough, N. (1995b) *Media Discourse*, London: Edward Arnold.

Fairclough, N. (1999) 'Global capitalism and critical awareness of language', *Language Awareness*, 8 (2): 71–83.

Fairclough, N. (2001) *Language and Power*, 2nd edn, London: Longman.

Ferguson, C. (1959) 'Diglossia', *Word*, 15: 325–340.

Feurer, H. (1996) 'The contemporary use of honorifics in Lhasa Tibetan', *Linguistics of the Tibeto-Burman Area*, 19 (2): 45–54.

Fishman, J. (1967) 'Bilingualism with and without diglossia; diglossia with and without bilingualism,' *Journal of Social Issues*, 23: 29–38.

Fishman, P. M. (1980) 'Interactional shitwork', *Heresies* 2: 99–101.

Fletcher, P. (1988) *A Child's Learning of English*, Oxford: Blackwell.

Foucault, M. (1980) *Power/knowledge: Selected Interviews Other Writings 1972–77*, New York: Pantheon.

Foucault, M. (1989/[1972]) *The Archaeology of Knowledge*, London: Routledge.

Fought, C. (2006) *Language and Ethnicity*, Cambridge: Cambridge University Press.

Fowler, J. (1986) 'The social stratification of (r) in New York City department stores, 24 years after Labov', New York University ms.

Fowler, R. (1991) *Language in the News: Discourse and Ideology in the Press*, London: Routledge.

Fox, G. (1993) 'A comparison of "policespeak", and "normalspeak", a preliminary study', in J. M. Sinclair, M. Hoey, and G. Fox (eds), *Techniques of Description: A Festschrift for Malcolm Coulthard*, London: Routledge, 183–195.

Franklin, B. (ed) (1995) *The Handbook of Children's Rights*, London: Routledge.

Frau-Meigs, D. (2006) 'Big Brother and reality TV in Europe', *European Journal of Communication*, 21 (1): 33–56.

Gardner-Chloros, P. (1997) 'Code-switching: language selection in three Strasbourg department stores', in N. Coupland, and A. Jaworski, (eds), *Sociolinguistics: A Reader and Coursebook*, Basingstoke, UK: Palgrave.

Giles, H. and Powesland, P. F. (1975) 'A social psychological model of speech diversity', in H. Giles, and P. F. Powesland (eds), *Speech Style and Social Evaluation*, London: Academic Press.

Gilleard, C. (2007) 'Old age in Ancient Greece: narratives of desire, narratives of disgust', *Journal of Aging Studies*, 21 (1): 81–92.

Gleason, J. (ed) (2008) *The Development of Language*, 7th edn, Boston: Allyn & Bacon.

Goffman, E. (1959) *The Presentation of Self in Everyday Life*, New York: Doubleday Anchor Books.

Gramsci, A. (2000) *The Antonio Gramsci Reader*, D. Forgacs (ed), New York: New York University Press.

Gray, J. (1993) *Men are from Mars, Women are from Venus*, London: Harper Collins.

Grice, H. P. (1975) 'Logic and conversation', in P. Cole and J. L. Morgan (eds), *Syntax and Semantics, vol. 3: Speech Acts*, New York: Seminar Press, 46–58.

Gross, D. (2009) 'Bubblespeak the Orwellian language of Wall Street finds its way to the Treasury Department', *Newsweek*. Online: www.slate.com/id/2214806 (accessed 2 May 2010).

Gumperz, J. J. (1997) 'Interethnic communication', in N. Coupland and A. Jaworski (eds), *Sociolinguistics a Reader and Coursebook*, Basingstoke, UK: Palgrave, 395–407.

Gumperz, J. J. (2003) 'Cross cultural communication', in R. Harris and B. Rampton (eds), *The Language, Ethnicity and Race Reader*, London: Routledge, 267–275.

Haeri, N. (1997) *The Sociolinguistic Market of Cairo: Gender, Class and Education*, London: Kegan Paul.

Hall, K. and Bucholtz, M. (eds) (1995) *Gender Articulated: Language and the Socially Constructed Self*, London: Routledge.

Halliday, M. A. K. (1978) *Language as Social Semiotic: The Social Interpretation of Language and Meaning*, London: Hodder Arnold.

Hanlon, M. (2009) 'Play Jobzilla Lingo Bingo!', *Mail Online*, 8 January. Online: www.dailymail.co.uk/news/article-1108836/Play-Jobzilla-Lingo-Bingo-It-win-500-.html (accessed 15 May 2009).

Hargraves, O. (2003) *Mighty Fine Words and Smashing Expressions*, Oxford: Oxford University Press.

Harrington, J., Palethorpe, S. and Watson, C. (2000) 'Does the Queen speak the Queen's English?', *Nature*, 408: 927–928.

Harris, M. and Coltheart, M. (1986) *Language Processing in Children and Adults*, London: Routledge.

Haugen, E. (1966) 'Dialect, language, nation', *American Anthropologist*, 68 (6): 922–35.

Hebdige, D. (1979) *Subculture: The Meaning of Style*, London: Metheun.

Henneberg, S. (2010) 'Moms do badly, but grandmas do worse: the nexus of sexism and ageism in children's classics', *Journal of Aging Studies*, 24 (2): 125–134.

Herring, S. C., Johnson, D. A. and DiBenedetto, T. (1992) 'Participation in electronic discourse in a "feminist" field', in *Locating Power: Proceedings of the 1992 Berkeley Women and Language Conference*, Berkeley: Berkeley Women and Language Group, 250–262. Also in J. Coates and P. Pichler (eds) (2011) *Language and Gender: A Reader*, 2nd edn, Oxford: Blackwell.

Hillier, H. (2004) *Analysing Real Texts: Research Studies in Modern English Language*, Basingstoke, UK: Palgrave.

Hilpern, K. (2009) 'This life; Kate Hilpern reveals what's in a name', *Daily Mail*, 19 September. Online: www.dailymail.co.uk/home/you/article-1213847/This-Life-Kate-Hilpern-reveals-whats-name.html (accessed 6 May 2010).

Hiroko, I. and Tsui, A. (2004) 'Gender and conversational dominance in Japanese conversation', *Language in Society*, 33: 223–248.

Hoey, M. (1986) 'The discourse colony: a preliminary study of a neglected discourse type', in M. Coulthard (ed), *Talking About Text. Birmingham: English Language Research Discourse Analysis Monographs*, 13: 1–26.

Holmes, J. (1984) 'Hedging your bets and sitting on the fence: some evidence for hedges as support structures', *Te Reo*, 27: 47–62.

Holmes, J. (1986) 'Functions of *you know* in women´s and men´s speech', *Language in Society*, 15: 1–22.

Holmes, J. (1987) 'Hedging, fencing and other conversational gambits: an analysis of gender differences in New Zealand speech', in A. Pauwels (ed), *Women and Language in Australian and New Zealand Society*, Sydney: Australian Professional Publications, 59–79.

Holmes, J. (2007) 'Social constructionism, postmodernism and feminist sociolinguistics', *Gender and Language*, 1 (1): 51–66. Also in J. Coates, and P. Pichler, (eds) (2011) *Language and Gender: A Reader*, 2nd edn, Oxford: Blackwell.

Holmes, J. (2009) 'Men, masculinities and leadership: different discourse styles at work', in P. Pichler and E. Eppler (eds), *Gender and Spoken Interaction*, Basingstoke, UK: Palgrave Macmillan, 186–210.

Holmes, J. and Meyerhoff, M. (1999) 'The community of practice: theories and methodologies in language and gender research', *Language in Society*, 28 (2): 173–183.

Holmes, J. and Meyerhoff, M. (2003) (eds) *The Handbook of Language and Gender*, Oxford: Blackwell.

Horvath, B. (1985) *Variation in Australian English: The Sociolects of Sydney*, Cambridge: Cambridge University Press.

Hudson, R. (1980) *Sociolinguistics*, Cambridge: Cambridge University Press.

Huffington Post (2010) 'Arizona ethnic studies classes banned, teachers with accents can no longer teach English', 2 May. Online: www.huffingtonpost.com/2010/04/30/arizona-ethnic-studies-cl_n_558731.html (accessed 2 May 2010).

Hymes, D. (1997 [1974]) 'The scope of sociolinguistics', in N. Coupland and A. Jaworski (eds), *Sociolinguistics: A Reader and Coursebook*, Basingstoke, UK: Palgrave MacMillan, 12–22.

Irwin, A. (2008) 'Race and ethnicity in the media', in N. Blain and D. Hutchison (eds), *The Media in Scotland*, Edinburgh: Edinburgh University Press, 199–212.

Itakura, H. and Tsui, A. B. M. (2004) 'Gender and conversational dominance in Japanese conversation', *Language in Society*, 33 (2): 223–248.

Jakobson, R. (2000) [1960] 'Linguistics and poetics', in L. Burke, T. Crowley and A. Girvin (eds), *The Routledge Language and Cultural Theory Reader*, London: Routledge, 334–49.

James, D. and Clarke, S. (1993) 'Women, men and interruptions: a critical review', in D. Tannen (ed), *Gender and Conversational Interaction*, Oxford: Oxford University Press, 231–280.

Jenkins, J. (1998) 'Which pronunciation norms and models for English as an International Language?' *English Language Teaching Journal*, 52 (2): 119–26.

Jenkins, J. (2003) *World Englishes: A Resource Book for Students*, London: Routledge.

Jespersen, O. (1922), *Language: Its Nature, Development and Origin*, London: George Allen & Unwin.

Johnstone, B. (2008) *Discourse Analysis*, 2nd edn, Oxford: Blackwell.

Johnstone, B. (2009) 'Locating language in identity', in C. Llamas, and D. Watt (eds), *Language and Identity,* Edinburgh: Edinburgh University Press.

Jolanki, O. (2009) 'Agency in talk about old age and health', *Journal of Aging Studies,* 23 (4): 215–226.

Kachru, B. (1992) 'Teaching World Englishes', in B. Kachru (ed), *The Other Tongue: English Across Cultures*, Urbana, IL: University of Illinois Press.

Kerswill, P. (2001) 'Mobility, meritocracy and dialect levelling: the fading (and phasing) out of Received Pronunciation', in P. Rajamäe and K. Vogelberg (eds), *British Studies in the New Millennium: The Challenge of the Grassroots*, Tartu: University of Tartu, 45–58. Online: www.teachit.co.uk/armoore/lang/dialect. PDF.

Kiesling, S. (2005) 'Variation, stance and style: word-final –*er*, high rising tone and ethnicity in Australian English', *English World Wide*, 26 (1): 1–42.

Kimmelman, M. (2010) 'Pardon my French: the globalization of a language', *The New York Times*, 25 April, Arts and Leisure (sec AR): 1, 21.

Kleyman, P. (2001) 'Media ageism: the link between newsrooms and advertising suites', *Aging Today*, March–April.

Koller, V. (2009) 'Analysing gender and sexual identity in discourse: a critical approach', research paper, Roehampton University, CRELL seminar series, 29 October.

Kress, G. and Hodge, R. (1993) *Language as Ideology*, London: Routledge.

Kuiper, K. (1991) 'Sporting formulae in New Zealand English: two models of male solidarity', in J. Cheshire (ed), *English around the World*, Cambridge: Cambridge University Press, 200–209.

Labov, W. (1964) 'Stages in the acquisition of Standard English', in R.W. Shuy (ed), *Social Dialects and Language Learning*, Champaign: National Council of Teachers of English.

Labov, W. (1966) *The Social Stratification of English in New York City*, Washington DC: Centre for Applied Linguistics.

Labov, W. (1969) 'The logic of non-standard English', in J. Alatis (ed), *Georgetown Monograph on Languages and Linguistics,* 22: 1–44; also in V. Lee (ed) (1979) *Language Development: A Reader,* London: Croom Helm.

Labov, W. (1972a) *Sociolinguistic Patterns*, Philadelphia: University of Pennsylvania Press.

Labov, W. (1972b) 'The linguistic consequences of being a lame', in *Language in the Inner City*, Philadelphia: University of Pennsylvania Press.

Labov, W. (1972c) 'Academic Ignorance and Black Intelligence', *The Atlantic*, 72, June: 59–67.

Labov, W. (1997 [1972]) 'Linguistics and sociolinguistics', in N. Coupland and A. Jaworski (eds), *Sociolinguistics: A Reader and Coursebook*, Basingstoke, UK: Palgrave Macmillan, 23–24.

Labov, W., Ash, S. and Boberg, C. (2006), *The Atlas of North American English: Phonetics, Phonology and Sound Change*, Berlin: Mouton/de Gruyter.

Lakoff, G. and Johnson, M. (1980) *Metaphors We Live By*, Chicago: University of Chicago Press.

Lakoff, R. (1975) *Language and Woman´s Place*, New York: Harper and Row.

van Leeuwen, T. (2004) *Introducing Social Semiotics*, London: Routledge.

Levinson, S. (1979) 'Activity types and language', *Linguistics*, 17: 365–399.

Lin, A. and Tong, A. (2009) 'Constructing cultural self and other in the internet discussion of a Korean historical TV drama: a discourse analysis of weblog messages of Hong Kong viewers of Dae Jang Geum', *Journal of Asian Pacific Communication*, 19 (2): 289–312.

Loviglio, J. (2004) 'Yet another age-fighting strategy: surgery for a younger voice', *Associated Press*, 18 April.

Lucy, J. (1997) 'Linguistic relativity', *Annual Review of Anthropology*, 26: 291–312.

Lucy, J. (2005) 'Through the window of language: assessing the influence of language diversity on thought', *Theoria*, 54: 299–309.

Majid, A., Bowerman, M., Kita, S., Haun, D. B. M. and Levinson, S. C. (2004) 'Can language restructure cognition? The case for space', *TRENDS in Cognitive Sciences*, 8 (3): 108–114.

Makoni, S. and Grainger, K. (2002) 'Comparative gerontolinguistics: characterizing discourses in caring institutions in South Africa and the United Kingdom', *Journal of Social Issues*, 58 (4): 805–824.

Maltz, D. N. and Borker, R. A. (1982) 'A cultural approach to male-female miscommunication', in J. J. Gumperz, (ed), *Language and Social Identity*, Cambridge: Cambridge University Press, 196–216. Also in J. Coates and P. Pichler (eds) (2011) *Language and Gender: A Reader*, 2nd edn, Oxford: Blackwell.

Martin, L. (1986) '"Eskimo words for snow": a case study in the Genesis and Decay of an Anthropological Example', *American Anthropologist*, 88: 418–423.

Mautner, G. (2005) 'The entrepreneurial university – a discursive profile of higher education buzzwords', *Critical Discourse Studies*, 2 (2): 95–120.

May, P. (2010) 'Clever startup names giving to too cute', *The Seattle Times*, 26 April: A 12.

McCafferty, K. (1999) '(London)Derry: between Ulster and local speech – class, ethnicity and language change', in P. Foulkes and G. Docherty (eds), *Urban Voices*, London: Hodder.

Mees, I. and Collins, B. (1999) 'Cardiff: a real-time study of glottalization', in P. Foulkes and G. Docherty (eds), *Urban Voices*, London: Hodder.

Menz, F. and Al-Roubaie, A. (2008) 'Interruptions, status and gender in medical interviews: the harder you brake, the longer it takes', *Discourse & Society*, 19 (5): 645–666.

Mertz, E. (1982) 'Language and mind: a 'Whorfian', folk theory in US language law, *Duke University Working Papers in Sociolinguistics*, 93: 1–21.

Mertz, E. (1998) 'Linguistic ideology and praxis in U.S. law school classrooms', in B. B. Schieffelin, K. A. Woolard and P. V. Kroskrity (eds), *Language Ideologies: Practice and Theory*, Oxford: Oxford University Press, 149–162.

Mesthrie, R., Swann, J., Deumert, A. and Leap, W. L. (2009) *Introducing Sociolinguistics*, 2nd edn, Edinburgh: Edinburgh University Press.

Meyerhoff, M. (2006) *Introducing Sociolinguistics*, London: Routledge.

Miller, L. (2004) 'Those naughty teenage girls: Japanese kogals, slang, and media assessments', *Journal of Linguistic Anthropology*, 14 (2): 225–247.

Mills, S. (1997) *Discourse*, London: Routledge.

Mills, S. (2008) *Language and Sexism*, Cambridge: Cambridge University Press.

Milroy, J. and Milroy, L. (1999) *Authority in Language: Investigating Standard English*, London: Taylor & Francis.

Milroy, L. (1980) *Language and Social Networks*, Basil Blackwell: Oxford.

Milroy, L. and Gordon, M. (2003) *Sociolinguistics: Method and Interpretation*, Oxford: Blackwell.

Mitchell, W. J. T. (1986) *Iconology: Image, Text, Ideology*, Chicago: University of Chicago Press.

Moir, J. (2009a) 'A strange, lonely and troubling death ...', *Daily Mail*, 16 October. Online: www.dailymail.co.uk/debate/article-1220756/A-strange-lonely-troubling-death--.html (accessed 2 May 2010).

Moir, J. (2009b) 'The truth about my views on the tragic death of Stephen Gately', *Daily Mail*, 23 October. Online: www.dailymail.co.uk/debate/article-1222246/The-truth-views-tragic-death-Stephen-Gately.html (accessed 2 May 2010).

Montgomery, M. (2008) *An Introduction to Language and Society*, 3rd edn, Oxford: Routledge.

Nunberg, Geoffrey (2002) 'Media: label whores', *The American Prospect*, 13 (8). Online: www.prospect.org/cs/articles?article=media_label_whores (accessed 20 July 2010).

Obama, B (2009) Inaugural Address. Online: www.whitehouse.gov/the_press_office/President_Barack_Obamas_Inaugural_Address.

Ochs, E. (1983) 'Cultural dimensions of language acquisition', in E. Ochs and B. Schieffelin (eds), *Acquiring Conversational Competence*, London: Routledge and Kegan Paul.

Ochs, E. and Taylor, C. (1992) 'Family narrative as political activity', *Discourse & Society*, 3 (3): 301–340.

Orwell, G. (1988 [1946]) 'Politics and the English language', in *Inside the Whale and Other Essays*, Harmondsworth: Penguin.

Padilla, A. (1999) 'Psychology', in J. A. Fishman (ed), *The Handbook of Language and Ethnic Identity*, Oxford: Oxford University Press, 109–121.

Pall Mall Gazette (1981) 'Literary notes, news, and echoes', Saturday 18 July, issue 8214 (sourced from Times Digital Archive).

Parfitt, T. (2006) 'Bizarre, brutal and self-obsessed. Now time's up for Turkmenistan's dictator', *The Guardian*, 22 December. Online: www.guardian.co.uk/world/2006/dec/22/tomparfitt.mainsection (accessed 7 April 2009).

Parker, T. (2004) 'Quest for Ratings', *South Park* episode, season 8.

Paton Walsh, N. (2006) 'Turkmenistan despot axes pensions', *The Guardian*, 4 February. Online: www.guardian.co.uk/world/2006/feb/04/nickpatonwalsh.mainsection (accessed 7 April 2009).

Patterson, K. E., Marshall, J. C. and Coltheart, M. (1985) 'Surface dyslexia in various orthographies: introduction', in K. E. Patterson, J. C. Marhsall and M. Coltheart (eds), *Surface Dyslexia: Neuropsychological and Cognitive Studies of Phonological Reading*, Hove, UK: Lawrence Erlbaum, 209–214.

Pauwels, A. (2003) 'Linguistic sexism and feminist linguistic activism', in J. Holmes and M. Meyerhoff (eds), *The Handbook of Language and Gender*, Oxford: Blackwell, 550–570.

Pichler, P. (2009) *Talking Young Femininities*, Basingstoke, UK: Palgrave Macmillan.

Pichler, P. and Eppler, E. (eds) (2009) *Gender and Spoken Interaction*, Basingstoke, UK: Palgrave Macmillan.

Pinker, S. (2008) *The Stuff of Thought: Language as a Window into Human Nature*, London: Penguin Press Science.

Poe, E. A. (1993) 'The purloined letter', in *Tales of Mystery and Imagination*, London: Everyman, 493–511.

Power, N. (2009) 'Bamboozle, baffle and blindside', *The New Statesman*, 28 May, 37 (4949): 49.

Preece, S. (2009) '"A group of lads, innit?" Performances of laddish masculinity in British higher education', in P. Pichler, and E. Eppler (eds), *Gender and Spoken Interaction*, London: Palgrave Macmillan.

Preisler, B. (1986) *Linguistic Sex Roles in Conversation*, Berlin: Mouton de Gruyter.

Pullum, G. (1991) 'The great Eskimo vocabulary hoax', in *The Great Eskimo Vocabulary Hoax and Other Irreverent Essays on the Study of Language*, Chicago: University of Chicago Press.

Rampton, B. (1995) *Crossing: Language and Ethnicity among Adolescents*, London: Longman.

Rampton, B. (1997) 'Language crossing and the redefinition of reality: implications for research on code-switching community', *Working Papers in Urban Language and Literacies*, paper 5, Kings College. Online: www.kcl.ac.uk/schools/sspp/education/research/groups/llg/wpull.html. Also in P. Auer (ed), *Code-switching in Conversation, Language, Interaction and Identity* London: Routledge, 290–317.

Reah, D. (2002) *The Language of Newspapers* (Intertext), Oxford: Routledge.

Reid-Thomas, H. (1993) 'The use and interpretation by men and women of minimal responses in informal conversation', unpublished M.Litt dissertation, University of Strathclyde.

Richards, I. A. (1965 [1936]) *The Philosophy of Rhetoric*, Oxford: Oxford University Press.

Ricoeur, P. (1994) *The Rule of Metaphor*, London: Routledge.

Rodriguez, G. (1991) 'The Talátur: ceremonial chant of the Atacama People', in M. Ritchie Key (ed), *Language Change in South American Indian Languages*, Philadelphia: University of Pennsylvania Press.

Romaine, S. (1997 [1990]) 'Pidgin English advertising', in N. Coupland and A. Jaworski (eds), *Sociolinguistics A Reader and Coursebook,* Basingstoke: Palgrave.

Romaine, S. (2000) *Language in Society*, Oxford: Oxford University Press.

Rosewarne, D. (1994) 'Estuary English: tomorrow's RP?', *English Today*, 10 (1): 3–8.

Sacks, H., Schegloff, E. A. and Jefferson, G. (1974) 'A simplest systematics for the organisation of turn-taking for conversation', *Language*, 50: 696–735.

Sankoff, D. and Laberge, S. (1978) 'The linguistic market and the statistical explanation of variability', in D. Sankoff (ed), *Linguistic Variation: Models and Methods*, New York: Academic Press, 239–250.

Sankoff, G. (2006) 'Cross-sectional and longitudinal studies', in U. Ammon, N. Dittmar, K. J. Mattheier and P. Trudgill (eds), *Sociolinguistics: An International Handbook of the Science of Language and Society*, Volume 3, New York: Walter de Gruyter.

Sataloff, R. T. (2005) *Treatment of Voice Disorders*, San Diego, CA: Plural Publishing.

Schieffelin, B. and Doucet, R. C. (1992) 'The "real" Haitian Creole: metalinguistics and orthographic choice', *Pragmatics*, 2 (3): 427–445.

Schiffman, H. (1996) *Linguistic Culture and Language Policy*, London: Routledge.

Schilling-Estes, N. (2007) 'Investigating stylistic variation', in J. K. Chambers, P. Trudgill and N. Schilling-Estes (eds), *The Handbook of Language Variation and Change*, Oxford: Blackwell.

Shenk, P. S. (2007) '"I'm Mexican, remember?" Constructing ethnic identities via authentication discourse', *Journal of Sociolinguistics*, 11 (2): 194–220.

Shon, P. C. H. (2005) '"I'd grab the S-O-B by his hair and yank him out the window": the fraternal order of warnings and threats in police–citizen encounters', *Discourse & Society*, 16 (6): 829–845.

Simpson, P. (1993) *Language, Ideology and Point of View*, Oxford: Routledge.

Sinclair, J. M. H. and Coulthard, M. (1975) *Towards an Analysis of Discourse: The English Used by Teachers and Pupils,* Oxford: Oxford University Press.

Slack, J. (2007) 'The language barrier: 2.5m workers only speak English as a second choice', *The Daily Mail*, 1 January: 18. Online: www.dailymail.co.uk/news/article-425775/2–5m-workers-speak-English-second-choice--today-open-door-30m-more.html#ixzz0YjoKz3EL (accessed 8 May 2010).

Spender, D. (1980) *Man Made Language*, London: Routledge.

Stuart-Smith, J. (2006) 'The influence of media on language', in C. Llamas, P. Stockwell and L. Mullany (eds), *The Routledge Companion to Sociolinguistics*, London: Routledge, 140–148.

Sturm, C. D. (2002) *Blood Politics: Race, Culture and Identity in the Cherokee Nation of Oklahoma*, London: University of California Press.

Suzuki, Y. (2002) *Nihongo-no-deki-nai-Nihonjin* (Japanese who can't use Japanese correctly) Tokyo: Chuokoron-Shinsha.

Swann, J. (1989) 'Talk control: an illustration from the classroom of problems in analyzing male dominance of conversation', in J. Coates and D. Cameron (eds), *Women in their Speech Communities*, London: Longman: 122–140. Also in J. Coates and P. Pichler (eds) (2011) *Language and Gender: A Reader*, 2nd edn, Oxford: Blackwell.

Talbot, M. (1992) '"I wish you'd stop interrupting me": interruptions and asymmetries in speaker-rights in equal encounters', *Journal of Pragmatics*, 18: 451–466.

Talbot, M., Atkinson, K. and Atkinson, D. (2003) *Language and Power in the Modern World*, Edinburgh: Edinburgh University Press.

Tannen, D. (1990) *You Just Don't Understand*, London: Virago.

Tench, P. (2003) 'Review: *Phonetics*, Peter Roach', *System,* 31: 417–428.

Thornborrow, J. (2001) 'Authenticating talk: building public identities in audience participation broadcasting', *Discourse Studies*, 3 (4): 459–479.

Thorsheim, H. and Roberts, B. (1990) 'Empowerment through story-sharing: communication and reciprocal social support among older persons', in H. Giles, N. Coupland and J. Wieman (eds), *Communication, Health and the Elderly*, Manchester: Manchester University Press.

Tollefson, J. W. and Tsui, A. B. M. (2007) 'Issues in language policy, culture and identity', in A. B. M. Tsui and J. W. Tollefson (eds), *Language Policy, Culture, and Identity in Asian Contexts*, Mahwah, NJ: Lawrence Erlbaum, 259–270.

Tout, K. (ed) (1993) *Elderly Care: A World Perspective*, London: Chapman & Hall.

Troemel-Ploetz, S. (1991) 'Selling the apolitical', *Discourse & Society*, 2 (4): 489–502. Also in J. Coates, and P. Pichler (eds) (2011) *Language and Gender: A Reader*, 2nd edn, Oxford: Blackwell.

Trudgill, P. (1974) *The Social Differentiation of English in Norwich*, Cambridge: Cambridge University Press.

Trudgill, P. (1983) 'Acts of conflicting identity: the sociolinguistics of British pop-song pronunciation', in *On Dialect: Social and Geographical Perspectives*, Oxford: Blackwell.

Trudgill, P. (1995) *Sociolinguistics*, London: Penguin.

Trudgill, P. (1999) 'Standard English what it isn't', in T. Bex and R. Watts (eds), *Standard English: the Widening Debate*, London: Routledge.

Truss, L. (2003) *Eats Shoots and Leaves: The Zero Tolerance Approach to Punctuation*, London: Profile Books.

Tsui, A. B. M. and Tollefson, J. W. (2007) (eds) *Language Policy, Culture, and Identity in Asian Contexts*, Mahwah, NJ: Lawrence Erlbaum.

Turner, G. (1973) *Stylistics*, Harmondsworth: Penguin.

Uchida, A. (1992) 'When "difference" is "dominance": a critique of the "anti-power based tendency" in language and gender, *Language in Society*, 21: 547–68.

Wahl-Jorgensen, K., Williams, A. and Wardle, C. (2010 forthcoming) 'Audience views on user-generated content: exploring the value of news from the bottom up', *Northern Lights*, 8.

Wardhaugh, R. (2006) *An Introduction to Sociolinguistics*, 5th edn, Oxford: Blackwell Publishing.

Wardle, C. and Williams, A. (2010) 'UGC @ the BBC', *Media Culture and Society*, 32(5): 761–80.

Warner, W. L. (1960) *Social Class in America,* New York: Harper and Row.

Warren, J. (1999) 'Wogspeak: transformations of Australian English', *Journal of Australian Studies*, 23 (62): 85–94.

Waugh, P. (2007) 'Immigrants told to learn English', *The Evening Standard*, 21 February: 7.

Wenger, E. (1998) *Communities of Practice: Learning, Meaning, and Identity*, Cambridge: Cambridge University Press.

West, C. and Zimmerman, D. (1977) 'Women's place in everyday talk: reflections on parent-child interaction', *Social Problems*, 245: 521–9. Also in J. Coates (ed) (1998) *Language and Gender. A Reader.* Oxford: Blackwell. Also in J. Coates, and P. Pichler, (eds) (2011) *Language and Gender. A Reader*, 2nd edn, Oxford. Blackwell.

Wetherell, M. (1998) 'Positioning and interpretative repertoires: conversation analysis and post-structuralism in dialogue', *Discourse & Society*, 9 (3): 387–412.

Whorf, B. L. (1954) 'The relation of habitual thought and behaviour to language', in S. I. Hayakawa (ed), *Language, Meaning and Maturity: selections from Etc., a review of general semantics, 1943–1953*, New York: Harper, 197–215.

Wierzbicka, Anna (2005) 'There are no "color universals" but there are universals of visual semantics', *Anthropological Linguistics*, 47 (2): 217–44.

Williams, A., Wardle, C. and Wahl-Jorgensen, K. (2010, forthcoming) '"Have They Got News for Us?" Audience revolution or business as usual at the BBC?', *Journalism Practice* (online from 14 April 2010).

Williams, A., Ylänne, V. and Wadleigh, P. M. (2007) 'Selling the "Elixir of Life": images of the elderly in an Olivio advertising campaign', *Journal of Aging Studies*, 21 (1): 1–21.

Winawer, J., Witthoft, N., Frank, M.C. Wu, L., Wade, A.R. and Boroditsky, L. (2007) 'Russian blues reveal effects of language on color discrimination', *PNAS*, 104 (19): 7780–5. Online: www.pnas.org_cgi_doi_10.1073_pnas.0701644104 (accessed 19 April 2010).

Wittgenstein, L. (1963) *Tractatus Logico-Philosophicus*, D. F. Pears and B. F. McGuinnes (trans), London: Routledge and Kegan Paul.

Woll, B. and Sutton-Spence, R. (2007) 'Sign languages', in D. Britain (ed), *Language in the British Isles*, Cambridge: Cambridge University Press.

Wooden, R. (2002) *Recasting Retirement: New Perspectives on Aging and Civic Engagement*, San Francisco: Civic Ventures.

Wray, A., Trott, K. and Bloomer, A. (1998) *Projects in Linguistics: A Practical Guide to Researching Language*, London: Arnold.

Wray, A., Evans, B., Coupland, N. and Bishop, H. (2003) 'Singing in Welsh, becoming Welsh: "turfing" a "grass roots" identity', *Language Awareness*, 2 (1): 49–71.

Wyse, P. (2008) 'Wyse words', *The Guardian*, 6 September. Online: www.guardian.co.uk/lifeandstyle/2008/sep/06/words (accessed 21 June 2009).

Yang, J. (2007) 'Zuiqian "deficient mouth": discourse, gender and domestic violence in urban China', *Language and Gender*, 1 (1): 107–118. Also in J. Coates, and P. Pichler (eds) (2011) *Language and Gender: A Reader*, 2nd edn, Oxford: Blackwell.

Zimmerman, D. H. and West, C. (1975) 'Sex roles, interruptions and silences in conversations', in B. Thorne, and N. Henley (eds), *Language and Sex: Difference and Dominance*, Rowley, MA: Newbury House, 105–129.

Index